Liang and Lin

Liang and Lin

Partners in Exploring China's Architectural Past

Wilma Fairbank

FOREWORD BY JONATHAN SPENCE

University of Pennsylvania Press

Philadelphia

Library of Congress Cataloging-in-Publication Data
Fairbank, Wilma.
   Liang and Lin : partners in exploring China's architectural past / Wilma Fairbank ;
foreword by Jonathan Spence.
      p.   cm.
   Includes bibliographical references and index.
      1. Liang, Ssu-ch'eng, 1901–   2. Lin, Hui-yin, 1904–1955.   3. Architects — China —
Biography.   I. Title.
NA1549.L53F35   1994
720'.92'2 — dc20
[B]   94-16414
                                                                    CIP

*For our grandchildren
and theirs*

Contents

Foreword

JONATHAN SPENCE

If we take only a distant, bird's eye view of the history of China in the twentieth century, it is often hard not to see it mainly as a century of colossal waste: wasted opportunities, wasted resources, wasted lives. How could there be purposeful national reconstruction when the agonies of foreign invasion and occupation were compounded by such viciousness in domestic politics? How could a balanced economy develop when the poverty of the majority was deepened by greed-driven and uncontrollable entrepreneurs at certain periods, or by the state's totalist extremism at others? How could individual acts of creation and intellectual exploration gain popular currency in a world of constant dislocations and fiercely unimaginative censorship?

The story of Liang Sicheng and Lin Whei-yin initially seems to support such melancholy reflections. Myriad layers of society's waste cluttered up and ravaged their lives, and at so many times the world simply gave them no room to breathe. But, as we ponder their story further, in all the moving and intimate detail provided by Wilma Fairbank, we become more conscious of the flashes of light that emanate from this strongly yet stressfully married couple. We hear bursts of laughter and the rattle of teacups in their living room jammed with friends. We see their patient scholarship slowly give back meaning to ancient architectural texts. We watch their skilled fingers guiding their drafting pens through the technical details in both Chinese and English, each written with equal elegance, and see vanished buildings regain their rightful place in a nation's consciousness. We sense the humor and fortitude that never left them even during prolonged and debilitating illness.

Both Lin Whei-yin and Liang Sicheng were born into the paradoxical China of the early twentieth century, where traditionalism crossed and co-existed with modernity. Lin Whei-yin's father was a talented political dreamer, a seeker of the new, who took two concubines to give him the children his principal wife could not. Lin Whei-yin, the elder concubine's only surviving child, received a good if informal education, and when her father was posted to England in 1920 as a director of China's League of Nations Institute he took the sixteen-year-old Whei-yin with him to be his companion and hostess. But when the poet Hsü Chih-mo fell flamboyantly in love with her her father took her back with him to China, so that she would be once more in the same environment as Liang Sicheng, the son of Liang Ch'i-ch'ao, to whom Lin Whei-yin had already been informally engaged.

Liang Sicheng had been born in Tokyo in 1901, during his father's enforced exile from the waning Ch'ing Dynasty. When the Ch'ing fell in 1912, the Liangs returned to China, where Liang Ch'i-ch'ao lived a life of intellectual eminence and of attempted political activism in the bewildering years of the early Republic. Sicheng was sent to a Westernized preparatory school and a Westernized college, while also being rigorously tutored in classical Chinese by his father, and made to translate H. G. Wells's *Outline of History* into Chinese. In 1923 an accident while riding on his new Harley-Davidson motorcycle, compounded by inept medical attention, left Sicheng partially crippled and forced to wear a steel back brace. Whei-yin, now formally engaged to Sicheng, had nonetheless renewed her friendship with the poet Hsü Chih-mo, who had returned to China as a lionized young poet. Together they arranged for Fritz Kreisler to give violin concerts in Peking, and translated for the Indian poet Rabindranath Tagore when he came to China on a lecture tour.

At Liang Ch'i-ch'ao's urging, Whei-yin and Sicheng traveled together to the University of Pennsylvania — engaged yet forbidden to marry until they completed their degrees. There, in the Beaux-Arts universe of 1920s Philadelphia, Sicheng studied architecture, Whei-yin studied fine arts, and both lived through a period of emotional and personal anguish that Liang Ch'i-ch'ao referred to as their private "Buddhist hell." Apparently strengthened, if not purified, they were at last married in Canada in 1928, returning after some further graduate work to be the first two professors at the newly founded school of architecture in Shenyang (Mukden).

When Wilma and John Fairbank, themselves newly married, met Whei-yin and Sicheng at a Peking party in 1932, the Japanese military aggression in Manchuria had forced the Chinese couple out of the Shenyang school. Whei-yin had had two children (a girl and a boy) and learned she had tuberculosis. Hsü Chih-mo, once again openly welcomed as a house guest, had died in a plane crash. Liang Chi-ch'ao too had died, after a tragically bungled kidney operation, and Sicheng had plunged into the scholarly analysis of early Chinese architectural texts, using former

Forbidden City carpenters and craftsmen as his exegetes. In this chaotic, work-filled, and ebullient period, the Liangs — on one prolonged occasion accompanied by the Fairbanks — embarked on the first intellectually orchestrated series of field trips in search of China's earliest surviving buildings that had ever been undertaken. Their greatest triumph was the identification, measuring, drawing, and photographing of the Fo-kuang Ssu, a wooden temple dating back to A.D. 857 in the Wutai Mountains area of Shansi province. But this was only one of numerous astonishing discoveries that were encapsulated after long years of work and interruptions in Sicheng's great book *A Pictorial History of Chinese Architecture*, lovingly reassembled from scattered fragments and edited into an integrated whole by Wilma Fairbank.

Though the Fairbanks' and the Liangs' lives inevitably diverged again in the later 1930s, Sicheng's and Whei-yin's friendship with Wilma and John continued by letter; one of the many treasures of Wilma Fairbank's memoir is that we hear Whei-yin's voice through the illness, the work, and the renewed misery and relocation caused by the full invasion of China by Japan in 1937, and the flight of the Liangs, first to Changsha and then to Kunming and Chungking in China's southwest. For Whei-yin this was not only a world of loss and horror but one of "delicate bare branches that scatter silver, small quiet temples, and the occasional bridge one can cross with romantic pride" (see p. 91 below). Rasping with tuberculosis and shivering with cold in dank lodgings, Whei-yin could still note how "the sun steals in curious angles into one's aching sense of awareness of quietness and beauty" p. 112).

The last year of the war briefly brought the two couples together in Chungking, but from then on they were never to be all together again. Civil War, Korean War, Cold War, and then death (in 1955 for Whei-yin, 1972 for Sicheng, 1991 for John) ended the meetings. But Liang Sicheng and Lin Whei-yin continued to try and do what they could for the architecture they had tracked and loved — to save the old Peking as a wooded, leaf-filled city, to keep it free from industry, to preserve the wondrous walls and gates as public parks for all posterity to love and enjoy. They failed. They were struggled against, tormented, humiliated. And then, posthumously, when it was all too late, showered with praise and recognition.

We remember, of course, what we want to remember, as well as what the sources let us. So we can continue to hold in our hearts, if we wish, the nightmare sight of Liang Sicheng in the Cultural Revolution, his face clouded in "utter humiliation and shame" as he stumbles among the jeering crowds with a black placard round his neck, declaring his "treason" to the people. But for me, thanks to Wilma Fairbank, that image is pushed aside by little Sicheng, swimming underwater in the sea off Japan, trying to tweak the beard of the self-proud philosopher K'ang Yu-wei, and by the formalistic and aesthetic elegance of his drawings and calligraphy. And instead of Whei-yin dying of tuberculosis in the chill Peking of 1955 as the last of the grand old walls came crashing down, I watch her smiling wryly in the crowded living room of her Peking home in 1932, amid children and friends and noise and laughter, an unfinished poem on her desk, the upcoming months' itinerary to unknown temples a millennium old dancing in her mind. And I see Liang and Lin jolting along, by train, truck, and mule cart, down mud tracks where city folk had rarely gone, until we and they climb at last among the roof beams of China's past, feel the cunning wood under our fingers, and marvel at the touch and precision of an art that might have been forever lost.

Yale University
November 8, 1993

Introduction

John King Fairbank spent his life interpreting China to the West from his Harvard base. He is often credited with having "almost singlehandedly created the field of modern Chinese studies in the United States in the years after World War II."[1]

In 1932, when he married me in Peking, I already shared his enthusiasm. We were graduate students in our twenties, he originally from South Dakota, I from Cambridge, Massachusetts, where we had met and fallen in love. Chinese art was my special interest. His was Chinese history in all its aspects.

We settled in a charming Chinese courtyard house in the eastern part of Peking, found Chinese teachers, and began our study of the language. In our spare time we explored the Palace in the Forbidden City and the Buddhist temples in the Western Hills. These were great sights, but to us even more impressive were the lofty walls and gate towers that then encompassed Peking itself. Within the walls a never-ending drama of life played out on the streets. Happy though we were, exploring together, we were merely onlookers at the fascinating scene.

Some two months after our wedding we met Liang Sicheng and his wife Lin Hui-yin. Neither they nor we were aware that years of close friendship lay ahead, but we were captivated from the first. They were young, devoted to each other, and at the same time responsive to our delight in their company. Whei (as she shortened her name for foreign intimates) was extraordinarily pretty and vivacious. Sicheng was more reserved. Courteous and reflective, he had a whimsical wit that came into play at odd moments. Both were bilingual and bicultural. Whei balanced her husband's restraint with an outpouring of talk and laughter. Trading stories of her recent college life in America, she soon learned that John and I had both studied at Harvard and that John had come to Peking from graduate study at Oxford. This inspired some anecdotes from her own year as a teenage schoolgirl in London.

As we were parting, she inquired where we lived. We were as startled as she to find that their house was not far from ours, at the end of our street close to the east wall of the city. They were young and they were near. We were enchanted by them.

From this beginning, the friendship developed rapidly. We soon learned that Sicheng, trained at the University of Pennsylvania in Western architecture, had embarked on a career as China's first architectural historian. This was to bring him international recognition in years to come. Whei was his helpmate in architecture, but it is the poetry she wrote throughout her life that keeps her memory alive today.

Both Sicheng and Whei were children of famous fathers and distinguished families. Through them and their friends many doors began to open for us. We were no longer just onlookers. And when, the next year, John joined the faculty at Tsinghua University, we felt we really belonged.

As the story unfolds, it will be clear that the four of us remained close through the years. That we should outlive them is not surprising. Their lives were spent in pursuing their idealistic goals, through decades of warlordism, nationalist revolution, Japanese aggression, bitter civil war, and the dictates of a harsh Leninist state until they were finally vanquished by their own serious illnesses. This tribute is written not only to recount the fate they shared with so many others but also to commemorate their achievements and the creativity, humanity, and humor that supported their courage.

A Note on Names

When Lin Hui-yin early discovered that English-speaking readers of her romanized name pronounced it "Hewey-yin," she switched its English spelling to "Whei-yin." Letters to intimates were signed just "Whei." Her preference for using more accurate and easily pronounced English syllables is followed for a few names that are constantly repeated. These include the names of her husband, Liang Ssu-ch'eng: (spelled Sicheng it evades the *soo* sound); their children; their close family friend Lao Jin (not Lao Chin); and even the name of the wartime refuge, "Li-juang" (for Li-chuang). These pages include varying romanizations of their Chinese names chosen by individuals; other people are cited according to the Wade-Giles romanization system as used in the West in the Liangs' lifetimes.

Acknowledgments

This book was written to introduce a unique Chinese couple to readers in the Western world. Though most of the words are mine, I have had important collaborators.

Noriko Kamachi translated from a Japanese source Liang's childhood memories.

Julia Lin translated from the Chinese Lin Whei-yin's elegy for her brother, a poem.

Chiang Yung-chen skillfully selected and translated relevant references to Liang and Lin from the papers (N.P.) of Liang's father, Liang Ch'i-Ch'ao.

Charles Child wrote of meeting Liang and Lin on their trans-Siberian return to China and sharing briefly in their homecoming.

George Dudley contributed comments on Liang's participation in the United Nations Board of Design, New York, 1947.

Lin Zhu in her extraordinary chapter takes the reader through Liang's sufferings and humiliations in the Cultural Revolution. Judith Zeitlin and Wu Hung translated it from the Chinese.

My most important collaborators are, of course, Liang and Lin themselves. Quotes from their letters to us over the years tell their story best.

Kind friends who have encouraged me to write what I know of Liang and Lin are too many to list. But the fellow student and lifelong friend of Liang, Shanghai architect Ch'en Chih ("Benjamin"), has been particularly helpful. I am very grateful also to Feng Yen-tsai, Leo Ou-fan Lee, Winston Hsieh, Hsiao Chien, John Israel, Jack Service, Jeannette Elliott, Bill Holland, Arthur and Betty Lou Hummel, and Nancy Hosea.

My husband's major part in the story is obvious. Our daughter Holly led me to Lisa Pedicini of the Vicky Bijur Literary Agency, who in turn led me to the University of Pennsylvania Press where Jo Joslyn and Alison Anderson have been very supportive.

WILMA FAIRBANK
April 1994

PART ONE

Preparations, 1901–1928

1. Favorite Son

Liang Sicheng's life was shaped by the eminence, ideas, and concern of his father, Liang Ch'i-ch'ao. Filial devotion of son to father was still the primary virtue expected of any Chinese boy, but in Sicheng's case there were special reasons for it. His father had leapt into fame as a leader of the reform movement of 1898, when Japan's unexpected defeat of China in 1895 and the imperialist powers' seizure of spheres of interest early in 1898 seemed to threaten the actual dismemberment of the Chinese state. In the summer of that year Liang Ch'i-ch'ao had joined his teacher, K'ang Yu-wei, in supporting the young Emperor's sudden attempt to save China through drastic reforms. When the effort was blocked by a conservative coup d'état, he had taken refuge in Japan. He was a young Cantonese of twenty-five at the time, a precocious scholar and activist, who through his influential writings was already on the way to becoming the foremost intellectual leader of his generation.

Liang Ch'i-ch'ao's stature as a reformer was due to the fact that only a scholar of the Confucian classics could undertake to modernize Chinese thought. It had to begin from inside Confucianism. In a series of periodicals that he published in Chinese while in Japan, Liang introduced Western learning to the Confucian scholars of the revolutionary generation in China.

In his late teens he had been married to a Kweichow woman, Li Hui-hsien, who was four years older than he. The marriage was arranged by her older brother, an examiner who had been dazzled by the brilliance of young Liang in the provincial examinations. Little is known of her other than that she was a conventional woman of her class. Her feet were, of course, bound, and so were her attitudes. Living with a husband who was discovering and penetrating a wider world, she was content to remain within the confines of her tradition. In 1893 she gave birth to their first child, a daughter Ssu-hsun, in Kuangtung. Five years later she took the child to Japan to join her husband in his fugitive exile.

It was a comparatively settled existence after the previous hectic months and years of Liang Ch'i-ch'ao's life. The daughter was cherished, but the pressing importance of having a male heir was obvious. The wife was soon pregnant again and bore the longed-for son, but he died at birth. By this time she was well along in her thirties and had contributed only a six-year-old girl to the family. Her primary duty was clear. She made a trip back to her Kweichow home to find a concubine who could help to assure the lineage. The young girl, aged sixteen or seventeen, whom she brought back to Japan was healthy and vigorous, but she was illiterate and had large unbound feet. She was a *ya-t'ou,* a bondmaid, bought at an early age and raised as a servant in the family's house. The wife had carefully chosen a concubine who would be able to produce sturdy children but who would also be aware of her inferior status in the Liang household and of her obligations to serve.

It was the wife, Hui-hsien, however, who did finally give birth to the son and heir. Sicheng was born on April 20, 1901 in Tokyo. He survived to assume the duties and responsibilities of eldest son, which were his throughout the difficult years ahead. Three years later the concubine bore a son, Ssu-yung. The boys were playmates in childhood and close friends in youth. As adults, both became distinguished scholars.

A second daughter, Ssu-chuang, completed the wife's offspring. The concubine continued to bear children up to 1929, when the death of the elder Liang was followed shortly by the death at birth of his ninth son. The father's life came to an end at the early age of fifty-six after years of extraordinarily prolific and influential writings. He had also fathered four-teen children, all of whom became useful citizens and a number of whom made outstanding contributions.

The concubine outlived the wife by many years. Throughout her life in the Liang household she was the mainstay who cared for everyone in sickness and in health and in return was much respected and loved by all the siblings. Having arrived illiterate in a family of scholars, she simply waited for her first child to start school, and then learned along with him. She learned to read and to read aloud with expression. She not only became expert at nursing and managing the household but learned to swim, roller skate, roll hoops, knit, crochet, play bridge and mah-jong, and administer acupuncture.

For Liang Ch'i-ch'ao the years of exile from 1898 to 1912 were crowded with activity. He continued to write, edit, and publish his political views; he studied the Japanese language and read Western books in Japa-nese translation. He traveled widely, visiting overseas Chinese in Hawaii,

Singapore, Australia, Canada, and the United States. Sicheng's memories of these years were of daily life in a peaceful family setting; playing with his brothers, sisters, and cousins; cared for by Japanese servants but attending Chinese schools. Extracts from an article he wrote for a Japanese publication in 1964 give us the story in his own words:

"My memory begins in Yokohama. My father was editing the intellectual review *Hsin-min tsung-pao,* and we lived on the second floor of the publishing office. I went to a kindergarten attached to the Ta-t'ung School, which was run by overseas Chinese. The teachers were all Japanese women. They were very kind and tender, like mothers and elder sisters.

"There are many earthquakes in Japan. Each time there was an earthquake, the Japanese maid took me downstairs in her arms because my mother, with her bound feet, could not easily go down the staircase.

"We moved to Suma when I was about six. There we lived in a villa owned by an overseas Chinese. Its large garden was open to a pine grove that stretched out to the sea. My father called the place 'Shuang-tao yuan' ('double-roar garden') because we could hear the sounds of both the surf and the wind in the pines.

"From the house we walked to the train to Kobe to attend the Kobe Tung-wen School together with my cousins. The conductors on the train were very kind. If we didn't go to school even for a day they were worried and asked us the next day what had happened."

In the summer vacation the family went to swim at the beach. A retired naval officer taught the children to swim with ease underwater. The father's mentor, K'ang Yu-wei, visited them one summer. His presence antagonized the children because he was always arguing loudly and vigorously with their father. They retaliated at the beach by swimming around him underwater trying to deliver surreptitious tugs to his beard.[1]

The overthrow of the Manchu government by the successful revolution of 1911 ended the reason for Liang Ch'i-ch'ao's exile. With his family he returned to China in 1912.

Their home in Tientsin was a large Western-style mansion in the Italian concession on the riverfront. Built of stone and gray brick, it had many rooms on two floors to house the growing family as well as relatives and visitors. There was an extension at the rear for kitchens, storerooms, sickrooms, and quarters for the numerous servants required to serve the family and maintain the household.

After their return from Japan, Liang had a second, even larger house added. Designed by Italian architects and built of white stone, it was three stories high. The upper floors were devoted to housing the scholar's library. On the main floor were a drawing room, hall, dining room, and other areas for receiving guests, but most important, of course, his study. The elder Liang had, in the Chinese scholar's tradition, selected for himself an esoteric or "insider"'s name to identify his writings. His choice was "Ice-drinking Elder" (Yin ping lao jen), and a plaque over the door of his new study named it "The Ice-drinker's Studio" (Yin ping shih). The ice-drinking motif was apparently taken from a tale by the philosopher Chuang-tzu:

> Confucius was asked for advice by Tzu-kao, an official who had just been appointed to a mission in which he had no confidence. The Master said, "Few works, big or small, are achieved with ease. If you fail at doing it, people may be angry with you. If you succeed you may fall ill from over-excitement after long worrying. Only those who have high virtue may be free from both these anxieties."
>
> Tzu-kao replied, "Yes, I have got my appointment this morning and am drinking icy water this evening, because I am white hot inside. I already suffer anxiety within and I fear I won't be free from anxiety without. Such double distress is more than I can bear."[2]

As he dealt with the uncertainties of the modern world, Liang Ch'i-ch'ao apparently recognized in the anxieties and ice-drinking remedy of the ancient worthy, Tzu-kao, a classic parallel to his own life work on the frontier of Chinese learning.

In the Tientsin house there took place a special family custom that Sicheng cherished. When his father was at home the daily practice was for the entire family to sit down together at 6:30 at a round table. "While the children hastily ate their supper in about twenty minutes, father and mother sipped wine. The wine-sipping was leisurely; for about an hour the father talked about the subjects on which he was currently writing—biographies of poets and others, history, political philosophy, the classics, Confucian scholars, and those of the other schools. At this period he was focusing again on Chinese studies. There was very little discussion of the foreign subjects that had concerned him at an earlier age."

A few years later Liang Ch'i-ch'ao's fourth son, Ssu-chung, when he was a student in middle school, put to his father the somewhat tactless question, "Why would a famous Chinese patriot live and build his study and library in a treaty-port foreign concession?" The father responded, "Do not confuse personal matters with international affairs. Next to my family, my chief concern at the moment is my library. I need my books, so I must try to keep them usable. They will be safer in a foreign concession in the nearest port city than in a fire-prone palace that some angry student could unwisely burn down. And to use my books, I must sometimes live near them."

Though his scholarship and his political involvements absorbed much of his attention, Liang took very seriously his role as a father. Personal affection played an important part in his treatment of his children, but he was also guided by the Confucian tradition that sons (and of course daughters) owed special filial piety to the father of the family. The elder Liang was confident of his superior wisdom and concerned to steer his obedient offspring in proper thoughts and behavior, to make sure that their education was appropriate to the careers he envisioned for them, and to see that they married well.

In a book of his letters and other personal writings assembled by his friend V. K. Ting (Ting Wen-jiang) after his death (Liang's *Nien P'u* or *Chronological Biography*, published in Taipei 1958), he makes evident that, though he loved all his family, his favorites were his first-born daughter and eldest son — Ssu-hsun, the Elder Sister, and Sicheng.

Elder Sister was eighteen when the family returned to China from Japan. It was high time to make plans for her marriage.

The husband Liang selected for her was a young overseas Chinese from Southeast Asia named Chou Kuo-hsien. Bilingual in Chinese and English, he had attracted the attention of K'ang Yu-wei at the age of nineteen and was employed by him as his secretary. He subsequently studied in Europe. Liang Ch'i-ch'ao hired him away from K'ang on his return to China, made him his interpreter and secretary, and arranged the marriage with Elder Sister.

In Confucian style a father was an autocrat who need not even consult his children when arranging their affairs. An extract from a letter Liang Ch'i-ch'ao wrote to Elder Sister a decade later[3] reveals that he had modernized the traditional practice of uniting two strangers in wedlock. "I am very proud of your marriage. I think my method is very good. First I carefully observe a person, then I introduce you to each other and let you decide for yourselves. The ideal marriage system I think." Elder Sister's first child, a daughter, was born in Peking in 1915. Chou entered the Chinese Consular Service and began a series of overseas assignments that took them to Burma, the Philippines, and Canada, among other places.

The geographical separation of father and daughter led to a continuing correspondence between the two. Liang's letters to her reproduced in the

Nien P'u show her to have been his confidante. He told her his observations and worries about the family and other personal matters and asked for her views. Although he was very much the traditional all-wise father in his relationships with his other children, with her he consulted on an even footing despite the two decades' difference in their ages. This suggests that she filled a need that neither his tradition-bound wife nor his busy caretaking concubine could meet.

In September of 1913 Liang Ch'i-ch'ao was appointed Minister of Justice. The large mansion and library in Tientsin remained the family home, but it now became necessary to establish a second base in the capital, Peking. A house of numerous courtyards at the edge of the Forbidden City on the north-south street Nan Ch'ang Chieh was made available. It was centrally located, adequate for the growing family and large retinue of servants, and a short distance from the office assigned him in the round battlement, Tuan Ch'eng, at the entrance to the Pei-hai (North Lake Park).

The move to Peking made a marked change in the lives of the children. It was the traditional practice in such families to have the children's elementary education provided by tutors in the home. Sicheng, his brother, and his cousins had attended a Chinese school during the Japan years. The modern-minded father decided that his eldest son, now twelve years old, must learn English and prepare to live in an international future. He was enrolled at a highly regarded Anglican school in Peking and spent the years 1913–1915 there.

The girls, too, were sent to a modern school that could prepare them for functioning in the wider world. Elder Sister was the pioneer. Her father insisted when she became engaged to the bilingual Chou Kuo-hsien that she learn English. An English woman, Miss Bowden Smith, ran a school for girls in Peking established with just this purpose in mind. Once Elder Sister had enrolled and proved its value to the family, the mother became an enthusiastic supporter. She made friends with the English headmistress and arranged for the younger sisters, the girl cousins, and even children of friends to attend the school.

Sicheng entered the preparatory school of Tsinghua College in the fall semester of 1915. The college had been founded with funds remitted in 1908 to China by the United States Congress from China's payments due for the Boxer Indemnity. These funds not only supported the six-year preparatory school and two-year college but also supplied fellowships for outstanding students to pursue further study in American institutions of higher learning.

The curriculum was similar to that of an American high school. English and science were stressed, but also art, music, and athletics. Some of the teachers were Americans and much of the teaching was done in English. Sicheng distinguished himself by his scholarship and artistry. He is not known to have had any prior training in drawing, painting, or music, but in his school years he developed the skill in sketching that was to be so useful to him later on. He was a member of the Tsinghua Art Club and became art editor of the 1923 college annual, *The Tsinghuapper,* for which he drew witty full-page ink drawings and occasional cartoons. In the student listings in the annual, he is identified first as an artist and man of letters and then as "highly musical." As for athletics, he was strong and healthy. He loved running, jumping, rope climbing, and gymnastics.

The Tsinghua campus was located several miles northwest of Peking. Transportation was a problem. Rickshas or bicycles were the fastest but too expensive for students. Donkeys and mule carts were available but inconvenient and slow. Such telephones as there were could not be used by students. They communicated with their families and friends by letter.

Sicheng's comparative isolation during this extended period may well have played a part in his reaction to his Tsinghua education. Looking back twenty-five years later Sicheng commented to me that these eight long years (of middle school and college) provided a good foundation in English and a general background knowledge of Western science and history, but that the educational standards were low and the curriculum "could have been telescoped into four years." His comment disregarded the lifelong benefits he won at Tsinghua from his participation and leadership in such extracurricular activities as art, music, and athletics.

2. Favorite Daughter

Lin Whei-yin was an artist by nature, an architect by training, and a poet by vocation. Like Liang Sicheng, she grew up under the influence of a powerful father, Lin Ch'ang-min. He was an artist and a romantic, and these two attributes were also dominant in her personality.

Lin Ch'ang-min was a well-known scholar and government official whose poetry and calligraphy were prized by his circle. Born in Hangchow in 1876, by the age of twenty-one he had passed the examinations for the *sheng-yuan* (lowest level) degree and begun the study of English and Japanese at the Hangchow Language School. A marriage was arranged for him, but when his wife bore no children he took a concubine to provide him with the necessary son and heir. She bore three children, a son and two daughters. The son died in infancy and the second daughter in childhood. Lin Whei-yin, born in 1904, was the sole survivor.

Like so many bright spirits of his generation, the father went to Japan for several years to attend Waseda University. He graduated with honors in political economy in 1909. Returning to China, he moved his concubine and daughter to Shanghai, where his political life began.

By this time Whei was five years old. She had been living with her mother in Hangchow, surrounded by adults but without father or siblings. She was a precocious child; her precocity may have led the relatives in the household to treat her as an adult and thus cheat her of her childhood. The return of her father must have delighted her, and her quick, bright, and sensitive character must certainly have fascinated him. Perhaps it was in the Shanghai years that they were able to grow close.

The family moved again in 1912, this time to Peking. There the father rose to high official positions in the various governments. But at some time in this period he faced the fact that there was still no son and heir to continue the family line. He took a second concubine, from Fukien, who bore him in quick succession a daughter and four sons.

A shadow then fell on the life of Whei-yin. The second concubine and her growing brood were housed in the large front courtyard of their Peking house. It was full of the noise and activity of happy children. Whei and her mother lived in a smaller courtyard at the back. Whei's mother was consumed by jealousy of the second concubine. That her successor should be the mother of four sons was reason enough, but that the father preferred her and did not disguise his preference was unbearably humiliating to Whei's mother. The sensitive daughter was caught between them. She shared the outraged confidences of the mother and at the same time cherished the father and was aware of his love for her. His second family admit that she remained his favorite.

A new and very important chapter in Whei's life began in 1919, when she was fifteen. Lin Ch'ang-min had developed a close friendship with Liang Ch'i-ch'ao. Each of them had spent some years in Japan and had held high offices in the post-revolutionary Peking governments. That they would conceive the idea of merging their families by a marriage between Liang's favorite son and Lin's favorite daughter is not surprising. In 1919 the two young people were "formally introduced." This was a notable departure from the traditional family practice of marrying two utter strangers, selected by go-betweens, who would meet for the first time during the wedding ceremony. Whei was fifteen and Sicheng was eighteen; according to tradition, marriage between the two at their tender ages would have been regarded as normal. But the elder Liang made plain to them that, though their fathers favored the match, the decision was left to them. Four more years went by before that decision was reached, and much was to happen to each of them in the interim.

In the summer of 1920 Whei-yin left Peking and went with her father halfway around the world to London. When the League of Nations was established after the end of World War I, the Chinese, like supportive groups elsewhere, created their own League of Nations Association. Lin Ch'ang-min was a co-founder and became director of the organization. He went on League business to London for an extended stay and took his favorite daughter with him for companionship. Whei's acquaintance with the English language obtained at schools in Shanghai and Peking made her useful as well as pleasant company. She resumed her studies in London at St. Mary's Collegiate School, a girls' seminary, and soon became bilingual.

Travelers from all parts of the world converged on London after the hostilities ended. As her father's hostess, Whei met numerous Chinese and other visitors who came to pay their respects to him. Her household encounters were undoubtedly as influential in her education as her formal schooling.

The most important of these visitors was Hsü Chih-mo, a young disciple of Liang Ch'i-ch'ao who came to the Lins with an introduction from his mentor. The son of a prominent banker in Chekiang, he had as a youth been trained in the Chinese classics. He had married in 1915 and fathered a son. Leaving his wife and child in the care of his parents, he had finished his college education in Peking and gone abroad in 1918 for advanced study in the United States. What to study seems to have been a problem for him. The first year he elected economics and sociology at Clark University in Worcester, Massachusetts. The second year he transferred to Columbia University in New York and took up political science. By his third year, the war in Europe was over and he could sail for England to start afresh. This time he was planning to study with his new idol, Bertrand Russell, at Cambridge University. He crossed the Atlantic in October 1920 only to learn when he reached London that Russell had not yet returned from a trip to China and, furthermore, had been expelled from Cambridge University some years before. Consequently, Hsü was "feeling deeply depressed and searching for new direction."[1]

Nevertheless, the characteristics of his personality that had in the past attracted Liang Ch'i-ch'ao were evident beneath his dejection. They were his discernment, his charm, his spontaneity, his humor, his creative zest, his dramatic presence. Above all, he became famous for his uncanny ability to find and gather kindred spirits and to ignite in those who surrounded him new concepts, new aspirations, and, not least, new friendships.

That Lin Ch'ang-min and Hsü were kindred spirits must have been obvious to both on that first meeting. Hsü became a constant visitor to the household. Relishing the responsiveness of his guest, Lin confided in him at length. Among other memories, he told of his early love affair with a Japanese girl during his student days in Japan. This may have awakened in Hsü his own romantic longings. The two men practiced putting these emotions into words in a playful exchange of "love letters," with Hsü taking the role of a married woman and Lin that of a married man.[2]

Hsü was nearly ten years older than Whei. As an "older man," his original attachment to the father, not the daughter, was understandable to both. It is even said that in the beginning he was "Uncle Hsü" to her. She had a delicate beauty that attracted immediate attention. Her artistic temperament so like her father's, her liveliness, her lightning perceptions, her literary bent were all enthralling to Hsü. He fell in love.

Listening to her talking of Hsü years later, I noticed that her memories were always linked with literary names—Shelley, Keats, Byron, Katherine

Mansfield, Virginia Woolf, and others. It occurred to me that in his devotion he may have assumed the role of teacher and guide, leading her into the world of English poetry and drama, the new beauty, new ideals, and new feelings that were captivating him at the same time. In this way he could delight in her sensitive reactions to the books he loved and the dreams he cherished. He could weave a spell.

I have the impression that she was entranced with Hsü's personality, his enthusiasms, and his ardent feelings for her. She was not, however, as some have imagined, a sophisticated woman at the age of sixteen. She was a schoolgirl living in her father's house. Hsü's passion for her did not call forth an equal response from the inexperienced girl. His entry into her life was a great adventure. But it did not tempt her to break out of the future course her family had chosen for her.

Through Lin Ch'ang-min, Hsü met Goldsworthy Lowes Dickinson, British litterateur and Sinophile, who, much taken with Hsü, arranged for him to enter Kings College, Cambridge, as a special student in 1921. Dickinson's familiarity both with Cambridge and with the principal figures in English literature past and present were to open a new world to Hsü. His restless pursuit of economics and political science gave way to a lasting commitment to the study and writing of poetry. At last his temperament had found the expression that would focus all his emotions and employ all his talents.

The romantic poet, Hsü, worshiped love and beauty but regarded freedom as equally important. He had found in Whei the very image of his dreams. He imagined that, spending his life with her, he could reach the peak of his creativity. Weighted against such a future, his obligations to his wife and child were light as a feather.

Picture, then, his reaction when he learned that his parents in China were sending his wife to join him in England. She arrived in the spring of 1921. They moved into a rented house in Sawston, six miles from Cambridge. He took a bus to the college each day to attend classes and use the library. He had arranged a mail drop at a local grocery to which Whei in London could mail letters, which he eagerly sought and promptly answered. His wife stayed through the summer and became pregnant. In the fall he recommended an abortion, left for London, and sent word that he wanted a divorce. She left soon after for Germany, where her second son was born and soon died.

It may have been at this point that he announced to Whei his intention to get a divorce and asked her to marry him. There is no question that she loved and admired him and was overwhelmed with gratitude that he had widened her horizons and awakened in her new emotions and new ambitions. But marriage? Sicheng himself told me that, whatever other confusions this episode may have roused, the years of living with her heartbroken mother made her recoil at the very thought of a divorce in which an unloved wife would be set aside and she would be expected to take her place.

Whei's father, who was also devoted to Hsü, apparently decided now that after more than a year in London the moment had come to leave the complications of life there and turn homeward with Whei. They embarked on a long journey by ship through Suez and the Indian Ocean and reached home in October 1921.

Relieved of both women, Hsü returned to Cambridge. "That was the time," he wrote, "I finally had the chance to draw close to the life of the real Cambridge, and at the same time I slowly began to 'discover' Cambridge. Never had I known such intense happiness."[3] His circle of friends there included Dickinson, E. M. Forster, H. G. Wells, I. A. Richards, Bertrand Russell, Roger Fry, Arthur Waley, and John Middleton Murry, who took him to meet Katherine Mansfield, an encounter that moved him deeply.[4] The special joys of this year were being alone with his friends, alone with his own thoughts, and alone with nature. These emotions found their expression in what was apparently his first outflowing of poetry. He also wrote a deeply felt panegyric to the university itself that began, "My eyes were opened by Cambridge, my appetite for knowledge was stimulated by Cambridge, my concept of 'self' was nursed by Cambridge."[5] The beauty of the ancient stone buildings and the peaceful green countryside bewitched him. He was at home in the English language. Reading the romantic poetry of Keats, Shelley and Byron, Wordsworth and Swinburne, intoxicated him. He was impelled to express in his own language the profound personal yearnings, ideals, and romantic dreams inspired in him by the great British poets.

Classical Chinese poetry he knew from his youth. He had of course used the vernacular language all his life, and a few young Chinese scholars were championing its adoption as a poetic medium. That Hsü should find poetry a natural outlet for his emotions is not surprising. His poems, springing both from these native fonts and from the Cambridge stimulus, were to attain an extraordinary influence in the next decade.

After a full year of exhilaration at Cambridge, he turned homeward and reached Shanghai on October 15, 1922.

3. Their Teens

Liang Ch'i-ch'ao went to Europe at the end of 1918 to attend the Versailles Peace Conference. From his base in Paris he spent several months of 1919 visiting England and touring the continent. He returned to China for what was to be the last decade of his life intent on devoting his main energies to reexamining all aspects of Chinese civilization. He was also worried that the Tsinghua education his sons were receiving, in its concentration on English and the natural sciences, was depriving them of the knowledge of Chinese culture in which he had been steeped at the same age.

The time had come to intensify the informal family educational process that the father had conducted through the years as a low-key evening ritual. The summers of 1920, 1921, and 1922 were devoted to this end. Liang Ch'i-ch'ao organized, in effect, a school of Chinese studies for a select student body consisting of his sons Sicheng and Ssu-yung, their cousins, and his younger disciples at his home in Tientsin. He devoted the mornings from 9 to 12 to lectures that were interrupted from time to time by students' questions. In the afternoon, from 3 to 5, the students prepared stencils from Liang's lectures and mimeographed the day's lessons. The lectures were later published.

The effect on his sons of this daily immersion not only in the ideas of their father but even in reproducing his notably expressive style was profound. Sicheng noted that his father's methodology in particular greatly influenced him and his brother. That both brothers went on to careers of great distinction in Chinese studies, Sicheng in the history of Chinese architecture, Ssu-yung in Chinese archaeology, attests to the wisdom and force of the father's teaching — as well as the extraordinary capabilities of the sons.

During his stay in England, the father had been impressed with H. G. Wells's *Outline of History,* which was widely popular in England and the United States at that time and was being translated into many languages. A Chinese translation was needed; he would have liked to do it himself, but, as he wrote Elder Sister, "because my English is not adequate, my sons volunteered." With the cooperation of a young historian, Hsu Chung-shu, the two brothers undertook this task in the summer of 1921 and were still at it in the following February.

Their father's motivations were several. He obviously wanted to expose his sons to world history as currently viewed in the West. At the same time, the assignment would be a rigorous test of their recently acquired English language capabilities. Finally, it would be valuable practice in developing their Chinese writing style. As he wrote to Elder Sister in the same letter, "Since I want to teach my two sons Chinese, this summer I have spent half-days, and even now two hours daily, correcting their translations. So though the translations are alleged to be by 'the kids,' they are actually by me. Sometimes I could accomplish only a thousand words in half a day, whereas if I wrote it myself I could write four thousand words in that time." The manuscript was completed by the end of March 1922. It was published in two volumes by the Commercial Press in Shanghai in 1927.

At this time Elder Sister and her family were living in the Philippines, where her husband was assigned as Chinese Consul General in Manila. Her mother had come from Tientsin for a visit and possibly for medical consultation. During her stay in Manila she had an operation for cancer. The father dispatched Sicheng to Manila in the summer of 1922 to bring her home to Tientsin. Writing to his father on his arrival, he reported that the mother was "completely recovered from her serious illness."[1] Freed from these worries, he proceeded, on orders from his father, to buy a British automobile for family use and, as a gift from Elder Sister, a Harley-Davidson motorcycle for himself. Both were shipped home as cargo on their vessel.

The return of Whei and her father to China in late 1921 reopened the question of her marriage to Sicheng. By the beginning of 1923 they had made up their minds. On January 7, Liang Ch'i-ch'ao wrote to Elder Sister, "Sicheng and Whei have promised to marry each other." He added an important note, "I told them that they should finish their studies before they are engaged, and once they are engaged they should marry soon. But the Lin family want them to be engaged immediately, and so do most of our friends. What is your opinion?"

Liang's advice was followed. The engagement was not announced until the autumn of 1927 and the marriage did not take place until March 1928. The father was concerned about Whei's education as well as Sicheng's. Birth control was not known or available. Starting a family in the first year of marriage would have disrupted the education of the young couple and involved them in expenses and responsibilities beyond their means.

The same week the elder Liang wrote another letter of cautionary wisdom. It was addressed to Hsü Chih-mo. Like many others, the father loved and admired the young poet who had long been his devoted disciple. Yet he was also well aware of the dangers posed by Hsü's unbridled "wild horse" temperament. Hsü had obtained his divorce in March 1922. The intention of Liang Ch'i-ch'ao's long letter was both to reprimand Hsü for abandoning his wife and to protect Whei and Sicheng from the disruption Hsü was quite capable of creating. Without mentioning Whei in his letter, he urged Hsü not "to build one's happiness upon others' suffering" and not "to pursue the perfect state of bliss in a dream."[2]

Whei still admired and loved Hsü, but her life was firmly joined to that of Sicheng. Fixed in that long-term decision, she could throw herself into the company Hsü was founding, the Hsin Yueh She, the Crescent Moon Society. This was a group of young writers active in the *pai-hua* movement, which promoted the now generally accepted use of the vernacular language for literary purposes.[3]

This was the start of Whei's writing career. She wrote her first poems, short stories, and essays. But her first published work was, according to Sicheng, a translation of Oscar Wilde's romantic prose poem, "The Nightingale and the Rose."[4] Where it was published I have not discovered, but it may have been in the literary supplements of certain Peking and Tientsin newspapers, which were important outlets for the group in the beginning.

Peking was in a ferment of cultural activity during the early 1920s and was particularly hospitable to cultural visitors from abroad. This development fired Hsü's enthusiasm for introducing Chinese audiences to Western artistic achievements. He and Whei were responsible for arranging the highly successful concert performance of Fritz Kreisler, the violinist, which for the first time brought a famous Western artist to the Chinese capital to perform leading works of Western classical music.

Sicheng was in his final year at Tsinghua and was scheduled to leave in June with classmates for advanced education in the United States on Boxer Indemnity fellowships. He planned to go to the University of Pennsylvania for training in architecture. This inspired decision he owed to Whei. As he told me many years later, she had a schoolmate in London who spent hours leaning over a drawing board drawing houses. Whei was fascinated. Her friend, in response to eager questioning, described the profession of architect. On the spot Whei decided that that was the profession she wanted, a lifework that combined daily artistic creativity with immediate usefulness. After her return to China, she had no difficulty in leading Sicheng to the same decision. He had always loved drawing and had thought vaguely of a career as an artist. Architecture made sense to him and pursuing it together made sense to both.

On May 7, 1923, Sicheng, Ssu-yung, and their next younger brother came in to Peking from the Western Hills for the anniversary demonstrations protesting the National Humiliation caused by the Japanese ultimatum of May 7, 1915, which had demanded — and achieved — control by Japan over the areas of Shantung Province formerly held by the Germans. The family's large courtyard house was on Nan Ch'ang Chieh, an important, centrally located north-south street. Its southern end, a short distance from the Liangs' house, opened into the busy east-west boulevard, Ch'ang-an Chieh, which skirts the front of T'ien An Men. About eleven A.M. Sicheng wheeled out his motorcycle, the gift from Elder Sister, and with Ssu-yung riding on the back headed southward to find the demonstrations. As they turned into the boulevard they were hit from the side by a big car. The motorcycle was overturned by the blow. It fell heavily, throwing Ssu-yung clear but pinning Sicheng to the ground. The official riding in the car ordered his chauffeur to drive on.

Ssu-yung, bleeding from his wounds, got to his feet and was shocked to discover his brother lying unconscious on the pavement. He ran home at once, frightening the family with his bloody appearance, and cried out, "Hurry! Save Sicheng! He has been badly hurt." A servant went to the rescue and carried Sicheng home. His face was bloodless and his eyes unmoving. After about twenty minutes he regained consciousness and blood returned to his face. His father leaned over him, holding his hand. "He grasped my hand and kissed my face," Liang Ch'i-ch'ao wrote "and said to me, 'Father, I am your unfilial son. Before you and mother fully give this body of mine into my keeping, I have already damaged it. Pay no attention to me, and especially don't tell mother. Where is Elder Sister, how can I see her?'"[5]

"At that time my heart was almost broken," wrote the father. "I could only say, 'It's all right. Don't worry.' When I saw blood returning to his face I felt comforted. I thought if he could live, even as a cripple, I would be grateful. Later the doctor arrived and gave him a comprehensive examination. He concluded there was nothing wrong above the waist, only his left leg was broken and he sent him to the hospital by ambulance." During this time Ssu-yung was busy caring for Sicheng with the others. Afterward he fell asleep, and the family began to worry about him; so he too was sent off to the hospital. There he was found to have only cut lips and a small bruise on his leg. The brothers shared a hospital room, Ssu-yung to be discharged in a week but Sicheng to stay there eight weeks.

At first the surgeons at the hospital informed the family that Sicheng did not need surgery because the bone was not broken. It needed only to be bound tightly and would then recover naturally. The diagnosis was incorrect, and proper care was fatally deferred. He had in fact suffered a compound fracture of the thigh bone. By the end of May he had undergone surgery three times. A hopeful letter from the father to Elder Sister reported that the leg was now completely aligned and Sicheng would "walk like a normal person." This was not to be. The left leg from that time on was notably shorter than the right. The inevitable effect was a lifelong limp and eventually a spinal weakness that required him to wear a back brace. For a man whose career was to involve long walking in the countryside and climbing over the roofs and beams of structures to examine them, these handicaps would be hard to bear.

Characteristically, the father took this opportunity to turn the enforced passivity of his lively eldest son to good use. Within two weeks or so of the accident he was pressing Sicheng to review the classics, beginning with the Analects of Confucius and the works of Mencius. "In these two months you ought to be able to digest and presumably memorize those passages that will be useful for self-cultivation. Next you must read completely the *Tso Chuan* and the *Chan Kuo Tse*. These two would enrich your wisdom and help your writing style. If you still have time read some *Hsun Tzu,* that would be even better."

These classics had been standard fare for examination candidates during the last eight hundred years. Here Liang Ch'i-ch'ao, the leader of reform, had evidently returned to his roots in Neo-Confucianism and at the same time decided that memorizing classics would be a useful addition to Tsinghua's nondescript curriculum.

Sicheng's mother was outraged at the official whose car had hit her sons and run. She called on the President of the Republic to demand that he chastise the official. In the end, it was decided that the chauffeur had been at fault, but until the President apologized for his underling the mother was not satisfied.[6]

The mother meanwhile had other worries. It was a hot summer, and the patient lay in bed stripped to the waist. His beautiful Whei, who had been devastated at news of the accident, came daily to see him in the hospital. Without any sign of the prescribed diffidence, she sat at the edge of his bed every afternoon to talk with him earnestly, to joke with or comfort him. His mother was shocked at the behavior of this generation. At the same time Whei won the respect and gratitude of Liang Ch'i-ch'ao by taking his dictation of letters to Elder Sister to keep her informed throughout this critical period. Elder Sister, too, we learn later, had her doubts about having this modern girl added to the family.

Sicheng was not discharged from the hospital until July 31, by which time his father had already decided, backed by the doctor, that his plan to go to the United States for advanced study that summer must be postponed for a year. "If your body has not completely recovered," his father wrote him, "you may get into troubles during your travels. It is not worth the risk. The journey of life is rather long; a year or a month doesn't matter. Don't be disappointed or worried, or let yourself get depressed. Your life has been too smooth. Small difficulties can be a good opportunity to develop your character. Moreover, if you prepare yourself during one year more in China nothing is lost as far as study is concerned."[7]

Sicheng duly deferred his departure to the summer of 1924. Whei was meanwhile continuing her writing, completing her schooling in Peking, and planning now to leave with him and enter Penn Architectural School at the same time.

Hsü Chih-mo had replied to Liang Ch'i-ch'ao's cautionary letter reprimanding him about his divorce with a long emotional letter of his own reiterating his ideals. In it he stated his resolve, "I shall search for my soul's companion in the sea of humanity: if I find her, it is my fortune; if not, it is my fate." Whei's name was not mentioned.

Liang Ch'i-ch'ao apparently concluded that the problem no longer affected his family; he spent much of the summer of 1923 with Hsü. They both taught at Nankai University in Tientsin, Hsü lecturing for two weeks on modern English literature. Hsü was writing poetry in the new vernacular style, and many of his poems had appeared in print. In the autumn of 1923 he characteristically gathered his kindred spirits to share the aesthetic delights of Hangchow's West Lake. His popularity and influence were growing. He accepted an invitation to teach at Peking University in 1924.

Liang Ch'i-ch'ao and Lin Ch'ang-min were moving spirits in the Lecture Association of Peking, which had sponsored the visits of Russell and others to bring to Chinese audiences the views of celebrated thinkers in the outside world. Hsü Chih-mo had from the first enthusiastically endorsed an invitation to the celebrated Indian poet, Rabindranath Tagore. He met Tagore's boat in Shanghai on April 12, 1924, traveled with him throughout his seven weeks in China, and acted as his interpreter, translating Tagore's English to Chinese. There was an immediate affinity between the two poets. Shortly after they met, they spent a memorable evening together in a boat on Hangchow's West Lake, where they composed and talked about poetry until dawn.[8] Tagore reached Peking on April 23, where he was warmly received by Liang Ch'i-ch'ao, Lin Ch'ang-min, Hu Shih, and many other leading intellectuals.

Tagore thought of his visit as symbolizing the ancient religious link between India and China. He had come to strengthen the unity of the two great countries in their Asian spirituality, which, synthesized with Western practicality, could, he maintained, become the foundation of a new world civilization. His audiences of students and intellectuals in Peking numbered in the thousands. Many were attracted by his renown as a recipient of the Nobel Prize for literature. The drawing power of his interpreter, the gifted poet Hsü Chih-mo, was surely a factor as well. Hsü persuaded Whei to act as co-interpreter during Tagore's stay in Peking. The two were in constant attendance on him as he moved from occasion to occasion among the welcoming or curious crowds. The romantic aura generated by Tagore himself enveloped them. With him, they became public figures. The sight of the tall, white-haired old sage flanked by this dashing young pair was turned into something of a legend.[9]

The high point of Tagore's Peking visit was a festive party held on May 8 to celebrate his sixty-third birthday. It was arranged by Hsü's recently formed Crescent Moon Society, which had taken its name from Tagore's book of prose poems, *Crescent Moon*. Four hundred of Peking's most distinguished citizens attended the party. After the speeches and gifts, the guest was honored with a performance of *Chitra*, a play that he had written in English. The cast included Whei as a princess and Hsü as the god of love.

The next morning Tagore delivered the first of seven lectures he had prepared. It elicited sharp criticism from some young members of the audience. His second lecture, the next day, encountered what was obviously organized opposition. Tagore was very disturbed when he discovered that leaflets had been distributed among the audience indicting him as a reactionary who preached spirituality but was indifferent to China's present difficulties.

Beginning in 1923 the left in China, led by the small Communist Party, had begun a vigorous campaign against the "cultural imperialism" of Christian missions. To these dialectical materialists, Tagore was like fresh meat in a lion's den. He announced that his next lecture would be his last, that he was canceling the remainder. Some two thousand turned up for this final lecture. Hsü Chih-mo and Hu Shih defended the poet, but, pleading physical and mental fatigue, Tagore left for a respite in the Western Hills that lasted for most of his final week.

May 20, the day of Tagore's departure, was a day of emotional farewells. The poet himself may have breathed a sigh of relief at escaping his radical tormentors. But he regretted parting from Whei, whose unfailing presence and youthful loveliness had gladdened his days. He wrote a poem for her:

> The blue of the sky
> fell in love with the green of the earth
> The breeze between them sighs "Alas!"

For Hsü and Whei the parting had a special poignancy. Hsü had confided to Tagore in private talks that he was still in love with Whei, and the elderly poet himself had interceded and failed to win her heart.[10] Yet in the last weeks she and Hsü had shared a time of intimate caretaking of their revered Indian sage. Together they had played public roles, dramatic and exciting, under the eyes of thousands, and sensed the sudden fame that Hsü's person and poetry had attained.

Whei left for the United States within the next month and did not return to China for four years. Hsü accompanied Tagore to Japan and after returning to China that summer plunged into still another romantic tangle.

4. Professional Studies

The Architectural School of the University of Pennsylvania in Philadelphia was in 1924 a stronghold of the Beaux-Arts tradition, dominated by a distinguished French architect, Paul P. Cret (1876–1945). Cret himself had entered the Paris École des Beaux Arts in 1896 and undergone its intensive training not only in all aspects of architectural design and construction but also in two other of the disciplines which he passed on to his students in the United States and which were to play an important part in Liang's subsequent career: the study in depth of the history of architecture and the mastery of clear and beautifully executed architectural rendering, including the necessary lettering. Cret had been invited to the University of Pennsylvania in 1905 as a recent graduate of the École des Beaux Arts who showed exceptional promise both as an architect and as a teacher. His early promise was more than borne out in later years when he won competitions with his designs of such handsome structures as the Pan American Union and Federal Reserve buildings in Washington and the Detroit Institute of Arts. He continued to play an influential role as teacher at the Penn Architectural School until his retirement in 1937.

Sicheng and Whei enrolled at the University of Pennsylvania for the opening of the fall term in 1924, as did Sicheng's close friend and Tsinghua roommate, Ch'en Chih. According to Ch'en's recollection, the three traveled together from China and spent the summer months at Cornell University in Ithaca, New York, taking preliminary courses and adjusting to the new environment. On July 7 Sicheng wrote home that he had selected for his summer school studies still-life painting in watercolor, outdoor painting, and trigonometry and hoped that with this preparation he could "become a second-year architectural student or even more advanced." Meanwhile he was awed by the famous setting of the university on a high ridge overlooking Lake Cayuga. "The mountains are clear and the water is brilliant. The place is extremely beautiful."

During that summer it became clear at home that Sicheng's mother was dying of cancer. By mid-August his father wrote to a friend that he had decided to ask Sicheng to come back to China "to repay adequately his indebtedness to her. . . . This disease is very cruel. She always needs someone to take care of her. . . . The concubine is pregnant and needs Sicheng's help."[1] Just a month later, on September 13, his mother died. Whether the son was actually ordered home is almost irrelevant. If he had taken the three-day transcontinental train trip and caught even the earliest available ship for the long sea voyage across the Pacific, he could not have arrived in time.

Whei, arriving with Sicheng and Ch'en from Cornell to begin their professional training at Penn, made the unsettling discovery that the Architectural School was for men only. The explanation leaked out: architectural students had to work on their drafting at all hours of the night, and the unchaperoned presence of women would be improper. She had no choice but to enroll with other women in the university's School of Fine Arts. It had been her enthusiasm for the profession that had inspired both Sicheng and Ch'en to come to Penn. That she herself should be denied the training was unbearable. In fact, she did not accept it. The university's records reveal that by the spring term of 1926 she was a Part-time Assistant to the Architectural Design Staff and for the academic year 1926–1927 she was a Part-time Instructor in Architectural Design.

How she managed to break through the regulations we don't know. Yet even in their first year Whei was attending classes with Sicheng. A young instructor in the Architectural School, later a noted architect, John Harbeson, reported that their renderings in India ink were "marvelous."

That first year saw an emotional struggle between Whei and Sicheng that broke out at times in bitter quarrels. Their great differences of personality and temperament would involve an adjustment they had to work out in the interval before their marriage.

According to fellow students, the Boxer scholars from China were regarded as very formal and dour, except for "Phyllis," as Whei was known there, and "Benjamin" Ch'en. She was exceptionally pretty, vivacious and quick-witted, fluent in English, and by nature deeply responsive to her surroundings. "Ben" Ch'en, who sang in the University Glee Club, was the most Westernized of the scholars and the most popular male. He was always laughing, very funny, and full of jokes.

As for Sicheng, was he formal and dour? There is no question that he was a serious and concentrated scholar then as throughout his life. That was his nature. His notions of the relationship appropriate to their "not quite engaged" status probably differed markedly from Whei's. She was relishing the freedoms of the United States, and her popularity among both sexes was intoxicating. She had left her family and the constraints of her culture and conquered in this new world. No wonder that she fought fiercely if Sicheng, feeling not only devoted to but responsible for her, tried to control her activities.

This mutual struggle Liang Ch'i-ch'ao reported to Elder Sister in strong language: "Sicheng and Whei have lived some months this year in a Buddhist hell. They have been through the hill-of-sharp-knives and the forest-of-dangerous-swords. This kind of hell-on-earth is more frightful than the thirteen torture chambers of hell . . . but if there is repentance, after punishment heaven can result." And he observed, "All of us are in this cycle of reincarnation. We don't know how many heavens and hells we go through in our lifetimes."[2]

Sooner or later they learned to make allowances for each other without sacrificing their individual and very disparate temperaments. During these student years, the characteristic differences in their ways of working asserted themselves. Whei, full of creative ideas, would start to draft a plan or elevation. As the work progressed, alterations and improvements would suggest themselves and be incorporated, only to be themselves discarded in favor of still better ideas. As the deadline approached for completion of the drawing, even more furious work and longer hours at the drawing board would be inadequate to turn in the neat finished drawing required. At this point Sicheng would step in and reduce the frenzied product to a clear finished presentation in his precise and elegant draftsmanship. This kind of collaboration, in which each contributed to the architectural work of the other according to his or her own special gifts, persisted throughout their professional life together.

Sicheng recalled an incident at Penn that had taken place shortly after his arrival in 1924 and made a lasting impression. Alfred Gumaer, Professor of Architectural History, was giving a sophomore course in which Sicheng was enrolled. After the first few lectures, he went up to Gumaer to tell him that he found himself very much interested in architectural history — that he had not known there was anything so interesting. Gumaer in response asked him about *Chinese* architectural history. Sicheng replied that he thought there was nothing written on it; the Chinese had never considered architecture an art and had never paid much attention to it. But he wondered. At that time all the students were studying period architecture. Sicheng did a few problems in Chinese architecture based on Ernst Boerschmann's book of photographs of characteristic Chinese building types.

Within a few years after Sicheng completed his architectural training in the United States, the Beaux-Arts tradition would be supplanted by the Bauhaus-International-style curriculum, with Walter Gropius, Mies van der Rohe, and others as the influential leaders. At times in the 1930s and '40s I heard Sicheng express a wistful regret that he had just missed this induction into the contemporary movements of architecture. Nevertheless, for an architect-scholar destined to lead a unique enterprise in recovering the history of Chinese architecture, there were aspects of his Beaux-Arts training that were crucial to his later success.

Sicheng himself mentioned examples of the problems in architectural history set for the students at Penn that proved very useful to him in his later work in China. Typical assignments were to finish an unfinished cathedral in its appropriate style, to design a triumphal arch according to its historical period without making original departures, or to restore ruined buildings. Helpful, too, were the measured drawings of Roman buildings made by Prix de Rome students that he saw in exhibitions. In his final year at Penn, Sicheng made an extensive study of the Renaissance architecture of Italy. By comparing plans, façades, and other architectural features, he traced the structural developments throughout the period. The significance of this training cannot be overemphasized. We do not have his Renaissance project for reference, but we do have the important analogous drawings he made in China within the next fifteen years, which illustrate his conclusions on the evolution of Chinese architecture. His skill in draftsmanship was of course very important in carrying out these assignments; as always he continued particularly to enjoy drawing.

During his student years, Sicheng's abilities were recognized by the award of two gold medals and other honors for his designs. Nevertheless he had periods of feeling inadequate, which he confessed to his father. The elder Liang's sententious advice was, "Immerse yourself in your work. You feel that your own talent does not correspond to what you expect and that the monotonous training you have been through in these years will turn you into a mere craftsman. I think if you have this kind of feeling, you will make some advance in this stage of your learning. I am pleased to hear it. Mencius says, 'A master can only teach you the basics. He cannot make you gifted.' Those who learn the basics will afterward become skillful if they have the potential. . . . Whether you will have great achievement and to what extent of course depends on your talent. All my life I have treasured two sentences of Tseng Kuo-fan [the late Ch'ing paragon of moral advice], 'Don't ask what your harvest will be. Just consider how much you put into cultivation.'"[3]

As for Whei, we have a brief picture of her as a student at Penn from an interview in January 1926 seemingly by an American fellow student writing for his hometown paper.

"She sat on a stool by the window overlooking a campus walk, perched in front of a desk in the drafting room, a small figure to be bent over a massive architectural problem which when hung in the judgment hall with 30 to 40 others will receive a high award. This is not a rash prediction; her work has always received the highest grades or occasionally second. Quiet but with a sense of humor, unassuming, personal achievements did not once enter her conversation.

"'I travelled all through Europe with my father. During my travels I dreamed for the first time of studying architecture. The splendor of the classics of the modern west inspired me, filled me with desire to carry some back to my country. We need the theories of sound construction which enable your buildings to stand for centuries.'

"'And then I went to school in England. The English girls don't become friendly right away like Americans. Their conventions seem to make them unnaturally reserved.'

"'What do you think of American girls? — Flappers.'

"Soft laughter replied. A dimple appeared on her cheek, smooth and delicately tinted. Her thin blue-black brows rose toward her dusky hair bobbed in strict collegiate fashion.

"'At first my aunts were not going to let me come to America. They dreaded these "flappers" and they were afraid that I might become influenced and start flappering too. I have to admit that in the beginning I thought them very silly but now I think that when you get beneath the top layer you will find them the best companions in the world. In China a girl is worth only as much as her family stands for. Here there is a spirit of democracy that I admire.'"[4]

In the middle of her student years at Penn, Whei suffered the loss of her dear father under bizarre circumstances. He was killed at the age of forty-nine by a stray bullet in Manchuria while escaping from a coup in Peking. His devoted friend Liang Ch'i-ch'ao had the sad duty of informing Whei in a series of letters reporting at first rumors and fears and finally the confirmation of his death. In letters then and later, he told them what they must already have realized, that all their future plans were affected. Lin Ch'ang-min's second concubine would return with her children to the family home in Fukien, but Whei's mother, in Fukien for the moment, would be for the rest of her life dependent on Sicheng for support. The necessity for him to find employment was therefore urgent. From this time forward the father bent his energies toward Sicheng's future, in particular to locating a position appropriate for him on his return to China.

Sicheng and Whei both completed their studies at Penn in 1927. He was awarded his Bachelor of Architecture degree in February and his Master of Architecture degree in June. She received her Bachelor of Fine Arts degree in February with high honors, finishing the four-year course in three.[5] Perhaps the prize they most treasured was that Cret employed them both as assistants in his office that summer.

With their studies completed, the time had come for their long-deferred formal engagement. Letters from Sicheng's father in Tientsin made clear that he took very seriously the need for observing all the traditional rituals. He called on a friend to arrange the comparing of horoscopes, to note the place and time of birth of each and the names for three generations. Two expensive ritual jades and a pair of seals were purchased as engagement gifts. The fact that the concerned couple were on the other side of the earth was not permitted to diminish the formality. "Because the wedding ceremony will likely be held in the USA," wrote the father, "we have to be especially solemn and careful about this engagement. In the morning after we get up we will have an audience with the ancestors reporting to them on this engagement. Both families will use the right forms to notify all the elder relatives and at noontime we will hold a banquet for the guests, followed by a happy banquet for the whole family in the evening." A copy of the memorial to the ancestors was mailed to Sicheng to keep.[6]

Young Sicheng was as concerned about his future as was his father. Penn had certified him as a trained architect, but he chose to devote some additional months in the United States to preparing himself also for teaching. At the moment he may have known that his father was pressing Tsinghua to employ him, though it had no architecture department. In any case he was aware that he would need for teaching a wider acquaintance with scholarly writings; he wanted particularly to find out what, if anything, was being or had been published in the West on his special interest, Chinese architecture. Consequently he applied in August 1927 for admission to the Harvard Graduate School of Arts and Sciences, describing his aim as "Research in Oriental architecture. The supreme importance of the study of the edifices and their preservation inspired my choice of subject." His application was accepted, and he left Philadelphia for Cambridge in

September 1927. Lin Whei-yin, who had long been enchanted by the world of theater, decided to go to Yale University's School of Drama for a course in stage design.

At some time during Sicheng's years at the University of Pennsylvania, his father had sent him a reprint of a newly rediscovered book, *Ying-tsao fa-shih* ("Building Standards"), written in A.D. 1100 by Li Chieh, Vice-Director of the Department of Works at the court of Emperor Hui-tsung of the Sung Dynasty. Published in 1103, it was a builder's handbook of rules for the construction of the palaces in the capital of Northern Sung. Before forwarding it to his son, Liang Ch'i-ch'ao had examined it himself and commented in his accompanying letter, "A thousand years ago to have a masterpiece like this . . . what a glory to the culture of our race!" Sicheng read the book at once but, he admitted later, without fully understanding it. He could see, however, that his father had opened for him an important gateway for researching the history of Chinese architecture.

Meanwhile he intended to acquaint himself through the Harvard library collections with other relevant works in both Western and Eastern languages. He devoted the first semester of the academic year 1927–1928 to intensive reading. Harvard's Lecturer on Oriental Art, Langdon Warner, helped him to find the principal books from which he could learn how Westerners approached Chinese art and architecture. Much of the material was familiar to him, but he was interested to learn how the courses and books on these subjects were organized — Arthur Waley and Ernest Fenellosa on Chinese painting, R. L. Hobson and A. L. Hetherington on Chinese ceramics, Berthold Laufer on jade, Osvald Siren on sculpture. As for Chinese architectural history, at that time the two pioneers in the West were Siren, who had written *The Walls and Gates of Peking* (London, 1924) and *The Imperial Palaces of Peking* (Paris, 1926), and Ernst Boerschmann, whose books were *Picturesque China* (New York, 1923) and *Chinesische Architektur* (Vols. 1–2; Berlin, 1925). Sicheng commented in 1947, "Neither knew the grammar of Chinese architecture; they wrote uncomprehending descriptions of Chinese buildings. But of the two Siren was better. He used the *Ying-tsao fa-shih,* but carelessly."

Sicheng also ransacked the Harvard library for Chinese-language books on architecture. The collection was very small, just beginning, and he reported that he found almost nothing except for pages here or there — for instance, in the *Ku-chin t'u-shu chi-ch'eng,* which had elaborate descriptions of temples. Among books by Japanese scholars he came upon several volumes on Buddhist monuments in China by Tokiwa Daijo and Sekino

Tai, of which the plates were already in print but the text had not yet appeared.

His months of reading at Harvard produced a large file of cards with notations of data he might need in the future as well as the beginnings of a bibliography. But he could see that as far as Chinese architectural history was concerned very little was known.

By February 1928, Sicheng had accomplished what he went to Harvard to do. Meanwhile Whei had, with her usual sparkle, made a special place for herself in the circle of aspiring stage designers at the Yale School of Drama. Her thorough training in architectural design and drafting enabled her to be more than a fellow-student; she was a friend in need, even a fairy godmother, for certain of her comrades as deadlines approached. Stewart Cheney, who was then in his late teens and later to make his mark in American stage design, was a special pet. Eight years afterward, in February 1936, she wrote that she had discovered from a copy of *Theater Arts Monthly* that "my Stewart Cheney has actually become one of Broadway's leading designers! Imagine, that little troublesome boy who always got into 'jams' or 'scrapes' with everyone and needed all my motherly protection is now a leading designer on Broadway and has *four* plays running at the same time."

Persuading her to cut short her stage-design course and leave her new friends may have been difficult for Sicheng. But he could now offer marriage. Whei accepted, and they proceeded together to Ottawa, where Elder Sister's husband was the Chinese Consul General.

They were married in the consulate on March 21, 1928. The date selected was the only date given on the memorial stele erected in Sung times for their great architectural-analyst predecessor, Li Chieh, and they chose it in homage to him. After the wedding they left at once for Europe.

5. Homecoming

Liang's father on the other side of the globe continued to offer paternal guidance to his newlywed son. He had handled the Chinese end of the engagement and marriage rituals. Now he was planning the itinerary of the return through Europe.[1] He was opposed to their returning via Siberia because Russia was "barbarous and dilapidated." Accidents might occur entering and exiting Russia. "To tour southern Europe is a primary objective and to go from there to Moscow to take the train home would be extremely uneconomic. . . . I have a plan for you." His plan was specific. They should go from Canada to the United States and then to Sweden and Norway, because "Scandinavia is full of character and interesting modern architecture," then to Germany to see ancient cities and Rhine castles, then to Switzerland for natural beauty, then to Italy. The stay there should be longer so that they could thoroughly understand the beauty of the Renaissance. At last they would embark in Marseilles for their return.

As an afterthought, he added, "It would also be a good idea to go to Spain. Liu Tsing-k'ai is Ambassador there and could take care of you. And you might go to Turkey to see Islamic architecture. If you do, you must observe post-revolutionary politics there for me." (There was no mention of London or Paris.)

A few weeks later he wrote Sicheng some additional thoughts:[2] "If you want to return via Siberia to save money you must let me know so I can help with arrangements. When you arrive in Europe I hope you will keep a detailed diary. If it has literary quality I could edit it and get it published. Enclosed are a dozen of my name cards; when you visit embassies in Europe you can use them."

Following this letter, communication between the father and the newlyweds was interrupted by two months of silence on his part. A sudden decline in his health had taken place. However, in a long letter to them written in April[3] he claimed, "My health has made much progress. Half a month ago I had a blood transfusion at PUMC [Peking Union Medical College] and the blood count was normal."

The two-month interval since the wedding had sufficed to bring him accounts of it from both Elder Sister and Sicheng himself in that period of mail delivery by slow boat to China. He commented, "The eldest son of the family has finished this great ceremony. You can imagine how happy the old people are. And happiest of all is the fact that I have always favored girls and now have a daughter-in-law whose loveliness equals that of my own daughters. . . . I am trying to plan for you but I want you to realize the difficulty. Even if you cannot find a good job don't be disappointed or demoralized. That would be the most dreadful enemy in our lives; we should not allow it to overtake us."

Not surprisingly, Sicheng's own studies during the previous few years had inspired in him his own objectives. He had apparently suggested to his father that he would like to study the history of "Chinese palaces." Liang Ch'i-ch'ao considered this gravely but was less than enthusiastic. He alleged that "90 percent of ancient architecture has been destroyed" and that current conditions made field research impossible. But he assured his son that he himself had some interesting ideas about Chinese architecture from literature. "Perhaps you could do research on the examples I could give you."

Having bestowed this faint encouragement, Sicheng's father urged him to turn to his secondary project — the history of Chinese fine arts. Here the father waxed ebullient. He envisioned himself outlining different artistic schools, recounting in great detail the character and temperaments of the various artists and their historical backgrounds and arranging for his son to visit and study private collections to which he had special access.

The all-wise paternal advisor gives way in the final paragraph to pleading for love and attention. "Your letters are far too few. Old men love their children. In convalescence the greatest happiness is to receive letters from you. I do hope you will constantly tell me what you are seeing during your trip (Note: even postcards are welcome) so I can travel while lying in bed. I also specially hope my new daughter will write to me."[4]

This wistfulness on the part of the invalid was spelled out to Elder daughter in one of his typically intimate letters to her written shortly thereafter.[5] He complained to her of Sicheng's unresponsiveness to his many letters for over the past few months giving guidance about jobs. "He has not said even a word about this in his letters," which are "far too few anyway. . . . It may be he does not agree with whatever I have been arranging for him. I feel I have been wasting my time and my love. In these respects he is really too young and inexperienced to understand."

On the contrary, Sicheng had reached the age of twenty-seven, had completed with honors four years of professional education, and had married. Those four years had been spent in a world away from his father, where every day he had to make unaided decisions. Independence of thought and action was expected from his American classmates by their families as well as by the university. Sicheng was Chinese to the core, raised to observe filial piety as the cardinal duty of a son, and he unquestionably loved and admired his eminent father. He was not, however, the young and inexperienced lad who had left his father's courtyard four years before. Liang Ch'i-ch'ao's distress at his son's apparent indifference to his guidance is poignant, but Sicheng may well have felt that until he could talk with his father face to face, mute restraint was preferable to argument by post.

Meanwhile, working in the dark, so to speak, Liang Ch'i-ch'ao had used his influence to lead Tsinghua University to consider (reluctantly) offering Sicheng a lectureship (in architecture?) and an opportunity to teach drafting. However, in April another possibility came to his attention, and the father quickly recognized its advantages. National Northeastern (Tung Pei) University in Mukden, Manchuria (now Shenyang) proposed to establish an architectural department, and the Dean of the Engineering College had asked Yang T'ing-pao, a gifted graduate of the Penn Architectural School, to head it. Yang, a schoolmate and good friend of young Liang's, was, however, already committed to a position in an architectural firm in Shanghai. He in turn recommended Liang Sicheng as uniquely qualified for the job. Knowing that the young couple were traveling in Europe, he promised the Dean to consult Liang Ch'i-ch'ao.

Liang quickly took action on his son's behalf. In a letter[6] to his eldest daughter, written on May 13 while the honeymooners were weeks away, somewhere in Europe, he rejoined, "Sicheng's job has been solved. Both Tung Pei and Tsinghua have offered him jobs. Tung Pei is the better because the prospect of launching an architectural career there is bright. He can organize a firm there and start in a small way, then gradually expand. Therefore before he answers, I have already made the decision for him, declined the offer from Tsinghua and accepted the Tung Pei position."

Meanwhile the honeymoon trip was taking the young couple to France, England, Switzerland, Italy, Spain, and Germany in what was to be their first and last joint visit to that continent. Like generations of young American architectural school graduates, they rushed from place to place trying to see in a limited time everything they had studied. They had hoped to have the entire summer for their European travels, but these plans were cut short by an urgent message from home.

They were, they thought, en route to a teaching position at familiar Tsinghua. Communications between China and Europe were so slow at that time and the newlyweds were so constantly on the move that news of the job change had not reached Sicheng a month after it had been settled. His father received a cable from him on June 9 asking what courses he would be expected to teach at Tsinghua.[7] The father replied, "Negotiations with Tung Pei have reached the final stage. It is a better place for you with regard to your future. Only the reference books are fewer than Tsinghua's. Tung Pei really needs you and Tsinghua is hesitant so I told the President to withdraw his proposal." He added, however, that the recent bombing in Mukden had resulted in chaos there and it was unclear whether the university could actually start the new semester. He urged Sicheng to return before August. By June 19[8] he had concluded that, though the situation in Manchuria was dangerous, Tung Pei would not be affected, and he wrote Elder Sister that he had already contracted for Sicheng a monthly salary of 265 yuan, making him among the highest paid of the faculty there.

Meanwhile, lying in his sickbed at the family home in Tientsin, he worried about the Confucian obligations the young couple would face on their arrival. They would have to perform the ceremony of presenting themselves to the ancestors, which would take eight to ten days' preparation at least. In addition they would have to go to Peking to visit the ancestors' graves. For discharging all these filial duties time was really too short. A trip to Fukien to enable Whei-yin to perform her filial responsibilities there would probably have to be postponed until the winter vacation.[9]

The urgency of reaching home sooner than planned dictated the means of travel. The Liangs decided to go to Moscow and take the Trans-Siberian Railway despite the father's distaste for "barbarous and dilapidated Russia." This choice resulted in an unexpected and happy encounter with a young American couple, Charles and Fredericka Child, who were fellow travelers on the long train journey. Charles Child's memory of this episode, written at my request in 1980, gives a vivid account of the Liangs' return to China.

"There are sometimes episodes or periods in a lifetime that seem to have a magical quality — a special never-to-be-repeated essence. Our short intense friendship with the Liangs had this quality — an open door to shared dreams.

"In the early summer of the year 1928 Freddie and I were on a Trans-Siberian train pushing slowly eastward from Moscow, stopping every now and then to take on water and a load of wood fuel. During these halts everyone would pile out onto the platform, mill about, walk up and down, barter with the locals for food, make tea.

"Standing out from a rather hairy and smelly mob of passengers like two butterflies circling a dung heap was this enchanting young couple. Aside from a natural reticence, they seemed to us to be radiating a certain irresistible glow and ardor. We fell into happy conversation almost at once, spurred on by a mutual euphoria — they because, they explained to us, they were returning home full of their American experience and eager to put it to work, and we because we were launching ourselves on a Grand Tour into regions whose arts and philosophies had long had a compelling attraction for both of us. Looking back, I can see that the monotony of the train journey and the linguistic barrier to communication with the other passengers were obvious spurs to friendship.

"But who can 'explain' love? It just happened — we were delighted with each other's company and found it easy to share ideas, plans, aspirations with a measure of intimacy.

"The train wallowed on through Omsk, Tomsk, Irkutsk, Baikal, and a hundred other stopping places, to its junction with the Chinese Eastern Railway, which we four boarded for the trek east and south through Manchuria to Harbin, Mukden, and Dairen on the Yellow Sea.

"We stopped over in Mukden to pay a ceremonial visit to a huge old library approached by an avenue bordered by stone-statue guardians. There was some connection with Sicheng's father; the magic name Liang produced great miracles of bowing and scraping as we pored over rarities of brushwork and illustration.

"From Dairen we took a Japanese boat across the Gulf of Chihli to Taku, the port of Tientsin. Then from Tientsin to Pekin, in the dusk and pouring rain on a slow-slow leaking train. The roof was covered with free-loading passengers, in spite of which the rain dripped down inside onto the folded newspaper hats we had made and onto a number of guttering candles stuck to seatbacks. Thus to Pekin, where the odor of tuberose in one nostril and shit in the other mingled with the cries of rickshaw men and beggars to give us a tumultuous welcome to the city of our dreams.

". . . In Pekin the incredible Liangs became our faithful guides. From Coal Hill to the Temple of Heaven, from the Jade Fountain Pagoda to the Tartar City, the Western Hills, restaurants, theaters, street fairs, shops, funeral processions and even to the senior Liang's secret walled garden and to exquisite meals with various uncles and aunts in a bewilderment of courtyards filled with caged birds, summer flowers, pools, trees, and to the endless chambers and courtyards of the Forbidden City. All was freely given, all was spiced with warmth and courtesy.

"The experience of friendship was strengthened and made memorable by long winding conversations midst the half-ruined glories of the Pei Hai, the Confucian Temple, and other haunting places, during which it gradually became apparent that coming back had been a shock and a let-down. It had become obvious, they said, that it was going to be extremely difficult — perhaps impossible — to find a way to be useful or to have any substantial influence, in spite of their training, on the chaotic and changing motherland of those years. The problem of melding the new with the old, both in the theater world and in architecture, as they came face to face with the complications of bureaucracy and indifference, seemed overwhelming. And yet 'Keep on! Keep on!' was the watchword.

"There were moments when elements of cynicism and bafflement surfaced. At such times we stoutly maintained, in spite of our own doubts and ignorance, that this was only a shakedown period, sure to smooth out in the long run. Nevertheless it was apparent that our friends felt like a pair of Rip Van Winkles. They had come back to a China suddenly unfamiliar and chaotic; still they seemed determined to find a role and make useful impacts which would somehow contribute their new skills and creative vigor to the surrounding melange. There would be marvelous hours filled with lyrical hope — others given to doubt.

"Phyllis was passionate, forceful, dramatic and quite funny: mad at Mei Lan Fang because he dared not sit down in her presence, joyous at the prospect of bringing traditional theater into the rhythm of the 20th century. Sicheng was urbane, humorous, resilient — appalled at the careless deterioration and destruction of old public buildings, bridges, walls, shops and private dwellings. Together they made a marvelous combination — a balance of temperaments and skills which even at that early stage seemed able to produce a whole far greater than the sum of its parts — a rare serendipity.

"Seen against that time of war lords, banditry, and chaos, they seemed to us, even with their talents and privileged social position, as if they might eventually sink without a trace in the gigantic Chinese maelstrom. At this point in their saga we had to leave for Kyoto and never saw them again."

At the same time the delighted father was reporting to his absent children[10] the return of Sicheng and Whei-yin after the long separation.

"Since the newlyweds arrived, the entire household has been filled with happiness. The first day when I saw Sicheng he looked rather exhausted. But in the past few days, with nourishment, he looks very spirited and handsome. The more I look at him the better I love him. The worries I have had during the past few years are all gone. The bride is very much at ease, fits in well and is vivacious. She doesn't have the hypocritical role-playing expression typical of the old families, nor does she have the disgusting airs of the modern type. It's just as though she were produced from the same mold as my children."

That the father's illness was very serious seems not to have been perceived by the family. He had a lifetime history of good health and had always been the unquestioned master of the household, responsible for all important decisions. Because he was aware that the entire family depended on him, he concealed from them the fact that in the early spring of 1928 he discovered blood in his urine. He himself recognized the risk this implied. Peking's German Hospital, to which he went for a check-up, assured him that they found no signs of malignancy. After his discharge he treated his continuing illness with Chinese medicine, but it did not help. He then entered the Peking Union Medical College Hospital, where, after a few days of testing, one kidney was diagnosed as cancerous. On March 16, 1928 he underwent an operation for removal of the cancerous kidney. However, he continued to have blood in his urine. The doctors ordered him to rest, saying the amount of blood depended on his overworking. Their only recourse was to give him blood transfusions once every two or three months.

The operation had taken place while Sicheng and Whei were traveling through Europe. The father's letter to them of April 26, which reported "much progress" in his health after a blood transfusion two weeks earlier, appears to have been intended principally as a reassurance that all was well. It was only a minor departure from his habitual fatherly advice and his continuing explorations of Sicheng's future career.

Even after the newlyweds returned home at the end of the summer, the delight of the reunion and the hurried preparations for the move to Manchuria seemed to take precedence over realization that the father's life was nearing its end. He continued his researches and writing as usual, but by November 12 he could no longer sit up at his desk. He took to his bed and died there on January 19, 1929.[11]

The death of the famous scholar Liang Ch'i-ch'ao at the early age of fifty-five was not only a cruel shock to his unsuspecting family but a major loss for his colleagues and disciples and for the innumerable readers of his works. Sicheng, his eldest son, assuming his own new responsibilities, prepared an account of the final months, weeks, and days of his eminent father's life for the public. It was printed two days after the death in the major newspaper *Ta Kung Pao*.[12] The very first sentence — "My father was very healthy, seldom ill" — had a special poignancy he could not know at the time.

Forty years later, in 1971, he learned from his own doctor the tragic circumstances of his father's untimely death. In view of Liang Ch'i-ch'ao's eminence, the leading figure at PUMC, Professor of Surgery Dr. J. Heng Liu (Liu Jui-heng), had been designated to perform the kidney operation. What happened was reported some time later in confidence by two PUMC interns who had been present at the operation. According to their report, "After the patient was wheeled into the operating room, the attending nurse marked with iodine the wrong side of the abdomen. Dr. Liu went on with the operation [removing the healthy kidney] without checking carefully the x-ray film that was hanging beside the operating table. This tragic mistake was discovered immediately after the operation, but it was kept TOP SECRET for the reputation of PUMC was at stake."

Ray Chang, in Shanghai, a close friend of the elder Liang and also of the two interns, who wrote this account to me, commented, "Up to now, this story is not well known in China. But I do not doubt its authenticity, for I learned from other people who knew Liu rather well that Liu was never the proud surgeon again after that operation."

It may be significant that Dr. Liu in November 1928, nine months after the operation on Liang Ch'i-ch'ao and six weeks before his death, agreed to leave surgery and PUMC to assume office as Administrative Vice-Minister of Health in the National Government. This move to Nanking is explained in Howard L. Boorman's *Biographical Dictionary of Republican China*[13] in these words: "J. Heng Liu believed and taught that public service was more important than private practice, however lucrative." He devoted his remaining thirty-three years to laying the foundations of a national health service.

PART TWO

Achievements, 1928–1937

6. A Professorship

Whatever doubts the Liangs may have had, the Tung Pei job presented an extraordinary challenge. What Penn classmate could have expected within a year of receiving his architectural degree to be invited to found and staff a department of architecture in a newly established university? Furthermore, this would be one of only two such architectural training centers in the entire country. The other, in the Civil Engineering Department of National Central University in Nanking, had been functioning only since the previous year.

The challenge for the young architects came not only from the university but from the vastness of Manchuria itself. Originally a preserve of the Manchus, who invaded China and ruled from 1644 to 1911, the great northern area was still a frontier territory in 1928 despite the immigration of large numbers of Chinese peasant-farmers. By that summer they were arriving from the crowded nearby provinces of Hopei and Shantung at the rate of 40,000 a week and Chinese families constituted 90 percent of the total population. Russia had first built railways to open up the region, but Japan's defeat of Russia in 1905 had given it control in South Manchuria. At the time the Liangs arrived, the presence of Japanese troops in the railway zone was the chief factor in the maintenance of order. It was along the railways that the Chinese immigrants settled, glad to escape from the ravages of the North China warlords. However, Manchuria had a warlord of its own, Chang Tso-lin, who ruled at the will of the Japanese. Not satisfied with his autocratic control of Mukden, he led his forces on four incursions down through the Great Wall to Peking, intending to defeat the roving warlords in North China and reorganize the government with himself as president. When the new Nationalist government at Nanking headed by Chiang Kai-shek sent its forces northward, Chang Tso-lin's final attempt to take power in Peking was thwarted. He left to return to Mukden by train on June 3, 1928, but before he reached there his train was bombed and he died of the wounds he received.

The complicity of the Japanese military in the bombing assassination was taken for granted, and further menace from that quarter threatened. But before the end of the year the old warlord's son, the "Young Marshal" Chang Hsueh-liang, had brought Manchuria, henceforth known as the Three Eastern Provinces, into political union with the rest of China. There was an uneasy peace in Mukden. For the moment tasks of normal living could be resumed.

Despite the insecurity, Sicheng's university career got off to a good start. He was named "Assistant Professor in Charge, Department of Architecture" on his arrival and promoted to "Professor in Charge" two years later. Despite his impressive title, the department consisted for the first academic year of two staff members only—himself and Whei. They both taught architectural design, and he gave an ambitious course on the history of Western as well as Chinese architecture.

When spring came to relieve the northern chills of Liaoning Province, there was a new happiness in the air. Whei was pregnant and on August 21, 1929 gave birth to a daughter. They named her Tsai-ping ("another ice-figure") in deference to her late grandfather's studio name, "Ice-drinking Elder."

In the summer of 1929 the architectural faculty added three young men who had also been trained at Penn—Sicheng's longtime friend Ch'en Chih ("Benjamin"), T'ung Chun, a native of Mukden, and Tsai Fang-ying. All were competent to teach a Cret-style architecture curriculum, and their shared background and friendship seemed to foretell interesting and stimulating cooperation in the years ahead. Moreover, the need for architectural planning, design, and supervision of construction that Liang had anticipated had at last been recognized. An active architectural practice centered in Mukden was required. The firm of "Liang, Ch'en, T'ung and Tsai, Architects and Engineers" was established.

The firm received two major commissions almost at once. The first called on them to design an entire campus for Chi-lin (Kirin) University in Chi-lin Province. Administration and classroom buildings and dormitories for that university were designed and constructed of granite and reinforced concrete, a complicated undertaking that was completed in 1931. The second was also a matter of designing an institution of higher education. The University of Communications (Chiao-t'ung Ta-hsueh) planned to construct a branch at Chin-chou in Liaoning Province. Buildings for this project were designed by the firm and constructed, but they were later destroyed in warfare. Whei was a full partner in the designing, and she and Sicheng also collaborated in the "community planning" for a park outside

Mukden, the Hsiao Ho Yen, and in designing private residences for wealthy Mukden warlord families.

Sicheng's fascination with monumental architecture of earlier periods continued. Mukden had been the Manchu capital from 1636 to 1644, before they established the Ch'ing Dynasty at Peking. In such spare time as he could find, he measured architecture of the Manchus' "Northern Tombs" in the outskirts of Mukden. The great tiled roofs upturned at the eaves and wooden substructures with non-bearing "curtain walls" resembled the mausoleums of the Ch'ing royal house in the Peking area. He tried his hand at making for the first time careful measurements of the buildings, field notes on which final drawings could be based. He had learned of the technique in studying architectural history at Penn and from seeing exhibits of drawings by Prix de Rome contestants. His experiment was a disappointment. He discovered that his measurements were inadequate for the requirements of the final drawings. As he commented ruefully, "They represented a stage in my groping for the techniques that I later developed." For example, he promptly abandoned feet and inches for the metric system.

He was also frustrated in his first attempt to preserve important architectural monuments. The mayor of Mukden decided to demolish its handsome Drum and Bell Towers as hindrances to traffic. Liang tried to save them by shaming the official with the argument, "Demolition is easy, preservation is difficult. Once they are gone they cannot be restored. Why do you choose to destroy them?" As was to happen all too often in later years, his advice was rejected.[1]

It had been a heady experience for the eager young friends who made up the firm to be designing entire campuses from the start. That they accomplished what they did, from the firm's founding in 1929 through 1930, is remarkable because the development of institutions of higher education ran directly counter to the Japanese imperial ambitions in Manchuria. By the beginning of 1931 the Japanese military encroachments became constantly more flagrant. It was clear that Chiang Kai-shek had no intention of using his troops to defy the Japanese Kuantung Army in Manchuria. Without military resistance China's northeast would obviously be lost to Japan.

Some time late in 1930 a diagnosis of tuberculosis forced Whei to leave Mukden for Peking to undergo treatment. Ch'en Chih left in February of 1931 to start a professional practice of architecture in Shanghai. After moving his family to Peking, Sicheng returned to his post in Northeastern University until the end of the 1930–1931 academic year. He then turned the department over to T'ung Chun and joined Whei in Peking for the start of a new career. By September 18, 1931, when the Japanese made their move to take over Manchuria, T'ung, a native of Mukden, was the only one of the ambitious young architects remaining. When soon thereafter the Japanese closed the university, he and other faculty members as well as many of the students made their way southward to Peking and other destinations inside the Great Wall.

7. In Peking

In the autumn of 1930 Liang Sicheng settled Lin Whei-yin, their little daughter Liang Tsai-ping, and Whei's mother into a typical Peking house near the east wall of the city at No. 3 Pei-tsung-pu Hutung. It was to be the family home for the next seven years. Within its high walls was a secluded but ample courtyard planted with several flowering trees. Along each of its four sides stretched long, one-story dwelling units. Pitched roofs of gray tiles covered these and the paved walkways that linked them. The façades that faced the courtyard had large windows and doors in which were set wooden lattices of elaborate design. Sheets of white rice-paper were pasted or furled against the interior of these lattices, to let in the light while protecting privacy. A central doorway at the north end of the courtyard led into the living room, which was larger than the other rooms and faced directly south. The Liangs replaced the paper in the wide lower sashes of some windows with glass to afford them a view of the trees and flowers in the courtyard and let in a flood of warm sunshine during the chilly Peking winter. But above each glass was a roll of paper that could be unfurled down in the evenings for privacy and insulation. Rooms along a smaller courtyard near the front entrance housed the servants and the household work areas.

Here Whei resumed her writing career. And here, too, Hsü Chih-mo reentered their lives.

While the Liangs pursued their architectural training in Philadelphia, Hsü had followed his romantic nature into near disaster. After parting with Tagore in Japan in the summer of 1924, he returned to Peking, the scene of his recent limelight appearances. He had divorced his wife but failed to win Whei to take her place. He surely saw himself still as the single-minded and intense seeker after perfect beauty, perfect love, spiritual freedom, creativity. It was inevitable that he would fall in love again, and this time he chose not a sensitive schoolgirl but a woman of the world, a reigning beauty in the elite society of the city. Lu Hsiao-man was a married woman. Her husband of four years was a high-ranking army officer. Her married state did not deter Hsü; if anything it was a spur to his passionate courtship. She was a public figure in her circles as he was in his. Their affair aroused such gossip and scandal in Peking that he was prevailed on to leave the city for five months in 1925. He returned to Europe and traveled widely there, all the while pouring out his emotions to her in fervent love letters. She obtained a divorce, and they were married on October 3, 1926.

Liang Ch'i-ch'ao had reported the occasion in a letter to his children far away in America. "Yesterday I did what I was not willing to do—acted as master of ceremonies for Hsü Chih-mo's wedding. His new wife was previously Mrs. Wang Shou-ching. She fell in love with Hsü and divorced Wang. It is extremely immoral. I have chastised Hsü several times without effect. Since Hu Shih and Chang P'eng-ch'un persuaded me to take this role, I delivered a lecture in the ceremony and sternly criticized the newly-weds. . . . Young people are excited by emotion, cannot control themselves, and destroy the safety net of convention. They fall into a trap that will cause them suffering. It is truly sad and pitiable. Hsü is really intelligent. I love him. This time I see him drowning. I want to rescue him. I really do my best to save him." He ended with a very personal note, "This is the way I felt and I particularly write this to Sicheng, Whei-yin, and Ssu-chung."[1]

What further news of Hsü's life reached Philadelphia in the next two years we do not know. His creativity seemed undiminished. His first book of poems had appeared in 1925. It was followed by a second two years later, as well as four collections of essays. In 1927 he left Peking for Shanghai to teach, and there he organized the Crescent Moon Book Company and began publication of *Crescent Monthly*. Through his publications, his teaching, and as always his wide circle of friends, he continued to exert an influence on other writers, although it was diminished by the growing interest in Marxism.

In the summer of 1928, when the Liangs came home to Peking after their long absence in the West, Hsü was traveling alone in England and Europe. As they moved northward to settle in Mukden, he returned, low in spirits, to his home base in Shanghai, where his teaching, his publishing company, and his *Crescent Monthly* required his presence. The death in January 1929 of Liang Ch'i-ch'ao, his revered mentor, was an irretrievable loss.

The next year Hu Shih invited Hsü to teach at Peking University. There he was near enough to Mukden to visit his friends from time to time. When Whei's tuberculosis flared up, he added his voice to the councils urging that she be moved to Peking for better hospital facilities and a milder climate.

The Pei-tsung-pu house became a second home to Hsü. He stayed there when his work brought him to Peking. For both Whei and Sicheng he was a treasured guest. His keen wit and ebullience revived in their company, and he loved to share with them his friends, those kindred spirits who still clung to him.

A Liang relative who as a young teenager in 1931 met him several times at their house has described her first impression of him. "He made a dramatic entrance, wearing a brocade long gown with a delicate British mohair scarf wound around his neck. An odd combination! All eyes were upon him. His appearance was rather effeminate but electric. The entire company was charged with his presence. Whei was vivacious and Sicheng was always cordial and welcoming."

Undoubtedly, Hsü's greatest and most lasting contribution to the Liang family at this time was the introduction of one of his dearest friends. Chin Yueh-lin (pronounced Jin) was professor of philosophy at Tsinghua University. "Lao Jin," as he was known to his intimates, was China's leading expert in the esoteric field of symbolic logic. Far from being the exotic wizard his specialty suggests, he was a tall, slim, tennis-playing intellectual, reserved but very articulate. He was several years older than the Liangs. They remembered the stories of his arriving in Peking as a young student from his native Hunan in the last days of the empire, wearing his hair plaited in the long braid the Manchu government required.

Chin had made rapid progress in his studies in Peking and won a scholarship for study in the United States. His first choice was the Wharton School of the University of Pennsylvania, preparatory to a career in economics or business. But as time went on his natural bent toward analysis and abstract thought led him to pursue various aspects of philosophy. His period of study abroad lengthened into a number of years and took him eventually to extended stays in Britain and Europe. His mastery of Oxford English was striking. On his return to China he was appointed to teach philosophy at Tsinghua University.

His private life was rumored to have included several affairs with ladies in the West, one of whom followed him to Peking for a short spell, but he never married. Instead he settled himself into a way of life that was to last to its very end. He attached himself to the Liang family. Inevitably, Whei was the central force that drew him. Her magnetism, which was felt by so many, supplied him with the swirl of humanity lacking in his esoteric mental environment. She, in turn, found that his wide experience of the world and his inborn wisdom made him the perfect listener as well as the admiring stimulant to her creativity.

He loved her of course, but unselfishly, open-heartedly. He had no intent to wrest her from her family. He was loved and trusted by Sicheng and the children and was, in effect, incorporated into the family.

On November 19, 1931, Hsü Chih-mo, then thirty-five, was flying from Shanghai to Peking to meet his teaching obligations at Peking University the next day. That evening he expected to attend a lecture on Chinese art and architecture that Whei was giving for some foreign visitors. She went to the airport to meet his plane. When it was overdue, she waited and waited. The plane had crashed in heavy fog into a mountain in Shantung, killing passengers and crew on impact. There was no way for immediate word to reach the Peking airport. When and where Whei learned of his death is not known.

If there was any way of mitigating the heartache, Hsü himself had left it to his friends in the still living words of his poetry. His passionate attachment to love and life was matched by a fascination with flying and with death.

> Hold me until I pass away,
> Until my eyes can open no more,
> Until I fly, fly, fly into outer space,
> Disperse into sand, into light, into wind.
> Ah agony, but agony is short,
> Transitory; happiness is long,
> And love is immortal:
>   I, I want to sleep. . . .[2]

His many friends and admirers drew together to comfort one another. Later they gathered each year on November 19 to share memories of him. On the fourth anniversary of his death, Whei addressed a message to him. It concluded, "Whether or not our works will outlast us depends on whether they will live among those we will never know. The readers of our work are scattered in time and place, in the solitude of many who are totally unknown to one another.

"Dear friend, you should not underestimate the importance of this kind of indirect existence. Many earnest people live on for you, the meaning of their lives increased. What is heartbreaking is the fact that for those closest to you your absence leaves a void that can never be filled."[3]

8. Architectural Historian

The humiliation and outrage felt by Chinese at the Japanese takeover of Manchuria in September 1931 provoked a lasting nationwide boycott of Japanese goods. Students and merchants led the resistance, but widespread participation in the boycott kindled a new level of patriotic fervor in the general population.

It was an irony of fate that Sicheng, whose boyhood in Japan had been a notably happy one, should be dealt by Japan the first harsh setback of his adult life. But, ironically, it was the brutal pressure by the hated Japanese military that catapulted him from his promising start as a busy practicing architect and teacher into a congenial new career.

On leaving Mukden, Sicheng had accepted a position with a little-known organization in Peking, the Society (later Institute) for Research in Chinese Architecture. Its official name was Chung-kuo Ying-tsao Hsueh-she.

The Institute was an outgrowth of a rich man's hobby. Its founder was an interesting man of Liang Ch'i-ch'ao's generation, Chu Chi-ch'ien. Born in Kweichow in 1872, Chu was a capable administrator who in his middle years had held a number of important posts in the Chinese government. In 1915 the President of the Republic ordered him as Minister of the Interior to repair Peking's palaces and restore city gates and certain old buildings. In supervising these enterprises, Chu associated closely with the master crafts-men who had been keeping the imperial structures in repair throughout their lifetimes. He learned from them much about Chinese architecture, and when he reached retirement he continued his interest in investigating its historical development. By chance he came upon a rare manuscript copy in Nanking's Kiangsu Provincial Library of the Sung manual *Ying-tsao fa-shih,* and had it printed. Sicheng prized his copy of the book, which his father had sent to him. The author, Li Chieh, as an official of the Imperial Court, had supervised construction and restoration of government build-ings and, like Chu in later years, consulted the workmen who, having the traditional skills to shape timber and erect buildings according to official instructions, "explained everything."

Discovering Li Chieh's book inspired Chu to establish his Institute for Research in Chinese Architecture. He gathered a group of old-fashioned scholars to search through books written in the classical language for literary references to Chinese architecture. None of the scholars had any knowledge of Chinese architecture. Chu himself was aware that the technical terms used by carpenters would have to be "decoded." The carpenters were generally illiterate; methods of construction were usually conveyed orally, from master to apprentice, and were regarded as secrets within every craft.

Clearly Chu's Institute had a need for professional leadership. A modern-trained architect with a background in Chinese classical studies was essential. Chu was a contemporary of Liang Ch'i-ch'ao and knew that Liang Sicheng had returned from architectural training abroad. Chu interviewed him in 1930 and proposed that he join the Institute as Director of Research.

When in 1931 it became clear that the Japanese military were to be unopposed in their takeover of Manchuria and that their prompt closing of the university was inevitable, Liang could with good conscience accept Chu's offer. His own enthusiasm for the study of Chinese architectural history and confidence in his preparation for the task put to rest whatever doubts he might have had. He was aware from the first that he was creating a new field of study by asking new questions others had disregarded. What are the stages of Chinese architectural evolution and how can they be discovered? Under Cret's curriculum he had learned the stages of Western architectural evolution. He had been required to master them in drawings and, after his years at the drawing board, his honeymoon trip through Europe with Whei had taught them both to recognize at sight structures characteristic of the various epochs they had studied.

From the first day he joined the Institute, Liang started taking the necessary steps to discover the evolution of Chinese architecture. He knew that the problem was to find dated structures from the earlier periods that had survived relatively untouched. But a more immediate problem was to establish a base line for his studies by discovering what he could of even earlier structures erected too long ago to have endured into the twentieth century.

Chu had established a headquarters for the Institute inside Tien An Men in one of the unused portions of the Palace. Presumably his longtime official connections obtained this perquisite for his project. Sicheng set up his office there and started at once a study in depth of the *Ying-tsao fa-shih*.

Chu's experience with the various editions must have been helpful to him at this stage. However, the strictly literary approach so congenial to Chu and scholars of his generation was inadequate from the point of view of a modern practicing architect like Liang. He needed to know the specific shapes and functions of the timbers named in the unfamiliar technical terms used by Li Chieh. The misunderstood illustrations to the 1925 edition of the book were grossly misleading as explanations of the text, which had itself been somewhat garbled through the centuries. Sicheng's study of the *Ying-tsao fa-shih* continued off and on through the ensuing years, though he found the treasures he extracted from the book "hard to quarry out."

From the start of his new career as an architectural historian, Sicheng was determined to search and discover what he termed the "grammar" of Chinese architecture. He recognized that throughout China's history the timber-frame had been the fundamental form of construction. The Great Wall and the many city walls of packed earth faced with brick were exceptions, as were barrel-vaulted tombs of brick or stone. But the relatively few free-standing monumental structures built of these more durable materials, such as pagodas, were commonly direct copies of timber-framed buildings. Sicheng was eager to learn the principles of Chinese timber-frame construction and the evolution of such building methods over the previous three thousand years.

By 1932 Tokiwa and Sekino, the Japanese archaeologists whose volumes of plates Liang had studied at Harvard, had published the accompanying textual volumes reporting their exploratory trips in the Chinese countryside. Sicheng himself had up to that time had no experience combing the countryside, but he was excited to read of the Japanese discoveries of sculptures found in Liao Dynasty temples in northern Shansi at Ta-t'ung and of a small temple in the Sung mountains of northern Honan, Chu-tsu An, erected in 1125, which was a close contemporary of the *Ying-tsao fa-shih*. The French Sinologist Paul Pelliot had recently published his photographs of the T'ang mural paintings he had discovered in the Buddhist caves of Tun Huang in the remote Chinese northwest. From studying the structures illustrated in these books and a few other publications, notably the T'ang period temples in Nara, Japan, Liang was able to reach some hypotheses regarding T'ang architecture, ground plans, types of buildings, temple layouts, roofs, and elevated platform bases on which buildings were erected.

Sicheng's first article for the Institute's *Bulletin,* published in March 1932, was devoted to assembling existing documentary data about T'ang temples and palaces. From the outset, he aspired to find a surviving timber-framed building erected in the T'ang Dynasty (A.D. 618–907). His article marked the setting of his course toward that end. That he would succeed was most improbable, since over a thousand years had passed and wood was a perishable material. Wooden posts and beams were vulnerable to insects, rot, and fire even when protected by wide, overhanging tile roofs. Perhaps humans were the greatest enemy. Religious persecutions of Buddhist sects periodically annihilated priests and monks and demolished the great buildings where they worshiped.

This documentary research was a helpful first step, but it did not solve the mysteries of the textually distorted *Ying-tsao fa-shih*. Going every day to his office in the Palace, Sicheng soon arrived at eminently practical next steps toward solving the problem. Like Li Chieh himself, he turned to the master craftsmen at work on the Palace buildings for help. In order to make the best use of their knowledge, he acquainted himself with a builder's manual of the Ch'ing Dynasty published in 1734, the *Kung-ch'eng tso-fa tse-li*. Though he concluded it was not in the same class with the earlier, Sung, manual, it served him well in his study of the Ch'ing imperial buildings that still dominated Peking. As he wrote:

"With the *Kung-ch'eng tso-fa tse-li* as the textbook, the carpenters as teachers, and the Ch'ing palaces in Peking as teaching material, the study of the methods and rules of Ch'ing architecture began to have a solid basis.

"The book, published in 1734 by the Department of Works, is in seventy chapters. They deal with calculations of building materials, and rules for 'big timber work carpentry.' Exact measurements of each structural part in buildings of twenty-seven different dimensions are tediously described. However, the terminology and location of each structural member are very poorly indicated. Without having the craftsmen to point out and explain the concrete examples, it would have been very hard to read the book. Rules for the most characteristic construction member in Chinese architecture, the *tou-kung* or bracket set, as well as the diameter and height of the columns and the curvature of the roofs are all described. Other chapters treat 'small timber work,' joinery, stonework, brickwork, tilework, colors, and so on."

Sicheng contrasted this "tedious description" of dimensions with the Sung manual, which establishes in a very logical manner basic rules and then provides the formulas for finding the exact measurements of each member according to grade.

He was fortunate in finding two old carpenters who had spent their lives maintaining the Ch'ing buildings of the Palace. In their company he examined in detail the complex interrelationships of the timbers. It was not simply a matter of the craftsmen "pointing out and explaining concrete examples," for he needed to know not only their terms for the various members but the location and function of each member in relation to the structure as a whole. Here in the Palace buildings he began the crawling and clambering that close examination and accurate measurements required.

9. Search for Surviving Buildings

Chu Chi-ch'ien, not surprisingly, failed to see the need for the field trips outside Peking that Liang was proposing. He had established the Institute to solve problems of architectural construction by literary means.

Sicheng, by contrast, was a man of the twentieth century. His education had encompassed both the important Chinese traditions and the Western scientific insistence on observation and testing. Most important, he was by nature a man of action and practicality who while still in his twenties had himself designed and overseen the construction of buildings in Manchuria.

Yet in one way he was unprepared for trekking through the Chinese countryside. After his return from Japan at the age of eleven, his school years had been for the most part confined to the cities of Peking and Tientsin and the railroad that connected them. Even the brief Mukden years were spent on a new campus at the edge of a city, and travel was again by railroad to Tientsin and Peking.

His city upbringing was not unique in this respect. Members of the modern-educated literate class clustered in the urban areas, where the institutions of modernization were developing. Modern businesses, industrial plants, hospitals, and universities were established in cities on the east coast or on inland waterways. Within the major cities themselves, public transportation in Sicheng's youth was limited to overcrowded and precarious buses or occasional streetcars. Coolie-drawn rickshas or, in some areas, carrying-chairs were the private autos and taxis of the day. Travel by bicycle was common and by foot was universal. There was a premium on living close to one's work and one's friends.

The traditional gulf between the literate upper class and the peasantry was then still wide. True, unemployed or underemployed peasants sought humble employment in the cities and regularly brought produce from the country to marketing centers, but the current seldom flowed in the opposite direction. The urban literati confronted not only limitations of transport but numerous other difficulties and even dangers. Local inns, established to shelter carters and perambulating salesmen, commonly had for bedsteads brick platforms (*k'angs*), infested by disease-carrying lice, and outhouses teeming with maggots. Roadside teahouses could provide delicious simple fare, but the cleanliness of the bowls, chopsticks, food, and water was often dubious. Throughout the 1920s and '30s there was also the risk of attack by bandits who lived by preying on unsuspecting travelers.

Sicheng's first field trip, in April 1932, was an unprecedented experience. The impetus came by chance from his good friend, Yang T'ing-pao, who had recommended him for the Mukden position. According to his account, "I happened to visit the Peking Drum Tower, which was then being used as a small public library and exhibition hall for mass education. There I saw, hanging on the wall of the great arched vault on the first floor, a photograph of an odd-looking temple building. Down below on the picture was clearly written 'Chi Hsien, Tu-le Ssu (Temple of Solitary Joy).' When I described to Sicheng how the brackets on the building looked, he got quite excited and called me a very lucky person to have come across such a picture."[1] Sicheng went at once to the exhibition. The large brackets in the Chi Hsien photograph reminded him of similar features in photographs published by the Japanese archaeologists Tokiwa and Sekino from their China travels. He guessed that these probably indicated an early building.

Inquiries revealed that a bus left Peking every morning at six A.M., scheduled to reach Chi Hsien, some fifty miles to the east, at eleven. Liang planned to leave as soon as possible in the autumn of 1931. His bags were packed and everything ready when news came that a river had burst its banks, making the roads impassable, and the journey had to be postponed. When at last the trip was rescheduled in April, Liang was accompanied by a younger brother, a member of the Institute, and a professor from Tsinghua who loaned the expedition instruments important to its work. The fact that this was a daring excursion of city folk into the unknown countryside was epitomized in the first night's telephone message home to Peking: "No bandits. Inn 15 cents a day for four."

"That memorable trip," Sicheng wrote, "was my first experience of traveling away from main trunklines of communications. The old Model T that would have been, were it in America, sold long since as scrap iron, was still made to run regularly — or rather, irregularly — between Peking and the little town. When we were a few miles out of the East Gate of Peking, we came to the Chien-kan River. Its main flow was reduced to less than thirty feet wide in the dry season. But the riverbed of very fine sand measures about a mile and a half from bank to bank. After crossing the stream by ferry-boat, the bus could not move even an inch in the soft ground. We — the passengers — had to help push the old buggy the entire width of the riverbed, while the engine roared into our eyes and noses. There were other difficult stretches where we had to get off and on the bus many times. It took more than three hours to cover the fifty-mile ride. But it was excitement and fun. I did not know then that for the next few years I was to get used to rides like that and think nothing unusual about them.

"The Kuan-yin Ke, or Hall of the Buddhist deity Kuan-yin of Tu-le Ssu, stands high above the city wall and could be seen from a great distance. From afar, one gets an impression of a building of great vigor and suavity. That was the first time I opened my eyes to so early a building important to Chinese architectural history."

The Hall had been built in A.D. 984 at the beginning of the Sung dynasty, but the land was then held by the Liao Tartars. The structure is two stories with a mezzanine floor. The brackets (which transfer the weight of the roof to the top of the columns) are large and simple. They are supported by slightly entasised columns and crowned by deep, overhanging eaves. The balcony around the upper floor is likewise supported by such brackets. Thus they form three decorative bands that are basically structural. These present a marked contrast to the straight columns and small crowded brackets of later periods. They resemble closely the architecture of the T'ang Dynasty paintings in the Tun-huang Caves.

The Hall houses a colossal clay statue of an eleven-headed Kuan-yin, sixty feet in height. It rises through a central void in the upper two floors. On each floor there is a surrounding gallery, at the levels of the waist and chest of the statue. It is the largest clay figure known to exist in China today. This Hall, together with the Gatehouse in front of it, which were Sicheng's two first finds, remained for a long time the oldest wooden structures in the Institute's record of discoveries.[2]

A prime importance of the Kuan-yin Hall from Sicheng's point of view was his opportunity to examine in detail a building erected very close to the date of the Sung construction manual, *Ying-tsao fa-shih*. In his descriptions he uses terms from this work. He carefully compares measurements of each construction member at Tu-le Ssu to measurements cited in the manual. The comparisons throw light on obscure passages in the manual and illumine the earlier development of Chinese timber construction.

In April 1979 the Tu-le Ssu Kuan-yin Hall and its Gatehouse were intact, forty-seven years after Liang's visit and two years after the terrible earthquake that killed untold thousands and destroyed many buildings in the cities of Peking and Tientsin. The town of Chi Hsien is closer to the epicenter, T'ang Shan, than either of those cities, yet the towering wooden structure of the Kuan-yin Hall, nearly one thousand years old, suffered only minor damage. This fact is an impressive tribute to the flexibility of its structural system.

One of the Chi Hsien teachers who had been a fascinated onlooker and to some small extent participant in the group's studies of the Kuan-yin Hall was the head of the county school. Sensing his interest, Sicheng talked with him about the special characteristics of the architecture of the Tu-le Ssu that proclaimed it to be of Liao date and pointed out how it differed from buildings of later periods. The teacher responded, "In my native town, Pao-ti in Hopei, there is a Kuang-chi Ssu which has very similar characteristics" and urged him to visit it. Liang commented later, "There we were in the middle of an investigation at one place and before it was finished we already had a clue about the next place to explore."

In June 1932 the Institute conducted its second field trip, to Pao-ti. There, after an arduous journey from Peking, Sicheng and his party found the Kuang-chi Ssu to be another Liao temple as the teacher had guessed. The big brackets and deep eaves immediately identified it as having features of the Liao period. They came upon its main Hall of the Three Boddhisatt-vas only to find that the Hall had been filled with hay to supply the horses of a cavalry unit stationed in the town. A group of workers were stacking hay, and the expedition could barely see the building through the dust-filled air. Inside, a line of statues — three great Boddhisattvas, a number of minor Buddhist deities, and eighteen Lohans — were hardly visible in the clouds of dust. In front of the main figure on the altar table was a pile of timber for coffins. In the haystacks were a number of stelae, the most important of which was dated 1025. The local people called it the "Divine Stele" and considered it the most famous sight in Pao-ti.

Overhead, according to Sicheng, "we saw that the building had no ceiling but what is called in the *Ying-tsao fa-shih* an 'exposed roof construction.' The beams, ties, and bracket sets were exquisitely made and interlocked, unlike those we knew from later structures. When we had arrived at Pao-ti we had felt rather hopeless, but here that feeling disappeared at once. We were all delighted. A few months earlier we had discovered Tu-le Ssu and now again we saw a Liao structure, built nearly a thousand years ago. What extraordinary luck!"

The measuring that began the next day was hindered by the haystacks. "We climbed on the hay and in the hay, strained ourselves to arrive at proper measurements, but were unable to be completely exact." Yet in the rear of the Hall the piles of hay, which reached up to the eaves, turned out to be very useful. "Here we could easily climb up and take exact measurements of the bracket sets, beams, and ties. Advantage and disadvantage go together."

As was typical, two other old buildings described in the local gazetteer in promising terms had completely disappeared. The Great Hall they studied was to suffer the same fate, either from destruction or from dilapidation. It lives on only in Liang's handsome drawing.

Later that same year the Institute's researches and fieldwork were enhanced by the addition to the staff of Liu Tun-chen (1897–1968), a native of Hunan province. (He romanized his name in his *Bulletin* reports according to its local pronunciation, "Liu Tun-tseng.") Having received an excellent training in classical Chinese as a youth, he was sent to Japan on a government scholarship for further education. There he completed middle school and graduated from the Department of Architecture of the Tokyo Engineering College in 1920. He remained in Tokyo an additional year to work for a Japanese architect and on his return to China found employment with another in Shanghai.

He was, however, a man of pronounced intellectual bent who soon found teaching architecture more congenial than practicing. He left Shanghai in 1925 for his native province to teach at Changsha Engineering College. He later joined the Soochow Engineering College, and when that institution moved to Nanking in 1927 he became a professor at National Central University. He married in 1930.

Liu had already developed a strong interest in Chinese traditional architecture. Encouraged by his wife, he made the serious decision to apply for employment in the Institute for Research in Chinese Architecture, though leaving his teaching post would involve a deep cut in salary. Chu and Sicheng discussed together the letter he wrote setting forth his qualifications. They had read several essays he had written, including one on "Horyuji and the Architecture of the Han to Six Dynasties in China." They were impressed with this and with his knowledge of Japanese scholarship on the subject. He would obviously be a valuable addition.

In August 1932 Liu moved to Peking and joined the Institute. He was a quiet, clean-cut man four years older than Sicheng. In recognition of this age discrepancy the small staff was reorganized. Sicheng, his junior in years but senior at the Institute, had been "Director of Research." This title was now changed to "Director of Technical Studies" and Liu was given a coordinate title, "Director of Documentary Studies." Yet since field research and documentary research were inseparable in their operations, each did both. They worked together as a mutually supportive team leading their younger colleagues through the following decade. In the course of his field trips during these years Liu made a number of important discoveries fully presented in several volumes published by the Nanking Institute of Technology.

The first joint operation of Liang and Liu was neither a field trip nor a documentary research. Through Chu, the Institute was asked to restore a two-story imperial library, the Wen-yuan Ko, that had been erected in 1776 in the southwestern part of the Palace in Peking. Its function was to house an extraordinary compilation of some 36,000 volumes of literary treasures from the past, the *Ssu-k'u ch'uan-shu,* which had been assembled at the order of the Ch'ien-lung emperor in the 1770s. By 1932 the beams that supported the bookshelves were discovered to have sagged heavily. The Museum authorities of the Palace asked the Institute to investigate and make plans for restoring the building.

Liang, with his colleagues Liu Tun-chen and Tsai Fang-ying, took careful measurements on which to base the necessary calculations. These demonstrated that the weight borne by the beams was about double the safe load. They recommended replacing the beams with girders of reinforced concrete. It was Liang's first experience of participating in plans for restoring an old building.

10. The Liang Household

The birth of a son to Whei and Sicheng in August 1932 was a matter for universal rejoicing. Westernized though they were in many ways, the Liangs were not impervious to the age-old Chinese exultation at producing a male child for homage to the ancestors and safeguard of the living. They decided to name the newborn son for the Sung Dynasty architectural genius both parents idolized. They had demonstrated their devotion to Li Chieh in their choice of their wedding date. Now, four years later, they turned again to his memory and named their son Tsung-chieh, "Follower of (Li) Chieh."

At the time, Whei was undergoing the pangs, possibly her first, of being housebound. Not that she did not have servants, but her household included a little daughter, the new baby, and, most demanding of all, a mother who was emotionally dependent on her and whose mind was as tightly bound as her feet. Chinese tradition held that she should content herself with ministering to her mother, her husband, and her children; hiring, training, and supervising her six or seven servants; keeping a sharp eye on the persons and wares of all outside purveyors who entered; in short, she was assigned the role of judicious household manager. These duties were calculated to consume most of her time and energies within her four walls. Household errands outside were delegated to servants. The lady of the house was expected to go out only on occasion to visit relatives, pay respects at funerals, or attend special celebrations.

Lin Whei-yin was of course a member of the transitional generation, in rebellion against the traditionally accepted restraints. She was Western-educated not only in England and the United States but also in China in her high-school years. She had lived abroad the free life of a student and had taught and designed with Liang in Mukden. Yet here at home everything conspired to clip her wings. No period at desk or drawing board was safe from interruption by children, servants, or mother. She was the prisoner, in effect, of these ten persons in her household, who turned to her for every decision. Naturally, this was partly her fault. Of all her varied interests, her concern with people and their problems was paramount. She was irked to be disturbed in the middle of drafting an architectural plan or writing a poem, but instead of defending herself she turned her attention to the immediate human dilemma.

This was the time of our meeting and my role in Lin Whei-yin's life developed out of these narrowed circumstances. She needed a congenial, sympathetic listener. The chance to use her English-language skills to tell me the vagaries of her daily life she found stimulating. In my turn, I was fascinated by her vivid anecdotes, which led me inside Chinese life from the threshold I had so recently crossed.

My entry into the life of the household was regarded with suspicion by the mother and the servants. Though I came by invitation, I was an outsider. My foreign features and dress proclaimed me different, safe to encounter on the street but within the four walls faintly ominous. Despite these misgivings my comings and goings were in time accepted.

As our friendship deepened I often went over to the Liangs' at the end of the day by bicycle or ricksha. A servant unbolted the twin heavy red-lacquered doors of the courtyard entrance. I would walk through the inner garden to find Whei. Settled in a cozy corner of the living room with cups of hot tea, we hastened to relate the stories or thoughts we had been saving for each other. Together we might analyze and compare Chinese and American values and ways of life, but then we would dart off into our many common interests in literature, art, and adventure, and yet again to sharing memories of friends the other had not known.

One of these was, of course, the gifted poet Hsü Chih-mo. She talked to me of him from time to time, and never ceased to miss him. I often thought that the wide range and escalating excitement of her conversations with me in fluent English may have been echoes of their effervescent exchanges, which had opened up for her a wider world from the time she was a young girl in London.

Hsü's friend, the philosopher Chin Yueh-lin, known by his nickname, "Lao Jin," was, in effect, an adopted member of the Liang family and lived in a small house adjoining theirs. A side door in the Liangs' living room gave access to Lao Jin's house across his narrow single courtyard. Through that door he was often sought to join the Liangs' gatherings. The flow was reversed on Saturday afternoons, when Lao Jin was at home to his cronies. At such times the Liangs passed through his narrow courtyard and entered the inner room to mingle with the guests, all of whom were their dear friends.

The company were a close circle of Lao Jin's academic colleagues. They included, among others, two political scientists. Chang Shiro was a man of principles, outspoken and impressive. Ch'ien Tuan-sheng was a sharp-witted analyst of Chinese government and deeply interested in international affairs. Chen Deison was a tall, dignified, and reserved economist. Somewhat older were two professors who had pioneered their fields in China. Li Chi, trained in anthropology and archaeology at Harvard, led the Academia Sinica's Shang Dynasty excavations. Sociologist T'ao Meng-ho (also known as L. K. T'ao) had received his training in London and headed the influential Institute of Social Research. These men, like architectural historian Liang and philosopher Lao Jin himself, were all modernizers, devoted to applying scientific method in the study of China's past and present. A number of the wives turned up on Saturdays too and took part in the lively conversations.

We were invited and in our early days in Peking attended at times with Whei as sponsor. We were welcomed by Lao Jin and tolerated by the others, who were of course talking, gossiping, and laughing as they swapped stories in Chinese. By the time John became their Tsinghua faculty colleague in our second year, and our Chinese-language skills improved, we had ceased to be outsiders.

Frequently the Saturday afternoon gatherings at Lao Jin's moved on to a Chinese restaurant. One such evening was memorable for an extraordinary story Whei told friends around the table. In the chaotic life-style of the Liang living room there was always much going on, particularly the loyal amah, Ch'en-ma, running in and out to deliver news of crises requiring Whei's decision. Every crisis, not only inside the household but in the immediate neighborhood, came in this way to Whei for a solution.

Whei's story began with the entry of Ch'en-ma one day to report excitedly that there was a gaping hole in the roof of the neighbors' house that abutted the Liangs' to the west, beyond the high wall of the compound. She explained that the occupants, who were too poor to pay for repairing it, hoped Whei would take it up with the landlord. As usual, Whei at once dropped everything to investigate. Talking with the landlord she discovered the family paid for three rooms only fifty coppers a month — ten cents' rent. The landlord explained that in the time of Emperor Ch'ien Lung two hundred years ago the ancestors of the present family had rented the property at a rent fixed to a certain amount of cash. Since the same family had lived in it ever since, by Chinese law the landlord could not raise the rent. Whei's lively and detailed account of the story ended with her giving the landlord a roof-mending contribution. We all laughed and applauded. "How typical of Whei to serve up for us this bizarre evidence of Peking's still-living past!"

Whei's living room, flooded with sunshine from the south, was often as crowded as Lao Jin's Saturday "at home," but with a far more heterogeneous throng. In addition to children and servants running about, there were relatives of various generations. Several Liang nieces in college at the time loved to bring their classmates to this animated household. There they often happened upon the poets and writers who came as admirers of Whei's published works and returned often for the charm of her company.

The celebrated novelist Shen Ts'ung-wen had grown up in the wilds of western Hunan, where he traveled widely and lived the life of a soldier. Now in Peking he was pouring out stories based on the observations of his early years. For a time he taught at Tsinghua, but in 1934 he was made editor of the Literary Supplement of *Ta Kung Pao,* where most of Whei's writings were published. He was almost the same age as Whei. She was captivated both by the artistry of his works and by the exotic world they portrayed — so remote from her own background. They developed a close friendship. She tended to mother him, and he, like a fond son, turned to her to settle problems or offer advice.

As one example, Shen was left alone for a short time in Peking when his young wife, to whom he was devoted, went south to visit her family. One morning he hurried to the Liang house nearly in tears to find comfort from Whei. He told her that he had been writing his wife daily, sharing with her all his feelings, moods, and thoughts. Then he showed Whei the letter he had just received from his wife, which had caused his misery. It was a sorrowful lament venting her bitterness at reading in his long frank letters his admiration and care for a young girl authoress in Peking. He defended himself to Whei. He could not even imagine any conflict between these feelings and his love for his wife. How could he help writing that he admired and cared for someone when he *does,* he just *does.* He can love so many persons and things, he just *does!*

For Whei, an emotional tangle even so minor as this was the breath of life. "If I wrote a story with just such situations and such arguments, one would think I invented the situation badly and that it was untrue to life! But here it is, take it or leave it! And of all people, that it should be he, the quiet, understanding, both 'feeling' and 'gutty' person, a novelist himself, a genius at that! And he has got himself into this scrape and is feeling just as hopeless as any young and inexperienced little boy in such matters. The poet in him rebelled and looked so lost and puzzled by life and its conflicts that I thought of Shelley and also remembered Chih-mo in his mad struggles against conventional sorrow, and I couldn't help feeling fondly amused. How utterly charming he was that morning and how amusing! And how old and tired I sat there, talking to him, scolding him, advising him, and discussing with him life and its inconsistencies, human nature and its charms and tragedies, idealism and reality! . . .

"Little have I thought before that people who have lived and been brought up in so different a way as he has would have such feelings I could so well understand, and be troubled by such problems as I have known in other contexts. This is a new and deep experience for me and that is why I think proletarian literature is nonsense. Good literature is good literature regardless of the ideology of the people. From now on I am going to have fresh faith in my writing as Lao Jin has been hoping and trying to convince me of its worth all along. Hurrah!"

11. Further Searches

It was obvious to Sicheng that his first two field trips, which had involved such complex travels and had located two very important Liao temples, were matters of lucky chance. "Since there existed no guides to buildings important in the history of Chinese architecture, we sought out old buildings 'like a blind man riding a blind horse.'" Characteristically, he soon set about organizing a careful methodology for the Institute's future operations to assure that other architectural treasures of the past still surviving in North China would not be overlooked.

Sicheng described the procedure that was followed from this time on. The Institute every year dispatched small teams of field workers headed by a research fellow on trips of two or three months to comb the countryside for ancient monuments. Every trip was preceded by careful preparations in library research. Local gazetteers and books on history, geography, and Buddhism yielded a list of promising structures. An itinerary was made up. Every item on the list had to be located, identified, and, if still existing, measured and photographed. Sicheng himself led most of these expeditions, though he was physically the least rugged of the group.

Before starting out the team notified the provincial government of their plans and purposes and asked to have the local *yamen* alerted. On arrival they usually paid a call on the officials at the *yamen* and asked permission to be assigned a room in a school.

"My experience," Sicheng commented, "was that local people were not interested in architecture. When I told them I was interested in antiquities they would guide me to their stone stelae inscribed in earlier times. They were interested in calligraphy . . . , impressed by the written word, not the carpenter's handiwork."

In their field explorations, the teams had to pay the greatest attention to wooden structures. They were actually racing with time, for these structures were all the while steadily disintegrating. Waves of new influences, stirring up the whims of a few men in a conservative town, could innocently deface a masterpiece by their efforts at "modernizing" an "old-fashioned" structure. Delicate window traceries and finely carved door panels were always among the first to suffer such outrages. Seldom did they come upon a real gem left in peace and beauty by nature and humans alike. Even a stray spark from an incense stick could reduce a whole temple to ashes. Often, inspired by literary sources with wonderful visions of old monuments, they would find, after hundreds of miles of anticipatory pilgrimage, a heap of ruins, with perhaps a few roof tiles and stone column bases for a reward.

"Our trips themselves were also adventures full of unexpected ups and downs. With physical discomfort taken for granted, we frequently enjoyed unexpected and unforgettable experiences of rare charm and delight. Generally the journeys, like odd kinds of prolonged picnics, were either extremely disconcerting or highly entertaining when we encountered comical but disastrous mishaps.

"Unlike the highly expensive expeditions of archaeologists, big game hunters, or any tropical or arctic scientific explorers," Sicheng continued, "the equipment for our trips was scanty. Besides instruments for surveying and photographing, our luggage consisted mostly of gadgets of the home-made order, designed and modified by our members as they accumulated experience. Knapsacks like an electrician's, to be worn while working perched precariously on top of any part of a building, were among our favorite treasures. They held anything from a spool of string to a telescopic pole that could be extended like a long, rigid fishing rod. Often we had to make camp, cook, eat, and sleep under such very different circumstances each day and night, and our means of transportation were so uncertain, ranging from the most ancient and quaint to the more usual and up to date, that what we considered essential could not help being peculiar.

"Aside from architecture we often came across subjects of artistic and ethnological interest—handicrafts of different localities, archaic dramatic performances in out-of-the-way towns, queer customs, picturesque fairs, and so on, but we had to economize our precious film. On most of my trips I was accompanied by my wife, herself an architect. But being also a writer and lover of dramatic art, she, more often than I, let her attention stray and enthusiastically insisted on some subjects for the camera at any cost. I was always glad after we returned from a trip to have the valuable pictures of scenes and buildings that would otherwise have been neglected."[1]

Sicheng's 1933 field trip to Cheng Ting in Hopei Province, some hours south of Peking by train, with his faithful draftsman, Mo Tsung-chiang, was a memorable expedition. Visible from a considerable distance was the

"Cheng Ting Pusa," a Buddhist figure that he described as a "colossal bronze statue of a forty-two-armed Kuan-yin, about seventy feet high, standing on a beautifully carved marble platform." A three-story hall had originally sheltered it, but when he visited Cheng Ting the upper portions of the building were all gone, leaving the statue standing in the open with all forty extra arms missing.

A stele at the site explained that it had been cast at the order of the emperor who founded the Sung Dynasty to replace a famous bronze statue destroyed several years earlier. The casting was done in seven sections beginning on the twentieth day of the seventh month of A.D. 971, but the date of completion was not recorded.

Sicheng noted, "The Kuan-yin statue had been renovated by the devout but ignorant abbot by covering the bronze with coats of paint in bright primary colors, giving it the appearance of an ugly giant doll. I had to comfort myself by thinking that the paint will not last very long, perhaps not more than a century."

The statue is only one feature of the complex of temple structures known as Lung-hsing Ssu, the lodestone that had attracted Liang to the site. Of all the buildings contained in the complex, the most important and most unique is the Sung Dynasty Mo-ni Tien (A.D. 1030). To anyone who loves Sung landscape paintings, it brings to life the familiar shapes of those temples hidden in the pine-clad hills that the painters loved to depict. Unlike the oblong temples of later dates, it is cross-shaped in plan and has a hipped gable on each of its four sides. Sicheng knew this style from paintings, but this was the only existing example that he had seen. Another feature of the temple complex is its Library building (c. 960–1126), which contains a towering "sutra cabinet," a revolving bookcase to hold Buddhist scriptures. To make room for the large heavy bookcase, to support its weight, and to accommodate its motion, many ingenious adaptations had to be improvised in the construction. Sicheng examined it with admiration and delight.[2]

In the fall of 1933 the Institute dispatched a number of staff members to Ta-t'ung in North Shansi Province, a frontier town just inside the Great Wall from Mongolia. It has two important groups of Buddhist temples of the Liao Dynasty. Japanese scholars had reported the Buddhist statues they contained, but the structures themselves had not been studied. Liu Tun-chen had a major role in directing the researches on the Hua-Yen Ssu and Shan-Hua Ssu temple groups. Whei chose to spend her time at the famous Yun-kang Buddhist caves nearby, where she could sketch and photograph architectural details carved in the living rock for evidence of the lost wooden architecture of the much earlier Northern Wei Dynasty (A.D. 450–500).

Sicheng, who was working with the others on the temple groups, had already planned to make a side trip with his faithful assistant, Mo, to a small town some fifty miles south of Ta-t'ung, which the Japanese wrote contained fine Buddhist images in an eleventh-century pagoda. Known originally from its locality as "the Ying Chou pagoda," the town's status had changed and it was "the Wooden Pagoda of Fo-kung Ssu at Ying *Hsien*" that was Sicheng's target. Before planning a trip to such a remote spot he had decided to inquire whether the pagoda still existed and, if so, in what condition. There was of course no access by long distance telephone, and he knew nobody in Peking who had ever been there. The idea occurred to him to turn to the postal service for help. He wrote a letter to the Ying Hsien postmaster asking him to have the best local photographer take some pictures of the pagoda and mail them to him in Peking. He offered to mail in return some appropriate gift from Peking that the photographer might designate. The scheme worked perfectly. The photographs arrived and showed the pagoda to be in good condition and essentially unaltered since its erection date, A.D. 1056. The heart of the photographer was also gladdened by a gift of the stationery he requested.

As the Institute's project of studying the Ta-t'ung temples progressed satisfactorily, Sicheng found the opportunity to slip away with Mo to Ying Hsien, which now appeared to him to be well within reach. The two men boarded a bus in Ta-t'ung for the ride southward only to discover when they reached the bus stop that they were still twenty-five miles from their destination. They had to hire a mule cart and suffer six hours of bumpy ride. "It was sunset time," Sicheng wrote, "when we reached a point about five miles west of the town. Most unexpectedly I saw ahead of me, at the far end of the almost straight trail, a sparkling jewel on a dark purplish background—the red and white pagoda reflecting the golden setting sun against the mountain beyond. It was dark when we reached the walled city—a miserable town on alkaline soil, poverty stricken, with only a few hundred mud houses and barely a dozen trees within the city enclosure. But it boasts the only wooden pagoda existing in China today."[3]

According to Sicheng, the bulk of the pagoda "towered over the city like a black giant. But on the southern side of the top floor was visible a light, a speck that penetrated the enveloping darkness. That, I found out later, was the 'ten-thousand-year-lamp' that had been burning there night and day for nearly nine hundred years."

He did not identify his source for this story, but the name must have mesmerized him. It seems entirely incredible that a fire, however small, had been burning night and day in all weathers inside the tower through those nine hundred years. Furthermore, the local economy could never have afforded the fuel bill!

When the pagoda was built, in A.D. 1056, the Sung Dynasty had been driven to the south, and part of North China was ruled by the Liao Dynasty—"barbarians" from beyond the Great Wall. Sicheng pointed out that the pagoda's construction is similar in principle to that of the earlier "high-rise" tower of Tu-le Ssu (A.D. 984): "Since each upper story is underpinned by a mezzanine story, it actually consists of nine tiers of superposed orders."

He had reason to remember the top of the pagoda in detail. "It is finished with an elaborate spire of wrought iron, secured to the corners of the uppermost roof by eight iron chains. I was up on that spire one sunny clear afternoon absorbed in measuring and photographing, when the clouds closed in rapidly but unnoticed. Suddenly a terrific thunderbolt struck nearby. Taken by surprise, I nearly lost my hold on the icy-cold chain two hundred feet above the ground."

In the course of his field researches, he examined and published many Chinese pagodas. He comments, "As an architectural monument, giving expression and accent to the landscape of China, nothing figures more prominently than the easily pronounced and remembered Chinese name *t'a,* for pagoda. From its first appearance till the present day, the Chinese pagoda has remained essentially 'a multi-storied tower surmounted by a pile of metal discs.' It is the happy combination of two principal components: the indigenous 'multi-storied tower' and the Indian stupa, the 'pile of metal discs.' By combination of the two components, the Chinese pagoda may be classified into four principal types: one-storied, multi-storied, multi-eaved, and stupa. Whatever its size or type, a *t'a* marks the burial site of a Buddhist relic or the tomb of a Buddhist monk."

The Ying Hsien pagoda is a matchless national treasure. Though many wooden pagodas were erected in China in earlier times, this is the only pagoda built of that vulnerable material to have survived to the present. In recent years it has been expertly restored and reinforced by specialists trained under Liang at Tsinghua University.

Thereafter, when Sicheng had located through gazetteers or other sources monuments that sounded promising, he made it a practice to write the local postmaster asking his help in obtaining a photograph of the building. He enclosed a small amount of money to reimburse a local photographer for his time and expenses. In this way he checked in advance a number of the easily available targets along the two trunk lines that ran south of Peking, the Peking-Hankow and Tientsin-Pukow Railways.

Library research and photographic ingenuities were immensely helpful, but a children's jingle was responsible for one of Sicheng's most prized discoveries. Like our Mother Goose rhymes it had a catchy rhythm (in the original Chinese):

The Tsang Chou lion, the Ying Chou pagoda,
The Cheng Ting Pusa, the Chao Chou bridge.

To him the lion meant nothing, but when he heard the familiar names "Ying Chou pagoda" and "Cheng Ting Pusa," he pricked up his ears. This innocent boasting of human creative works in North China went straight to his heart. Whoever it was had invented the rhyme shared his passions for architectural treasures of the past. He was inspired to seek out the bridge for himself.

Located about thirty miles southeast of Cheng Ting in southern Hopei Province, the town of Chao Chou, like Ying Chou, had changed its status and become known as Chao *Hsien*. In 1934 Liang went by rail from Peking to Shih-chia-chuang and made the side trip to Chao Hsien. There finally, as he wrote, "I encountered the third of these landmarks, the astonishing and superb An-chi Ch'iao [also known as 'Great Stone Bridge'], an open spandrel bridge of the Sui Dynasty (A.D. 590–618)!" He quotes an eighth-century citation by a T'ang Prime Minister who had in his time been equally excited over the discovery: "The stone bridge over the Hsiao River at Chao Chou is the work of the Sui builder, Li Chun. Its construction is so strange that nobody knows how it was built. Just look at the ingenuity with which the stones are handled! They are dressed into perfect forms, and these well-fitting blocks interlock with one another, forming a lofty arch without the help of columns — how astonishing ! . . . They are laid in lime mortar and held together by iron keys. The two ends are penetrated by four arches, for the purpose of reducing the forceful onrush of the ferocious current. Without great wisdom and foresight [of the builder], the construction would not have been possible. The balustrades and the posts are carved in the forms of dragons and beasts, winding, crouching, interlacing and flying as though alive."

The translation is Sicheng's and he comments, "As to the statement that 'its construction is so strange that nobody knows how it was built,' it is an evidence that the construction of the bridge is truly the work of a genius. It is not the stereotyped structure of the ordinary artisan following the tradition of the period in which he is living." Additional citations emphasize that even as early as the T'ang Dynasty the bridge was considered extraordinary.

The vaults, of both the main span and the open spandrels, were built in the Roman way by placing a number of separate strings of arches side by side, in this case twenty-eight strings altogether. The bridge is 115 feet long between the points where the two ends now emerge from the banks of the river. Sicheng noted that "The clear span, if excavated from the banks, would be considerably longer. But our attempts to find its spring line by excavation at the abutments failed when we reached the water level seven feet below the dry riverbed." He adds that "My disappointment at my failure was only rivaled by that of the local onlookers, who had anticipated confirmation of the folktale with which they were all familiar, namely, that "the stone circle completes itself underground."

Liang's delight at discovering this unique Chinese construction, designed and built a millennium earlier than its nearest European equivalent (in France), led him to linger at the site, confirming his measurements, excavating for further information, and photographing from all angles. The bridge had not only survived for some 1,300 years but was still in active use.

At Chao Hsien he also found a "Little Stone Bridge," a twelfth-century imitation of its great neighbor. He published his studies of both in the Society's *Bulletin* the same year.

While Sicheng was finding his extraordinary bridge, I was on a field trip of my own in the neighboring province of Shantung during which I also discovered some treasures of early Chinese architecture. As a student at Harvard I had particularly admired the rubbings of the Han Dynasty engraved slabs from the Wu family tombs in Shantung. Sets of the inked paper rubbings of the designs engraved on these stones in the second century A.D. had reached scholars in Europe and the United States, whose publications in Western languages made them world famous. One of my first acts on reaching Peking had been to purchase a set for myself. Since then I had spent hours poring over them. The round horses and chariots were delightful. Conventionalized human figures filled the elegantly composed scenes. The rank of each was clear from his costume. In my ignorance, I marveled at the unique aesthetics but knew nothing of the famous stories portrayed.

I wanted to see the Wu slabs for myself; my spoken Chinese by this time was adequate for travel purposes and ordinary conversations. An American woman friend was happy to go with me for company on our trip of nearly two weeks. Much of this time we spent exploring other parts of Shantung. But our destination, the Wu graveyard in the southwest corner of the province, was remote, reached by a change of train, then a jitney bus, an overnight stop, and finally a long walk.

The Wu stone slabs, gathered in no particular order inside a small building at the site on a vast plain, were of many shapes and sizes. Some were engraved on one side only. Some had engravings on front and back or front and side. There were free-standing pillars. Most surprising to me were the large slabs that had gable-shaped tops. The exhibition of stone engravings I had expected to find turned out to be no art exhibit but a collection of constituent parts of buildings. Architecture! What sorts of buildings? Above ground or underground? How many? Might it be possible to reconstruct them?

The idea fascinated me at the time, and I did in fact undertake the task after my return to Cambridge several years later. Studying the publications on the subject was stimulating. I was shocked to realize how ignorant I had been on my visit to the site. My hypothetical reconstruction involved four steps: (1) to assemble as full a set of clear Wu rubbings as I could find; (2) to photograph them at a uniform scale; (3) to excise the unapt margins; and (4) to move the photographs around on a table top, like jigsaw puzzle pieces, until gables matched, decorated borders met, and the rear and side walls of three open-faced shrines were completed to the best of my ability. I published my effort in a thirty-six page article in 1941 that explained all my choices and decisions.[4]

Because the rubbings were world famous and my architectural reconstructions were the first to be proposed, I achieved a reputation in certain limited scholarly circles. It was exhilarating. My interest in the aesthetics of Chinese art had now been joined to an appreciation of structural relationships in such archaeological survivals as the Wu slabs. The influence of the Liangs was clear. I was deeply indebted to them.

12. A Joint Expedition in Shansi

Liang's dream of finding a timber-framed temple of T'ang date surviving in the twentieth century had still not been realized despite his widespread searches in North China. He knew by now that if it existed at all it would be found in some out-of-the-way place where it would have escaped those evil human and natural influences that threaten architectural destruction.

The mountainous province of Shansi, west of Peking, where he had already done some exploring in the north, was a likely target for his search. When he heard that John and I were planning to spend the summer of 1934 in central Shansi and that we hoped he and Whei would visit us there, he could accept our invitation free of qualms that he would be neglecting his primary goal.

They came in August, to find us snugly settled near Fenchow (now Fenyang) in an old stone flour mill beside a rippling stream, the Yu-tao Ho. Dr. Arthur Hummel, a good friend, turned over to us for that summer a mill that had been a family refuge for them for many years. He was a much-admired missionary scholar and historian who had been recently made Chief of the Orientalia Division of the Library of Congress. The mill was a rambling one-story building enclosing a pleasant square courtyard. There had formerly been many such mills along the course of the stream, but the development in Fenchow of a flour-milling industry using modern machinery had spelled the end for most of them, including ours. That some were still in use was proven by the noodles locally available, which, often delicious, were nearly always gritty from the grindstone.

The narrow valley through which the stream rushed down from the nearby mountains was crowded with poplars. Their dappled shade, the gurgling water, and the thick stone walls of the mills guaranteed a blissful coolness to the inhabitants during the torrid North China summer. Foreign missionaries had discovered the place and made a mini-resort for themselves at the far upper end of the valley. There they could gather from other parts of North China for a refreshing summer reunion before returning to their scattered and often lonely outposts.

We took with us from Peking Chinese texts and papers, dictionaries and other books, boxes of "character cards," blocks of watercolor paper, paints, and — by special arrangement — a Chinese informant, formerly a minor official in the Peking government, who could aid my husband in his studies of Ch'ing documents. An utterly urban type, he was miserable in the countryside. He scorned the local folk and regarded their dialect as "the twittering of birds." Faithful to his duties during the day, he endured them only by looking forward to a generous cupful of Fenchow's fiery liquor at sunset. He was a trial — for us — but also a gifted raconteur. After his sundown cup he entertained us with court gossip and other tales of the old days. We hung on his words; they were, after all, in Chinese. The arrival of the Liangs brightened his life enormously, but they had not made their long trip to comfort him. When, shortly, we four began our architectural explorations, he gladly returned to Peking.

We were all fascinated by the dominant local domestic architecture — cave dwellings in the loess cliffs. The loess soil characteristic of much of northwestern China had been formed over untold centuries by dust blowing from the Gobi Desert. The homogeneous particles cling tightly to one another, making an easily worked medium for excavation. Best of all, when carved or cut away, the loess separates in vertical cleavage instead of slithering down in talus slopes. The walls of our valley were steep loess cliffs in which numerous individual barrel-vaulted rooms, and even dwellings of several such rooms, had been hollowed out and lined with bricks. These formed our neighboring villages, from which the peasants climbed to the level tops to plow and sow their crops.

The flat-topped cliffs, on either side of the valleys carved by streams from the mountains, reminded me of the mesas of northern New Mexico. The lay of the land was very like the approaches to Los Alamos with the Jemez Mountains above, and down the valleys the sweeping view across the plain to the Sangre de Cristo range on the far side.

The life of the valley had a number of simple but clever expedients. Little boys led the family goats on leashes from one grazing spot to another. The rushing stream was no barrier to them. Goats and boys both crossed without risk on ingenious "bridges" of two or three logs wedged side by side and thickly covered with a layer of sod. As for the adults, preparing the soil, weeding, and harvesting were all manual tasks. American home gardeners could learn from them a Chinese technical advance. While they leaned down to the planted rows with a small curved weeding blade in the right hand, they supported their weight with a foot-long stick held in the left: Result, progress with less backache.

Whei was the author of the *Bulletin*'s report on this field exploration. Like every newcomer to the valley, she first commented on the surprising presence of flowing water in this arid area. It has, of course, its legend. "It is told that once at this place the horse of the Sung Emperor T'ai Tsung pawed the ground with his hoof, and up welled a spring of fresh water that relieved the thirst of three exhausted armies. The water of this spring has not stopped flowing since, but now, a thousand years later, it feeds tens of mill-wheels."

Our time with Sicheng had been relatively limited in Peking, but at Yu-tao Ho he was one of us. We four ate three meals a day together, and discovered the first day that he loved hot, peppery dishes. This quiet, self-contained man scintillated at the table. Our mealtimes were hilarious. The rest of the day he devoted to studying the architecture of the region and exploring for old buildings, or preparing to do so by consulting the local histories and maps he had brought with him. He worked out a proposed expedition for combing eight *hsien* (counties) from the provincial capital, Taiyuan, about ninety miles north of us, down to Chao-ch'eng, a small town south of us along the Fen River.

We four happily explored nearby temples on foot or donkeys and hired the missionaries' car for covering a wider area. John and I soon became adept at the simpler tasks of measuring while Sicheng was photographing and making notes and Whei was recording the important inscriptions from temple stelae.

In the start of her article Whei discusses some of the nearby temples and reveals an interesting discovery. She describes the Lung-t'ien temple as having a long north-south axis with a gateway building at the southern end. So far, very normal. Here, however, after we passed through the barrel vault in the gateway building we looked back and saw above the vault an open stage facing inward toward the courtyard. Whei comments:

"Many of the temples we have visited in central and southern Shansi have such buildings with stages. The stage is an elevated platform above the arched entry, surrounded on three sides by walls but open on the (inner) front. It faces (but does not protrude toward) the main hall of the temple. In the center of the stage are columns extending upward to the ridge of the roof that facilitate the division of the stage into front and back areas. In the left wall is a door from which a stone staircase of some ten steps leads down to the courtyard. In this temple the rear wall of the stage has the same function as a screen wall, to screen off the courtyard from evil influences."[1]

Troupes of Chinese opera performers traveled through the countryside to entertain the villagers. It was an age-old practice that had made the operas familiar and popular everywhere. The temple stage facing an interior walled courtyard provided appropriate spaces for performers and audience.

Sicheng regarded our local searches as useful training for us but was eager to press on toward greater goals. A little more than a year earlier, Sung editions of Buddhist sutras — some of the earliest printed works in existence — had been found in Kuang-sheng Ssu, a temple near Chao-ch'eng, some seventy miles south of us along the Fen River, making the name of the temple widely known to scholars. If the contents were Sung, the buildings of the temple might also be of Sung date. It was an exciting challenge.

The distance seemed trivial. We planned to hire a car and be there in less than a day. What we did not know in our secluded valley was that men were already at work truncating the road south. The Shansi warlord, Yen Hsi-shan, was expecting a military invasion by Chiang Kai-shek's Nanking government troops advancing northward to take over his province. To counter this threat, Yen had slyly purchased an entire German army narrow gauge railway, tracks and rolling stock, a vestige of World War I. The only road of entry for an army from the south lay along the east bank of the Fen River. Yen decided to outwit Chiang by having his provincial troops lay the railway tracks on the roadbed itself. This scheme was calculated to block entry of standard gauge rolling stock and at the same time thwart access by motor traffic.

Warnings, when they finally reached us, failed to weaken our determination to go to Chao-ch'eng. We did manage to hire from the missionaries a car with a cheery American driver and load it with cots, bedding, tinned food, architectural gear, and personal luggage. But summer rains had turned the loess roads to gumbo. By sunset we had gone only ten miles and had not even reached the bank of the river. We unloaded the car and wished the driver Godspeed on the return journey. Nearby was a temple we had photographed a few days earlier on one of our carefree architectural explorations. We moved our belongings there and set up our cots on the veranda of the open courtyard where the four walls of the temple could protect us from the excited crowd outside. They soon found that the parapet of the high town gate opposite was an excellent vantage point from which to keep us in view, but by that time we were too exhausted to care.

On day two we hired two mule-drawn carts, crossed the river by ferry, and managed to cover fifteen miles to Chieh-hsu. There in the late afternoon we first encountered Yen's narrow gauge railroad. It was a shocking sight. The rusty tracks, streetcar size, were laid on dirt embankments dumped on the highway. Since the roadbed had not been tamped or rolled, the tracks wavered from side to side and up and down in a distressing way. No workmen were visible. This section was apparently considered completed; we would catch up with the current construction further south. Here the railroad lay along the very brink of the river bank, forcing our crude open carts, each hardly more than a four-plank floor on four wheels, to thread their way along a narrow pathway in a ditch behind the tracks.

We put up at a good inn and explored the city. The temples were disappointing, but the streets and houses gave us the impression of a transplanted central Italy. High crenelated walls lined the narrow streets, and great arches marked the intersections. We had glimpses through open doorways into some of the two-story residential courtyards, but no time or opportunity to study them in detail. Later we learned that these high-walled mansions had been the original homes of the nineteenth-century Shansi family banking firms that sold letters of credit, especially to officials who wanted to transfer funds from one to another part of China. This obviated the need to send shipments of silver bullion under convoy and gave rise to a new financial class.

At Ling-shih next day we finally encountered the railroad builders at work. Now our problems multiplied because we had to compete with Yen's soldiers for our needs. The only wheeled vehicles that could take us further south were rickshas. They were narrow enough to use local paths and the pullers could cope with local contingencies. All had been commandeered for the railroad building, but a wily innkeeper found us three at an exorbitant price. We shifted our luggage onto them and set off on foot. We needed a stopping place for the night, but the temples we came upon were full of the laborer-soldiers and the local inns were frightful. By the time we reached Chang-chia Chuang some eight miles further on, it was getting dark and we were exhausted. We could go no further. The high walls of the village houses now looked to us more inhospitable than charming.

Desperate, we picked a village gate tower as a public refuge and, carrying our luggage up, took possession. Hullabaloo ensued. There were soldiers in residence and they were indignant. At last a flustered major appeared and offered us a room in a private house in exchange for our vacating his premises. We accepted. That night we slept in a lofty upstairs room of one of those high-walled mansions we had been admiring from the exterior. Its windows opened on a secret garden to the north, and its door, to the south, gave onto a balcony overlooking the interior courtyard with its elaborately carved columns and brackets. Presumably it had been commandeered by Yen for his officers from one of the wealthy Shansi banking families.

The next morning we were eager to push on to the south. But the major turned up. Obviously impressed by Sicheng's gentlemanly ways and famous lineage, he insisted on guiding us through a leisurely tour of the town. Parting involved an exchange of formal courtesies that further delayed us. Not until mid-morning did we manage to get away. Trucks bringing supplies for the railway builders had ploughed mudholes into bottomless jelly, and blasting for railroad curves had covered our pathways with rocks and debris. One ricksha damaged a wheel. In these chaotic circumstances progress was slow. The pullers stopped to rest and eat every two hours. By nightfall we were still seven miles from Huo Chou.

The ricksha men realized, as we were to discover, that over rough ground in the dark this would be a four-hour pull. They refused to go further. Since there was no hope of a decent place to stay within the distance, we bribed the men to go on and hired a child with a lantern to guide us. We ourselves walked the whole distance, slopping through the mud. A miracle: when we arrived at the city gate at eleven P.M. it was still open. Inside, in an opium den, we found a man who could guide us to the China Inland Mission Station, where we knocked loudly and yelled our identities. The great gates were unbolted for us by a kindly old Chinese bible-woman. She raised our spirits for the moment with heaping bowls of noodle soup, and we fell into our cots dead tired.

Our missionary hosts were the Trickeys, a hospitable and devout English couple with six smallish children. The friendly welcome as much as the cleanliness and order were soothing to our spirits. We stayed two days with them, paying, of course, for our food and lodging, while it rained some more. It was a blessed respite for us after our thirty-mile walk in the mud. Sicheng, dedicated and indomitable, explored the town of Huo Chou (Huo Hsien) in the rain and found some beautiful and important temples, several of Yuan date, which he showed us later. The most interesting was of course occupied by soldiers, so investigation was impossible.

The Trickeys sent us off to Chao-ch'eng with their blessing and suggested we stop overnight there with another missionary, Miss Romke. The rain had stopped and the countryside was green and beautiful in the sunlight. We were in high spirits to be approaching our goal. By this time we were all becoming seasoned walkers — Sicheng, too, despite his lameness from his boyhood accident.

This section of the road had to be heightened drastically to form an embankment suitable even for this flimsy railway. Teams of soldier-laborers shoveling at the nearby cliffs were filling baskets with the loess soil. Other soldiers transported the loads, one basket on each end of a carrying pole, across to dump on the roadbed, and then retraced their steps. A total of several hundred men were involved in these two related operations. It was a sight to remember — a reminder of those other throngs of men who had by unaided muscle power built the Great Wall and the ubiquitous city and village walls, and achieved such other engineering feats as the Grand Canal.

Sicheng, ever hopeful, had read in the local gazetteer that the city of Chao-ch'eng had a temple dating from the T'ang Dynasty. Entering the city gate at the end of the day we went directly there. No. His hopes were dashed. It was considerably later in date and not particularly interesting. We left for the China Inland Mission Station of the lone lady evangelist, the elderly Miss Romke. She gave us, unexpected visitors though we were, a warm welcome and baths before supper. She was surrounded by simple peasant women whom she had rescued from injustices, death threats, or starvation. Their devotion to her was plain in their faces. She, however, even while recounting to us their stories, took no credit herself. Her radiant face expressed devotion to the Lord who had accomplished these miracles.

We still had some fifteen miles to go, from Chao-ch'eng to our ultimate goal — the site of the Upper and Lower Temples of Kuang-sheng Ssu at the southern end of the Huo Shan range. This involved leaving the river and the soldiers behind. It was a refreshing change that morning. The good weather held and for much of our long day we could see on a distant hilltop the pagoda of the Upper Temple beckoning us on. Not until we almost stumbled upon it at the foot of the hill did we see the Lower Temple in the last flash of the setting sun. Its grandeur, graceful proportions, and huge *tou-kung* brackets promised an architectural treasure to reward our efforts.

By this time we were thoroughly exhausted. Our spirits were lifted by the Buddhist monks, who greeted us, fed us, and permitted us to set up our cots wherever we chose. The Liangs selected the interior of the main hall, where they could sleep in the shadows of the great Buddhas and study the overhead construction at first light. We preferred the open platform on the parapet of the small side Bell Tower, where we could look up at the brilliant stars.

In the bright morning sun we could see that the spirits of wind and water which are the arbiters of Chinese geomancy had provided a fitting site for this beautiful old temple. Behind it, to the north, it was protected from harsh winds by the slope of a hill. Below it, just outside the front gate, underground streams gushed forth into a pool of crystal clear water.

Water spirits in China are dragons. Where such clear springs as these are found there must be a dragon king, and one expects to find his shrine nearby. Sure enough, alongside the Lower Temple overlooking the pool was the Lung Wang Miao, "Temple of the Dragon King." It was an impressive sight in its own right. Much larger than the usual dragon shrines, it was double-eaved, set on a high platform, and surrounded by a continuous porch beneath the lower eave. Inside, the image of the Dragon King (more king than dragon) sat on his throne, but our attention was excited by the mural paintings around him on the walls. They depicted secular subjects, not the usual religious themes. One in particular was a scene of a theatrical performance. It showed costumed actors whose faces were painted in conventional patterns, prototypes of the elaborate facial designs seen in Chinese operas of later periods. Its inscription gave the date corresponding to A.D. 1326 in the Yuan Dynasty, when Chinese drama was taking its ultimate shape. Its relevance for study of the subject is obvious.[2]

Though news of the discovery in 1933 of the rare A.D. 1149 Buddhist scriptures at Kuang-sheng Ssu had led the Liangs to hope that the temples themselves might have been erected at that date or near it, they concluded from their inspection that both temples were fourteenth-century constructions, late Yuan or early Ming. A unique architectural feature caught their attention, first in the Lower Temple. Whei described it thus: "The Front Hall is five bays long with a hip and gable roof. . . . An interesting peculiarity of this building is that two of the columns that would normally define the separation of the bays in a regular grid are missing. These are the interior column on each of the front [south] corner bays. In place of these columns the roof is borne by big longitudinal beams extending from the gables to the central bay and, in the transverse direction, by unusually long and thick *ang* [cantilevers] prolonged obliquely until they meet, abutting each other at an upper beam." Sicheng was delighted with the originality and ingenuity of the fourteenth-century "architect" who had designed this framing of the beams for the support of the roof, and commented that he had not seen elsewhere such organic use of the wooden frame.

Climbing the steep path to the Upper Temple, we reached a glorious panorama visible from the southernmost spur of the Huo mountain range. The approach to the temple took us through two great gateway buildings. Beyond the second gate we came upon the tall pagoda in the center of the courtyard. This odd placement was typical of T'ang Buddhist architecture; later periods normally had two pagodas in such a courtyard, one on each side of the temple's central axis. The Liangs were not surprised to learn that both Kuang-sheng Ssu temples were originally built during T'ang times but were destroyed in an earthquake in A.D. 1303, to be rebuilt in 1319, perhaps copying to some extent the original construction. They pointed out to us here the same inventive framing of the beams that they had admired in the Lower Temple. All of us enjoyed the beautiful Buddhist sculptures, which presided over the halls.

The pagoda, octagonal and thirteen stories high, was entirely sheathed in highly colored glazed tile, which sparkled in the sunlight. As we were examining the great Buddha enthroned on the ground floor, the first steps of a staircase leading upward in the interior caught our eyes. We decided to climb up, never imagining what a bizarre adventure it would turn out to be. The stairway was dark, the brick steps were narrow and shallow, and the risers were steep. The only light came from a small opening to the sunlit exterior at each story, some three feet high and two feet wide, through the thick outer wall. We groped our way up in single file. At the top of the first flight, we were startled to find that there were no landings. When you bumped your head against a blank wall you knew you had come to the end of one flight of stairs. You had to turn around there and step over empty space onto the first step of the next flight. To steady you in the precarious maneuver, hand holds had been provided by removing a brick here and there in the wall. It sounds formidable, but the construction was so precise that as we climbed we soon learned just how to cross the gaps and where to reach for the hand holds. At intervals we could crawl out on hands and knees to the small apertures to look at the superb view from this extra height. Who designed this unique interior, or when, we did not discover. The only date connected with the pagoda appeared to be 1515, in the Ming Dynasty, when it was recorded that the pagoda received its coating of glazed tile.

Descending to the Lower Temple to bid the monks goodbye and pick up our luggage, we asked them to explain the freshly whitewashed walls in the principal temple halls. We were well aware that this would be an embarrassing question. They told us that in 1927 the monks had sold the frescoes on both end walls of the Main Hall to a curio dealer to enable them to repair the temple buildings. Seeing our dismay, they defended the action by saying the buildings were so dilapidated at that time that the frescoes would have been lost in any case. Was this just a sly tactic to assure architectural researchers that preservation of the buildings was the worthy motive for the sale? We knew that a number of leading museums in the United States and one in Toronto had on display frescoes from Shansi temples they had reputedly bought from the Japanese dealer Yamanaka. Were all these monks accepting money in exchange for artistic treasures in order to save buildings?

The trip back to Yu-tao Ho took several more days but was not quite so arduous as the trip south had been. We had time and occasion to discuss this and other aspects of the experiences we had shared. The architectural treasures we would carry in our memories were the temples, and in addition our night in the two-story mansion with crenelated walls in Chang-chia Chuang, an unexpected gift. We all prized our chance to live for a few hours in the interior of the great house, and to explore this example of a seemingly unique domestic architecture developed in that locality of Shansi.

As for the expedition itself and our human encounters with others en route, our reactions varied. John and I enjoyed the contacts with the missionaries, who, so far from home, were bringing their message to a not widely responsive population yet continuing, single-minded. For us these were brief hours within the "domestic architecture" of missionary life. Sicheng, on the other hand, was distressed at depending on foreigners for cleanliness and order in his own country. His national pride was repeatedly hurt by behavior that did not come up to his standards, such as the zany grading of the roadbed and laying of the tracks by Yen's soldiers, the peevish ricksha men asserting themselves by stopping to eat for one hour of every three, and the monks selling temple frescoes abroad — art treasures of China torn away, very possibly for private gain. Whei, as always, was keenly sensitive to her surroundings. When she was rested she responded to beautiful views and humorous encounters with utter delight. But when she was tired or for some other reason fell into one of her black moods, she could be unbearable. A difficult situation would be a strain for all of us, but she alone would rail loudly at the frustration of the moment. It was a shock to me who had been trained by my parents since childhood to "be a good sport for the sake of others." I began to wonder. She was facing the actuality and protesting vigorously. I, as a "good sport," was quietly and passively waiting it out. Who was right? Well, perhaps both or perhaps neither. We were two very different individuals, products of two very different upbringings.

The unforeseen demands of this expedition had been physically exhausting, particularly for Whei with her precarious health, but also for Sicheng with his lame leg. John and I recovered quickly, but what the long-term effect on them would be was difficult to assess. When we parted in Fenchow, they still had one more beautiful temple compound to explore, Chin-tzu near Taiyuan on the route of their homeward journey.

In another week or two, we would also be returning to Peking and settling as before into our house in their neighborhood. The weeks together, sharing daily joys and tribulations, had fostered a lasting intimacy.

13. Japanese Encroachment

Before the end of 1934, Sicheng had the satisfaction of receiving from the Commercial Press his two volumes on Ch'ing structural regulations, introduced by Whei's preface. One volume presented the text of the Ch'ing manual as Sicheng had edited and reorganized it.[1] The other interpreted and explained the text as he understood it from his painstaking examinations and instruction by the craftsmen.[2] The research for these volumes, completed two years before, had been a fundamental first step in his determination to master the evolution of Chinese architecture. He had educated himself; now the book would spread his understanding to others. He presented us with a beautifully boxed gift copy. We could not miss the pride and joy shining through his usual quiet, controlled demeanor.

The publication of his book established Sicheng as China's outstanding architectural historian. Word of the Institute's travels off the beaten path and the architectural discoveries located on those field expeditions had begun to spread. First, personal friends had come to the office to see what was going on. Then reports in the Institute's *Bulletin* brought a wider group of Chinese visitors. As the *Bulletin* began to reach Europe, Britain, and the United States, architects and interested individuals from afar turned up to see the base of operations, ask questions, and express admiration. Among the many who sought Sicheng out was Professor George Rowley, head of the Art Department of Princeton University. His interest in Chinese art and architecture had inspired him to visit Peking, and there he was much impressed by both Liangs.

Sicheng and Whei treasured not only the great buildings they discovered but also the exquisite carvings and decorative details that enhanced their beauty. For some time Sicheng had been planning to compile for future architects and historians a reference guide to such details. It would be illustrated with photographs of surviving examples, preserving in this way the handicraft artistry threatened by industrialization. Between 1935 and 1937, Sicheng with his gifted student and colleague Liu Chih-p'ing completed ten portfolios that treated platforms (terraces and pedestals), stone balustrades, carved shop fronts, brackets, glazed tiles, pillar bases, eave patterns, consoles, and caisson ceilings.

Early in 1935 the Nanking Government decided that the Temple of Confucius at Ch'u Fu in Shantung required restoration and preservation. Sicheng's knowledge and skill made him the obvious choice to advise on this important matter. By July he presented to the Government his survey report with its proposed restorations and estimated costs. In the same year he was made advisor to the Peking Municipal Committee for Preserving Cultural Relics. Numerous temples, halls, towers, and gates in the city were restored or reinforced. Sicheng was kept so busy at renovation that his primary goal, to explore the countryside for buildings surviving from earlier periods, had to be regretfully set aside.

While Sicheng was away on an advisory assignment, Whei made the shocking discovery that her TB had returned. Doctors of the PUMC hospital urged her to take to her bed and stay there for three years. She settled for six months only and employed a trained nurse to move in, care for her, and run her house so that she could stay at home with her family. Protected by the nurse from her own tendency to spend her energies dealing with the many minor crises around her, Whei was able to concentrate on her writing. She tried to capture the fleeting dreams, sensations, and insights that constituted her many moods.

"Hearing a melody I was familiar with when I was a very young girl on board the boat across the Indian Ocean homeward — somehow moonlight and dancing performances, tropical stars, and sea air all crowded into my mind and that little bit known as *youth,* which lasted like a short breezy moment of a song, came to haunt me like a vision, half sad and half twinkling, but loaded my heart only with a sense of loss."

By midsummer, Whei's principal literary critic and advocate, Lao Jin, reported that "She has just finished a short story, reeling off rhythmically one beautiful scene after another until the climax is reached and subsiding into something distant and sublime," but there was an ominous suggestion that Whei's sheltered six months had come to an end. "She is of course worried about things, if not any one thing in particular, she is sure to be worried about everything in general. She is about to take a trip to Peitaiho [the northern seaside resort]."

About a week later Whei reported from the Liang family house at the seashore, "I can't find fault with the weather here. Peace and health and wealth are actually physically visible everywhere, and such a *sea!* Still, I run into more relatives by marriage than is good for me. I feel myself dispersed into bits and can no longer assemble them again into any sense or integrity. I have written Sicheng to persuade you two to come for a weekend trip."

We were not able to go. Later Whei explained that, though our absence was a disappointment, it was also a relief. The concubine grandmother, Liang Ch'i-ch'ao's second wife, who ruled the house and to some extent ruled the large Liang family, was adamant that we must not come. Her only objection to us was that we were a young couple. If we slept together in the Liang house a terrible accident might take place—a baby intended for the Liangs might get to us by mistake.

After her months of bed rest and her seaside vacation, Whei should have returned to Peking with new health and an optimistic outlook. Instead, she encountered a crisis. Her young half-brother, Lin Heng, a quiet and serious teenager, had come from Fukien to live with the Liangs while preparing to enter Tsinghua for training as an engineer. Whei was fond of him, but in her absence relations between her mother and the boy had taken a bad turn.

The mother's resentment was deep. The son and heir she had borne for her husband had died. But the second concubine had produced several sons and won his affection. Now one of those sons who had replaced her dead boy was living under the same roof with her as a healthy teenager. She found it intolerable. Whei was caught in the middle.

"For the last three days my own mother has been driving me into human hell. I am not using the language too strongly. On the first day I found my mother feeling faint. There was a general disturbance in the house. I had to dig into the past with my half-brother trying to establish an understanding to make the present close contact possible and bearable.

"That left me exhausted and worn, almost wishing I was dead or hadn't been born in such a family as mine by the time I went to bed. . . . I know I am a happy and lucky person really, but the early battles have injured me so permanently that if any reminder of them arises I become only absorbed in the past misfortune."

A tragedy was looming for China that would overwhelm those past misfortunes. The Japanese militarists, masters now of Manchuria, were moving south of the Great Wall. They craftily avoided out-and-out invasion but terrified the countryside with their large trucks and planes. In 1934 they got Nanking government agreement that the area stretching south of the Wall from Peking to Tientsin would be a demilitarized zone. There they set up a Chinese puppet regime. The success of this limited "peaceful" move inspired the Japanese in 1935 to expand their bloodless conquests by making a vast neutral zone covering five North China provinces from Shantung to Suiyuan. An agreement with the Japanese, signed by the local Peking commander, Sung Che-yuan, on orders from Chiang Kai-shek, made this new "neutral zone" official. The exultant Japanese officers rapidly moved to incite a separatist movement to create a puppet autonomous state, "North China-land" (Hua-pei-kuo).

The atmosphere in Peking was tense. The Japanese "took" Fengtai, the important railroad junction between Peking and Tientsin, "just for practice in case of war," and later drove two trucks full of armed men to the more distant Paotingfu "to test the trucks."

For the Liangs it was a bitter reminder of Mukden days when the Japanese had staged an annual insult of "practicing taking over the city." To face again the disgrace and humiliation of passively yielding Chinese territory to the Japanese was hard to bear. Whei's reaction was, "I know that all those I love among our friends have moral guts, but we all lack the naive fervor, some blunt active physical force that will push things somehow. I wish you knew my oldest and dearest friend Chih-mo. But a small airplane chose to kill him. He *did* things, fought for things, more than he talked about them — and he talked a lot at that! He was such a refreshing element among the balanced and the sane." In contrast to Whei's ruminations, Sicheng prepared himself to face the reality: "There is no place in China for architectural research in this generation. . . . The times call for action of a more elemental sort, and an education that has prepared one for something else should be thrown away without a thought in the face of the bigger issue."

In the end it was not the generation of Hsü Chih-mo and Liang Sicheng but the young students of Peking who took action against the Japanese pressure. The leaders were students of Yenching and Tsinghua universities — a number of them from Manchuria. They secretly organized their fellow students in the colleges and middle schools of the city to stage a great demonstration. The American journalist Edgar Snow and his wife helped the organizers and arranged for a number of other foreign journalists to be present. On December 9, as Snow reported,

Thousands and thousands of blue-clad youngsters marched and sang their way to the Forbidden City in defiance of both their own police and conservative parents. . . . Largely unprepared and puzzled by the presence of foreigners, the

> local police made only half-hearted and spasmodic attempts to interfere. . . .
> Suddenly the political gendarmes, in black leather jackets, led by a nephew of
> Chiang Kai-shek . . . pushed into the throng and indiscriminately clubbed boys
> and girls alike.[3]

Lin Heng, Whei's teenaged half-brother, was badly beaten and missing
for over twelve hours. Sicheng spent most of the night searching for him
among the many injured students in Peking hospitals. Whei spent the
evening telephoning for news of her brother. She got no news of him but
plenty about the last bunch of students marooned outside one of the city
gates, who were shamefully beaten, some almost to death, or hurt and
chased with whips and other weapons until they scattered to some schools
outside. Finally in the middle of the night Lin Heng managed to get a
message through to her. She dashed out in a car to a far corner of the West
City to find him and bring him home. After his recovery, the boy, saying
nothing of his intention to the family, turned away from his engineering
education and took the entrance examination for the Airforce Academy.

Among the thousands of students in that first demonstration was
another family member, Sicheng's half-sister Ssu-yi, one of the Yenching
University leaders. They learned the next day that she had also been heavily
beaten with a scabbarded sword. For her, too, the shock of the experience
was a lasting one. She became in later years an ardent and active Communist Party member.

This first demonstration had an electric effect on an entire generation.
Demonstrations began all over the country. Soon many teachers joined in.
On December 16 thousands of students again demonstrated in Peking and
Tientsin. Many were injured and nearly two hundred arrested, but a week
later a third demonstration was held. This one called for the first time for
an end to civil war in China and a united front to resist Japan. The student demonstrations and their call for assistance were accompanied by a
strengthening of the existing boycott against Japanese goods. Tokyo was
shocked. Not prepared for war at the time, they recalled General Doihara,
who had masterminded the Mukden coup and was directing the moves to
detach North China. Both the Japanese foreign ministry and the war office
issued denials that they had any intention of using force to annex North
China. The Japanese had to face the fact that to achieve their aims in China
would require a major invasion. By the time that invasion came, Chiang
Kai-shek would finally have no alternative but to commit the nation to all-
out resistance.

14. Interval of Reprieve

The Japanese government's disclaimer in late 1935 of hostile aggression in North China was seen to be no more than a temporary reprieve. However, for the next year and a half, until the sudden invasion of July 1937, life in Peking could return to a semblance of normalcy.

In the meantime, the government universities had been led by the apparent imminence of a Japanese takeover of Peking in late 1935 to prepare for moving to the south. Tsinghua University was packing up its scientific instruments. Faculty received orders to withdraw from the library those books that were important to them, and students were seen going back and forth out of the stacks with their long gowns padded with books they were removing. John commented sorrowfully, "The best college library in China is being scattered to the winds."

Chu Chi-ch'ien had no intention of leaving Peking. But Sicheng knew that to save the Institute's precious collections from destruction or from falling into the hands of the Japanese, they had to be packed for moving to a safe hiding place. With the help of the staff, the process was begun.

Meanwhile the Liangs themselves realized that if Tsinghua went south, Lao Jin and all their closest friends would be moving with it. From their Mukden experience, they could see all too clearly what lay ahead for Peking under the Japanese and they wanted no part of it. So they, too, initiated their own personal packing.

"Sicheng and I have been straightening our old papers and things for several hours now. Such an amazing lot of odds and ends piled up along the track of life! Looking over and back through that pile of our past, built around so many people and so many lovelinesses that are now being threatened, we found the task too depressing for words. Especially because we are at present hung sadly at the pessimistic end of the line, with a very vague future ahead. . . .

"If our national calamity were more spectacularly swift or brutal, we would be compelled to meet the situation in some way or other, immediately and actively. There would be difficulties and hardship, but we would not be sitting here with fists aimlessly tightened and our 'face' threatened every minute with disgrace."

As they packed to escape to the south, we were packing for departure to England and the United States. Since our student years in China had to end with 1935, we had picked Christmas day for our departure.

We had not foreseen the sudden deepening of the Japanese menace as autumn came. Sicheng and I had begun a project we had been considering for some time — to translate some of his architectural research articles from Chinese to English. His English was so clear and straightforward that he hardly needed me, but my presence gave him self-confidence and I could catch minor errors. We both enjoyed it, and I promised to help find a publication outlet in America.

On November 21, 1935 Whei was shocked to learn that the *Ta Kung Pao* in Tientsin, the outstanding paper that through its literary supplement had become the publishing medium of the foremost contemporary writers, was being suppressed by the Japanese for an indefinite period. In its place, the puppet *United Asia Herald* was established. Whei received a copy inviting her to contribute to the literary supplement. She was outraged to find that there were some fifty Chinese on its staff. "Why can't they realize what they are doing?" Sicheng threw the paper into the stove.

Our closest friends were facing an immediate crisis; we were outsiders. They made a point of keeping us in touch with developments, but our participation in the gloom was helping neither them nor us. On a sudden inspiration I introduced Whei to horseback riding.

From time to time John and I had ridden ponies imported from Mongolia by sporty foreigners for playing polo. (The only Chinese one saw on horseback in Peking were occasional cavalry units.) Stable boys delivered the saddled ponies just outside whatever city gate was specified. From there one rode off to explore the countryside. In those days the great plain was cultivated right up to the city walls. Scattered among the fields were low-lying mud villages connected by sunken roads worn deep in the loess soil. Sitting on horseback, in the sparkling air, one could see clearly the blue western and northern hills that ringed the plain, but also in the foreground occasional pagodas and, marked by shade trees, deserted temples or tomb compounds. Our exploring took us across country to visit these tempting goals, or sometimes for a swift gallop in either of the two uncultivated areas, the ruined "Old Summer Palace" — the Yuan-ming-yuan — to the west or the grassy northern area framed by an embankment, which was the last trace of the Mongol city wall.

Whei had liked ambling on a donkey in Shansi and told us she had done it often. On horseback she was amazing. Evidently all that donkey riding had given her confidence and a "seat." She was as thrilled over the sensitive response of the horse to a touch of the reins as she was by the same quality in human beings. She came back with her cheeks aflame and her black eyes shining from riding against the crisp cold wind. Far from endangering her health, the exercise was good for her body, and her spirit reveled in the beauties of the countryside. Our scheduled departure was only six weeks away and the crisis was ever-present, but we managed frequent rides up to the last moment. Whei found some riding boots, a warm jacket and pants, and a snug fur hat, and played with gusto what was a new role for her — equestrienne.

After our departure a letter from Whei brought our past two months to life again:

"I have been much younger and alive and 'peppier' since you two have run around with us and imparted to me new vitality and outlook on life and the future in general, so much so that I am gratefully astonished myself each time I recall everything I did this winter.

"You see, I was biculturally brought up, and there is no denying that bicultural contact and activity is essential to me. Before you two really came into our lives here at No. 3, I was always somewhat lost and had a sense of lack somewhere, a certain spiritual poverty that needed nourishing and that your 'blue notes' more than restored. And another thing; all my friends in Peking are older and more serious-minded people. They don't supply much fun themselves but often turn to Sicheng and me for inspiration and fresh something. How often I have felt drained!

"The *picnics* and *riding* this autumn or rather early winter (and the Shansi trip too) made a whole world of difference to me. Imagine if not for all that, how was I to survive all the excitement and confusion and depression of our frequent national crises! The riding was symbolic, too. Outside the gate of Ch'i-hua Men, which had always meant for me only Japs and their targets, now I can see the country lanes and vast flat open wintry atmosphere, delicate bare branches that scatter silver, small quiet temples and the occasional bridge one can cross with romantic pride."

No letters came from Sicheng, but we knew that the reprieve won by the students' demonstrations had brought the partly packed-up Institute alive again. He was involved in putting on a major exhibition of the Institute's architectural researches at the new Municipal Museum in Shanghai. Whei reassured us, "Sicheng is a constant entity so even if you may hear less often from him than from me you know he is here the same as ever and very sweet and gentle and lovely as he has always been — with a lot of lovely work (which I have really helped in my way though no one would ever believe its truth)."

Not surprisingly, when Whei next wrote us, her life was again full of family complications.

"March has been a windy month for me . . . mostly with sisters-in-law. I can quite envy Wilma for having married an only child (not to say he is John). . . . One sister-in-law [the Yenching student demonstrator] was to be arrested and has to be hidden and sent off by various tricky ways to the south. Another sister-in-law [recently widowed] with child arrived with a Cantonese amah to stay permanently. And they have to have quarters out of my already packed household! And a lot of time out of my already unspareable time! General noise and hustle-bustle. Thirdly, my eldest sister-in-law blew in in the middle of the night to take her Yenching daughter away. The mother kept saying nasty things out of pure jealousy while the girl was in tears. She complained that the girl came from college to town without her knowledge during the tense political student situation. 'Since she is so fond of coming out to her uncle and aunt why didn't she let them pay for her college education,' etc. As she left, the irate elder sister threw her final bombshell, that she did not want her daughter to have radical ideas of love and marriage from associating with her uncle and aunt who have a friend radical enough not to believe in marriage — meaning Lao Jin!"

A happy break in April was the arrival in Peking of the American architect and urban planner Clarence Stein and his charming wife, Aline Mac-Mahon, a well-known actress. Whei wrote, "We fell in love with them and they with us quite simultaneously." When Sicheng had to be in Shanghai for an exhibit, Whei took them to the Summer Palace and around the back hill to see the blossoms. Lao Jin went along and wrote us his observations.

"They are remarkable people in a way. Though I have very little communication with them, I can see arresting qualities in them. Particularly Mr. Stein. He is very sensitive, very reserved, very retiring, and almost always liable to be absent-mindedly interested in what he experiences at the moment. About a week ago we went to the Summer Palace and when we reached the Garden of Wit and Humor, where there is a pond with pavilions and walks around it, Mr. Stein seemed to rise ethereally and with gleaming eyes, and in the spirit of both awe and appreciation, he murmured 'Oh — oh — oh . . . what floating architecture.' It is so nice to see reality, and I had no desire any more to disturb him out of his trance merely for the purpose of carrying on a polite, conventional conversation."

Sicheng was stimulated through Clarence Stein to read and think about urban planning, a subject that was to play an important part in his life in later years. Meanwhile, in the brief cessation of Japanese pressures in North China he was determined to pursue his field studies.

"The love and preservation of antiquity are no business of the Japanese warlords though their nationals normally should share with us the special love and respect for our old culture, from which they derived their own. Even as early as 1931 and 1932, most of my trips were abruptly disrupted by the renewed booms of Japanese guns, each time drawing nearer than the last, meaning business. It was quite evident that the days we could work in North China were limited. Before we were prevented from doing so, we decided to put our entire effort in that part of the country."[1]

By early autumn, Sicheng and Whei were off together on another field trip, this time to Lung Men, famous rock-cut Buddhist cave carvings. Whei wrote:

"I am sitting right under the largest open-air rock-cut cave of Lung Men with the nine largest statues sitting and standing in various calm and dynamic poses staring at me (and I at them!). . . . I am overwhelmed with that kind of awe which comes only through this kind of magnificent experience."

And soon after, they were in Kaifeng and planning a tour of twenty-three counties of Shantung.

"We are again on our way between heaven and hell like the trip in Shansi. We rejoice over all the beauty and color in art and humanity and are more than often appalled and dismayed by dirt and smells of places we have to eat and sleep (necessarily *well* in order to have strength to go on). I have never lost sight of Wilma's famous quote, 'Nao-yi-nao, Lao-yi-lao' (constant yammering makes one old) — in fact I cling to that sagacious outburst in order to keep my youthful appearance and complexion. . . . This trip reminds us continuously of the happy time we trod the mud together to Ling-shih [Shansi]."

15. Triumph and Disaster

The Liangs' discovery in the early summer of 1937 of the prize they had long sought — a still extant wood-frame structure of T'ang date — was their crowning achievement as historians of Chinese architecture.

Their expedition to the Wu-t'ai Shan area was inspired by their study of two plates of T'ang murals in cave 117 in the volumes on the famous Buddhist caves *Les Grottes de Tun-houang* by the French Sinologist Paul Pelliot. The murals show conventionalized panoramas of the sacred Wu-t'ai mountains with their Buddhist temples identified by name. The Liangs' repeated disappointments on encountering wealthy or famous Buddhist temples that had been rebuilt or fundamentally altered through the years led them to plan on seeking out the unknowns. For the purpose Sicheng had mapped a route around the mountain massif. This decision proved basic to their success.

Sicheng, Whei, and Mo Tsung-chiang left Peking in June 1937 by train for Taiyuan, the Shansi city nearest to their goal. Heading north from Taiyuan they rode comfortably in an automobile for the first eighty miles. At the town of Tung-yeh they changed to mule litters, each borne by two mules — fore and aft — to enter the Wu-t'ai mountains.

Following the "uncustomary route" for only a few miles, they were rewarded by coming upon their first find, which turned out to be their greatest. It was Fo-kuang Ssu, the "Temple of Buddha's Light," built in A.D. 857.

Sicheng reported their first impressions.[1]

"The temple stands on a high terrace on the mountainside facing a large courtyard in front and framed by twenty or thirty very old pines. It is a majestic building. Only one story in height, it has large, strong, simple brackets and a far overhanging eave, which at a casual glance at once tells its very old date. But could it be older than the oldest wooden structure we had yet found?

"The huge doors were at once thrown open for us. The interior, seven

bays in width, was more than impressive in the twilight. On a large platform, seated statues of Buddha and his numerous attendants rose before us
like an enchanted deified forest. At the extreme left end of the platform was
a seated figure of a woman in secular dress, a life-size statue but very small
and humble amid the group of deities. She was, the monks told us, the
wicked Empress Wu. The entire group, though glaring with fresh color
from a recent renovation, was without doubt of the late T'ang period. But,
if these were the original T'ang clay figures unharmed, the building that
covered them could not but be the original T'ang structure. Obviously any
rebuilding would have damaged everything under it.

"Next day we started a careful investigation. The brackets, the beams,
the checkered ceiling, the carved stone bases of the columns were all
anxiously examined. One and all yielded to us their unmistakable late T'ang
characteristics. But my greatest surprise came when we climbed into the
dark space above the ceiling; there I found roof trusses built in a way I knew
only from T'ang paintings. The use of two 'main rafters' (to borrow the
terms of a modern truss) without the 'king post,' just the reverse of later
methods of Chinese construction, was overwhelmingly unexpected.

"This 'attic' was inhabited by thousands of bats, which clustered
around the ridge purlin like a thick spread of caviar, thus preventing me
from finding a possible date written thereon. In addition, the timbers were
infested with millions of bedbugs that live on the bats. The upper side of the
ceiling, on which we stood, was covered with a thick layer of fine dust,
deposited there perhaps during the past few centuries and strewn with little
corpses of dead bats here and there. In complete darkness and amid the vile
odor, hardly breathing, with thick masks covering our noses and mouths,
we measured, drew, and photographed with flashlights for several hours.
When at last we came out from under the eaves to take a breath of fresh air,
we found hundreds of bedbugs in our knapsack. We ourselves had been
badly bitten. Yet the importance and unexpectedness of our find made those
the happiest hours of my years of hunting for ancient architecture.

"Frescoes must originally have decorated the walls of the Hall. But the
only frescoed parts preserved today are the 'frieze' — the plastered portions
above the lintel and between the brackets. Different sections of the frieze
have paintings of very different standards of draftsmanship and evidently
very different dates. There is a section painted with Buddhas in medallions
that bears the date corresponding to A.D. 1122. Alongside it is a section
painted with Buddha and attendants, definitely older in date and superior
in artistic merit. The analogy of this section to the murals of the Tun-huang

Caves is most striking. It can be of no other date than the T'ang Dynasty. Though merely a strip of wall, occupying a position of minor importance, it is the only T'ang mural painting I know of in China proper outside the Tun-huang Caves.

"On the third day of our work in the Main Hall, my wife noticed on the bottom of one of the beams very faint indications of calligraphy in Chinese ink. The effect of this discovery on our party was electric. There is nothing we like better than the dates of a building actually written on its beams or carved in stone beside it. Here was this glorious T'ang structure, the first we had found—but how was I to report its date? The T'ang Dynasty had lasted from 618 to 906. Now the timbers that bore the faint traces of calligraphy would soon give me the much desired answer. While the rest of us were busy with the problem of arranging for a scaffolding to be erected between the valuable statues for the purpose of cleaning the beams and studying the inscriptions close at hand, my wife went directly to work. Straining her head back, she tried her eager eyes on the beams from various angles below. After some time of such strenuous efforts, she was able to read a number of dubious names with long, official titles of the T'ang Dynasty. Of these, the most important was on the beam to the extreme right, only partly legible then: 'Donor of the Hall of Buddha, *Sung-kung* of Shangtu, Woman Disciple of Buddha, Ning Kung-yu.'

"Donated by a woman! That this young architect, a woman, should be the first to discover the donor of China's rarest old temple to have been a woman seemed too unlikely a coincidence. She feared she might have misread some of the less decipherable characters by too lively an imagination. But she remembered having seen similar names with official titles on the stone *dhanari* column that stood on the terrace outside. She left the Hall in the hope of verifying her reading from the column inscription. There, to her great delight, she found, apart from the long list of imposing officials' names, the same phrase, clear and distinct: 'Donor of the Hall of Buddha, Woman Disciple Ning Kung-yu. The column bore the date 'The 11th year of Ta-chung, T'ang Dynasty,' which corresponds to A.D. 857.[2]

"Then it dawned upon us that the small figure of a woman in secular dress, sitting humbly at the end of the platform, whom the monks called 'Empress Wu' was none other than the donor, Lady Ning Kung-yu herself.

"Assuming that the *dhanari* column was erected soon after the completion of the Hall, the date of the building can be closely ascertained. It is earlier by one hundred and twenty-seven years than the oldest wooden structure previously found. It is the only wooden building of T'ang date we have yet encountered in these years of search. Moreover, in that one Hall, we have T'ang painting, T'ang calligraphy, T'ang sculpture, and T'ang architecture. Individually they are extremely rare but, collectively, unique."

The Liangs and Mo worked at Fo-kuang Ssu for a week, examining, measuring, photographing, and recording the building complex in detail. Before leaving the temple grounds, Sicheng made a report of his discoveries to the Provincial Government of Shansi and to the National Commission for the Conservation of Antiquities, of which he was a member. He and Whei bade farewell to the Abbot in high spirits and promised to return the next year with funds from the Government for a large-scale restoration. They made a general investigation of the better-known regions of the Wu-t'ai Shan but found few edifices worthy of further investigation. They finally left the mountain area by mule litter along the northern path to Tai Hsien, "a magnificently planned city," where they settled down temporarily in a state of euphoria from their extraordinary find. They needed an interval to organize and review the mass of data they had collected.

"There," wrote Liang, "we worked in blissful contentment for a few days. On the evening of July fifteenth, after a hard day's work we were given welcome bundles of newspapers from Taiyuan that had been delayed by a flooded highway. When we relaxed into our camp cots and started to read the headline, 'Japanese launch severe attack on our positions near Peking,' the war was already a week old. After no little difficulty and detour (via Ta-t'ung) we managed to return to Peking."

The "double seventh" — the seventh day of the seventh month — July 7, 1937, is remembered with bitterness in Peking. On that day the Japanese military finally made their move to take over Peking and ultimately, they expected, all of China. It began with an encounter between Japanese troops and Chinese local forces at the Marco Polo Bridge on the outskirts of Peking. This was a Japanese feint similar to their first moves in Manchuria, intended to make full-scale invasion and conquest appear unavoidable in the eyes of the world. The local defenders fought on through the ensuing weeks without help from Chiang Kai-shek. He was in Nanking hoarding his German-trained troops for resistance at some future time, instead, unspec-ified. By July 29 Peking was occupied by the Japanese and the fighting came to an end.

The Liangs' spirits plunged from triumph to despair as they made their devious way home through the northern route, avoiding Japanese and puppet troops. But both of them were activists. The fact that the crisis demanded planning and decisions left them scant leisure for despondency. They needed all their energies to cope with such questions as: Where shall we go? And when? What are the basic necessities for us, the two children, and grandmother? How do we pack? What do we leave behind — not just things, but servants, relatives, friends, responsibilities? The packing that had been initiated in the fall of 1935 was now completed in earnest.

Sicheng was of course deeply concerned how to preserve the treasures of the Institute — drawings, photographic negatives and prints, models, research notes, files, and library. Since the founder, old Mr. Chu, still had no intention of leaving Peking, the future of the Institute, if any, was up to Sicheng himself. So while Whei dealt with the household, sorting and packing, burning some leftovers, selling or giving away others, and throwing out most of the rest, he co-opted Liu Tun-chen and other colleagues to help pack up the top-priority materials of the Institute for deposit somewhere in safekeeping. These included all the negatives, though he packed the prints and basic data to carry with him in hope of future work. He mailed to me for publication several articles he had written in English on his discoveries.

Kunming in the far southwestern province of Yunnan was their first choice as a place of refuge. Meanwhile representatives of the two leading universities in the Peking area, Peita (Peking University) and Tsinghua, had, in concert with Tientsin's important Nankai University, decided to merge their faculties, students, and whatever equipment they could move in an associated "university in exile." Their solemn purpose was to continue offering first-quality higher education to Chinese youths despite the Japanese militarists' aim — well known from their policies in Korea, Taiwan, and Manchuria — to limit the intellectual development of conquered peoples. The immediate plan was to establish the associated university in the central China city of Changsha, Hunan.

August in Peking was a month of frantic planning, packing, consulting with intimates, and waiting for the appropriate and possible moment to depart. But time suddenly ran out for Sicheng when he was approached by Japanese authorities, asking him for advice and inviting him to form a Chinese-Japanese Friendship Society. Preposterous! Did they think that his childhood decade in Japan would make him a willing tool? Clearly he must hurry away before they barred his departure.

Figure 1. Liang Ch'i-ch'ao with his children in Tokyo, c. 1905; Sicheng and Elder Sister holding Ssu-chuang.

Figure 2. One of the headings Liang Sicheng drew for the 1923 *Tsinghuapper*.

Figure 3. Lin Whei-yin with her father, Lin Ch'ang-min.

Figure 4. Hsü Chih-mo, innovative poet, c. 1924.

Figure 5. Liang Sicheng, May 1923, seriously injured at age 22 when a car sideswiped his motorcycle.

Figure 6. Rabindranath Tagore in Peking with, among others, Liang Sicheng, Lin Ch'ang-min, Lin Whei-yin, and Hsü Chih-mo.

Figure 7. Lin Whei-yin, poet at work.

Figure 8. Lin Whei-yin receiving the Bachelor of Fine Arts degree
with high honors from the University of Pennsylvania, February
1927.

Figure 9. Honeymooning in Europe, April 1928.

Figure 10. Logician Chin Yueh-lin ("Lao Jin" to his intimates), c. 1933.

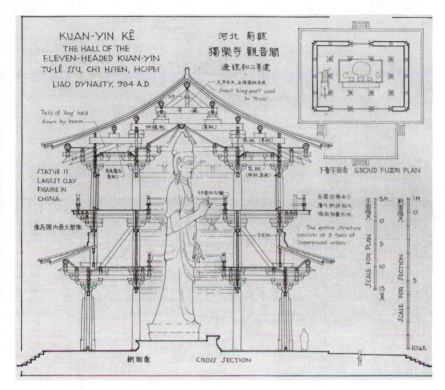

Figure 11. The Kuan-yin Hall of Tu-le Ssu, Chi Hsien, Hopei, A.D. 984 (Liao).

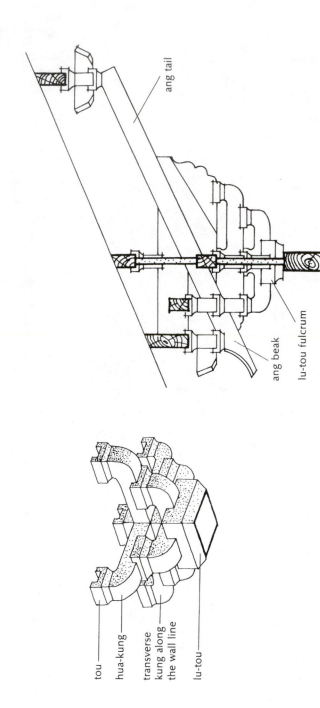

Figure 12. Chinese bracket sets. Left, the complex set; right, a bracket set in place atop a column. A long cantilever arm (*ang*) balanced on the fulcrum extends down from the inner superstructure through the bracket to support the wide overhang of the roof.

ang tail

ang beak

lu-tou fulcrum

tou

hua-kung

transverse
kung along
the wall line

lu-tou

Figure 13. Fairbanks and Liangs at tea at Lao Jin's home, Peking, 1934.

Figure 14. The pagoda of Fokung Ssu, Ying Hsien, Shansi. Built in A.D. 1056 (Liao), it is China's only surviving wooden pagoda.

Figure 15. The Chao Chou bridge, 30 miles southeast of Cheng Ting, Hopei. Erected c. A.D. 600, it is the world's first known segmental and open spandreled stone bridge.

Figure 16. Liangs and Fairbanks on their 1934 field trip, heading south in mule carts along a typical "sunken road" worn down in the Shansi loess.

Figure 17. (Left) Pagoda of Upper Kuang-sheng Ssu, near Chao-ch'eng, Shansi. It was built in the fourteenth century (Yuan) to replace a T'ang pagoda destroyed in an earthquake. (Right) The stairway that winds around the pagoda's interior has no landings. At the end of each short flight, climbers step over a gap to the first step of the next flight.

Figure 18. Lin Whei-yin and Liang Sicheng on the Temple of Heaven, Peking, 1936.

Figure 19. Lin Whei-yin just back from a wintry horseback ride, 1935.

Figure 20. The great T'ang Buddhist temple Fo-kuang Ssu (A.D. 857), Wu-t'ai mountains, Shansi, the prize at the end of the Liangs' search.

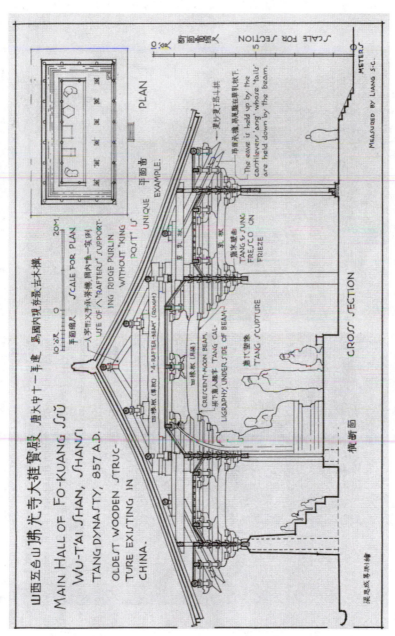

Figure 21. Cross section of the main hall, Fo-kuang Ssu temple, drawn by Liang Sicheng.

Figure 22. Liang family with three close Peking friends — Chou Peiyuan, Chen Deison, and Wu Youshun — all noted academics, Kunming (?), c. March 1938.

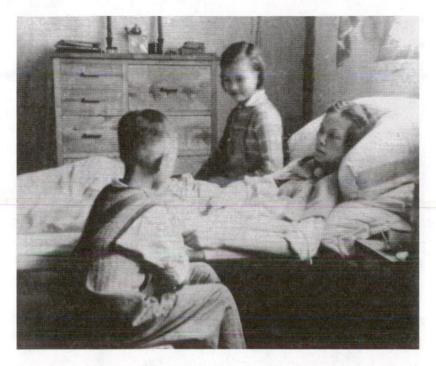

Figure 23. Lin Whei-yin, bedridden in Li-juang, with her children, c. 1941.

Figure 24. Mo Tsung-chiang and Liang Sicheng in the Li-juang workroom, drafting architectural illustrations for the *Pictorial History,* c. 1943–1945.

Figure 25. Liang Sicheng as a member of the United Nations Board of Design, standing between Le Corbusier (France) and Oscar Niemeyer (Brazil) among other distinguished architects, New York, 1947. Photo courtesy of the United Nations.

Figure 26. Liang Sicheng participating in the planning of the United Nations headquarters, New York, 1947. Photo courtesy of the United Nations.

Figure 27. Liang Sicheng's proposal to make Peking's city walls and gates into a continuous public park for the health and pleasure of the people.

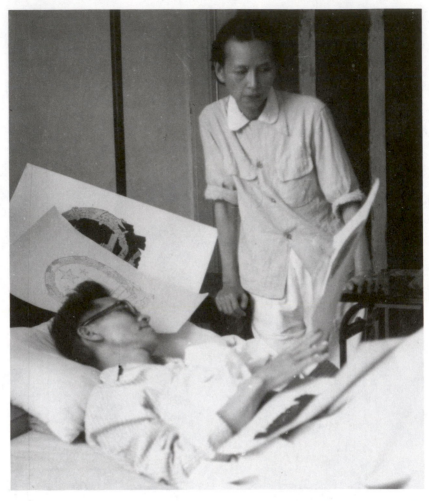

Figure 28. Liang Sicheng, hospitalized, designing new national emblems with Lin Whei-yin.

Figure 29. Wedding of Liang Sicheng and Lin Zhu, June 1962.

Figure 30. Postage stamp issued in 1992 to commemorate Liang Sicheng's life's work as China's architectural historian.

Survival in Wartime, 1937–1945

16. Escape

On September 5, 1937 the Liangs left Peking for Tientsin on the first leg of their escape route. The party included, in addition to the two children and the grandmother, Lao Jin and two Tsinghua professors. The Liang family home in Tientsin's Italian concession was a welcome refuge. There Sicheng was able to negotiate the safekeeping of the Institute's accumulation of negatives and other treasures in the locked vaults of a British bank. A hastily scrawled note reported, "So much has happened we don't know how to begin telling. Anyway we are safe, came to Tientsin a week ago and are leaving by boat to Tsingtao and via Tsinan to wherever we can reach after five changes — preferably Changsha — with as few air raids as possible in between. Then the war will be won and over for us for ever and ever."

Lao Jin later wrote about the trip: "No unusual difficulty was encountered but the usual kind was quite formidable. We zigzagged our way to Hankow and finally arrived at Changsha the first of October. The combined university opened on the first of November."

From the time they reached the overcrowded city of Changsha, air raid alarms were frequent. Hurrying to basements or dugouts became routine though up to November 24 no bombs were dropped. On that day through negligence there was no alarm signal. The Japanese planes were in the air above while the people below had no warning that they were targets.

Whei wrote:

"Our house scored almost a direct hit from a bomb during the first air raid on Changsha. The bomb dropped fifteen yards away from the door of the house in which we had three rooms as our temporary home. We were all home at the time — grandmother, two children, SC and I. Both children were sick in bed. No one knows how we managed not being blown to bits. Our house was in pieces just as we hurried down stairs after hearing some hellish crash and boom from the two bombs first dropped further away from us. By sheer instinctive action each of us had picked up one child and rushed for the stairs. But before we reached the ground, the nearest bomb exploded. It blew me up with Hsiao-di [son] in my arms and then threw me down again on the ground unhurt. Meanwhile the house started to crack and every bit of the much-glassed door and panels, roof, ceilings, all came tumbling, showering down on top of us. We rushed out through the side door and were on the street choked with black smoke.

"While we were running toward the joint university's dugout, another bomber started to descend. We stopped running, thinking there was not a chance for us to get away this time and we preferred to be close together rather than leave out a few to live to feel the tragedy. This last bomb did not explode but dropped at the end of the street on which we were running. All our things — very few now — are being excavated out of the glassy debris, and we are staying temporarily with friends here and there.

"In the evenings you will find the old Saturday friends wandering here and there looking for a bit of family warmth in those houses where wives and children have come to share the 'national crisis.' Before the bombing we still gathered to eat together, not in restaurants but enjoying my own cooking on a little stove in that three-room suite in which we did practically everything that used to spread out over the entire No. 3 Pei-tsung-pu Hutung. Much laughter and sighs over the past were exchanged but as a whole we still kept up our spirits.

"We have decided to leave this place for Yunnan. . . . Our country is still not well organized enough to give any of us any *active* war work, so we are really war *nuisance* so far. So why not clear out and go further back to the corner. Some day even that place [Kunming] is going to be bombed, but still we have no better place to go at present."

Whei's phrase, that lacking active war work, "we are really 'war nuisance,'" though mentioned only in passing, reflects an emotion that was widespread and much discussed among the friends in Changsha at the time. The Chinese government was well aware that persons with education and advanced technical skills were a vital resource for China's future and that they might represent as few as 2 percent of the total population. That scholars should not be soldiers but should be preserved as a class for the purposes of the state was a Chinese policy hallowed by centuries of tradition. So students and scholars in Government universities were, with few exceptions, confined to their institutions while the actual fighting against the Japanese was left to unlettered farmboys and the urban proletariat, who were too often conscripted into the army by force.

Meanwhile the intellectuals who were being protected from loss of life and hoarded for future use were far from contented. Living as they were, researchers, teachers, and students alike, under government control and dependent on government funds for bare existence, they had no option but to obey. Inevitably true patriots, denied a meaningful role in the war effort, experienced mounting frustration, guilt, and anger.

"We are packing *again* for the difficult ten-day trip by bus to Yunnan," Whei wrote. "Except for those that are here, everybody we know and every member of every family are scattered in different places and without news of each other."

Their own dear "family member," Lao Jin, was one of these. His branch of the Associated University was temporarily established at Nan Yueh, some distance from Changsha. News of their bombing had taken a week to reach him and he was still in Hunan five weeks after they had departed for Yunnan. He wrote us, "I am entirely lost when detached from the Liangs."

When the Liangs squeezed their family of five onto an overloaded bus for the pre-dawn departure from Changsha for Kunming on December 8, they had no way of knowing that they were leaving one mass migration for another. Large numbers of refugees from Canton and other parts of the southeast were also heading for Kunming or the designated wartime capital, Chungking.

In the small town of Huang Hsien on the western border of Hunan where it meets Kweichow, the Liangs' journey came to an abrupt stop. Up to that time Whei, riding with her small son on her lap through days of bitter cold, had been elated by the glorious scenery of western Hunan, about which Shen Ts'ung-wen had written. Arriving at Huang Hsien they learned that all buses onward had been commandeered to move aviation school cadets and mechanics. Ordinary travelers had to wait there for an indefinite period.

At this crucial moment Whei came down with acute bronchitis, which threatened to develop rapidly into pneumonia. The dirty little inns of the town were overcrowded with refugees. Sicheng was desperate. Walking along a dark, slushy street in great anxiety, he suddenly heard sounds from a nearby inn of somebody playing a violin beautifully. "That musician must be from Peking or Shanghai," he thought, and knocked on the door. Inside he came upon a roomful of eight cadets from an Airforce Academy who were awaiting transportation to Kunming. He told them of his grave problem — serious illness and no place to stay. The young airmen welcomed the family and moved in together to make room for the newcomers.

As a further miracle, among about a hundred travelers who had also stopped in the little village waiting for buses was a woman doctor who had been trained in an American mission hospital in Japan but had made a special study of Chinese herbal medicines. She gave Whei Chinese medicine available there, administered according to Western medical principles. So for two weeks Whei lay in "a little room partitioned off by thin boards from charming and vigorous young Cantonese aviation cadets, hideous vulgar local prostitutes, swearing gamblers, rough Shantung-dialect military officers, and chauffeurs of different provinces and temperaments who must necessarily drink and gamble with the prostitutes of that inn in order to have energy to drive through the dangerous route the next day." The children meanwhile had their father for a playmate. He taught them to read maps, took them for walks along the river, and showed them how to "skip stones."

The intimate friendship with the eight airmen that began here was to last through their final training at the Airforce Academy in Kunming and later war service as pilots. Their parents were all in the occupied areas. They made the Liangs their family and the Liangs regarded them as younger brothers and loved them all.

After two weeks Whei's fever ended, and shortly a sixteen-seater bus turned up headed for Kunming. "We resumed our journey," Whei wrote, "in desperate circumstances which started at one A.M. with fighting in the dark to get ourselves and our belongings (few enough) onto the bus. Twenty-seven passengers were packed in by the time it took off at ten A.M. It was a windowless, starterless, and 'everythingless' affair that puffed and shook and had difficulty even climbing a flat stretch of road let alone high and dangerous mountain ranges." By the end of the day the grandmother had chills and fever, but there was no recourse; they had to continue with this broken bus. It finally stalled on top of a wild Kweichow mountain famous for bandits — out of gasoline. The family, holding the children's hands, numb with cold, continued on foot up the mountain path in the gathering dark. "Again, miraculously enough, we reached a group of houses on the side of a high cliff and were taken in for the night."

Here Whei scrambled the rest of the trip into one characteristic paragraph. "After this, there was episode after episode . . . of broken cars, unexpected stops, filthy unattractive inns to put up in, . . . with occasional magnificent scenery to make one's heart more twisted than ever in the face of it. The jade mountain streams, autumn red leaves and white reeds, sailing clouds above, old-fashioned iron-chain bridges, ferries, and pure Chinese old cities are all the things I'd like to tell you in great detail, mingled with footnotes of my own peculiar emotional reactions at the time if possible."

Somehow, through all these "episodes" the family ultimately reached Kunming in mid-January of 1938. The "difficult ten-day trip" they had prepared to undergo when they boarded the bus in Changsha had taken just short of six weeks.

17. Settling in Kunming

Kunming is the capital of Yunnan Province, which borders on Burma to the west and south. The city is so distant from the east coast metropolises of Peking, Tientsin, Shanghai, and Canton that before the war it was hardly known and rarely visited by the modernized Chinese of those areas. The French had built a narrow gauge railway to the city from the Indo-China port of Haiphong in the early twentieth century with hopes of profitable mining in the back country. That railway became for a time soon after the Japanese invasion a godsend for refugees from the east coast of China heading for the southwest who could afford the ship and railway passages.

For the Liangs, who had come the hard way from Peking by inland routes, Kunming's bright sunshine, mild climate, and beautiful setting of lakes and mountains were heartening. Though the climate was warm and welcoming, the people of Yunnan tended to be cold and critical. They regarded the east coast refugees from the Japanese invasion as simply invaders themselves—foreigners who spoke strange dialects and arrived almost empty-handed to disrupt the tenor of life here. Both national humiliation and national pride were unfamiliar to this provincial population. What concern of theirs was Japanese aggression in the remote eastern provinces? This attitude aroused righteous indignation in the refugees, who had refused to collaborate with the Japanese invaders.

The outlook for the Institute was bleak—no funds, no president, no staff. For the moment if it existed at all it was in the determination of Sicheng himself to reestablish it here. Meanwhile the cost of living was constantly rising and the dwindling of funds with no future means of support in sight was frightening. For a bare living Sicheng and Whei turned to their architectural skills and began designing houses "for the vulgar rich and the profiteers." Their employers were a distasteful lot and the pay erratic. This forlorn attempt to support the family in such chaotic circumstances came to an end in mid-1938, when Sicheng suffered a violent attack of spinal arthritis and muscle cramps that crippled him for six months. On his recovery, his determination was rewarded. The Institute for Research in

Chinese Architecture was set shakily on its feet again in Yunnan. Y. T. Tsur (Chou Yi-ts'un) was named president, and the China Foundation allotted a small stipend for the next year, assuming that Liang would direct research as heretofore. In addition the Chinese government had indicated that he would be called upon to experiment with cheap construction of university buildings using local materials. The principal change was clearly in Liang himself. From the deep discouragement of his previous letters, he now had hope. His Institute would continue, his family could eat, and best of all, his special abilities were now needed in Kunming.

By early March of 1938, there began to be scattered arrivals in Kunming of teachers and students of the Associated University now moving on from Changsha. Some, at least, came via the narrow gauge railway from Haiphong. Among these was Lao Jin. There was a joyful reunion with the Liang family for him and others of the close friends. Whei wrote us that "I like to hear Lao Jin's and [Chang] Shiro's familiar laughs. It helps me to bear the war somehow. And this means we are the same people still."

Three days after he arrived, Lao Jin wrote us a letter about his first impressions. "If you were here you would see an enormous number of familiar faces in unfamiliar circumstances. Some of them have one suit or one robe, exactly the one that is on them and not anything folded in a suitcase. Others manage to share a house. Chang Shiro and family preceded me. The Academia Sinica is coming too; Liang Ssu-yung and Li Chi will be here in a few days, and Y. R. Chao has been here for a few days already. I suppose there will be a sort of miniature Peking life here just as there was in Changsha, only it is one that is materially inadequate. The possible exception is the weather. The sun is gorgeous and there are spots that give you a taste of Italy, as Whei pointed out to me yesterday." As for Whei herself, he described her after the long separation as "the same charming, vivacious, expressive, exciting, and excited person—no more words with the ex-prefix that I can think of—that she was. The only difference is that she has not got much chance to bubble or to smile, because in the present state of national affairs there are so few things to bubble over or to smile at."

He concluded, "As a matter of fact we are more or less in a grave state of mind. There are imprisoned in our hearts yearnings, hopes, and anxieties which are not expressed, which need not be expressed because everybody is aware of them, and which form an undercurrent of emotion when outwardly we are concerned with the house, the food, and the one hundred little details that form what we call ordinary life. For those who belong to the University group, the question of the exact location of the University is still undecided. There are an enormous number of obstacles that are human as well as difficulties that are natural. The attempt to keep higher university education alive is by no means easy, but I suppose we will manage it somehow."

The young cadets who had befriended the Liangs in Huang Hsien had completed their training in the Airforce Academy in Kunming. They invited Sicheng and Whei to attend the ceremony as their parents. This occasion was followed by frequent air raid alarms and finally a major raid by twenty-three Fiat bombers in two different groups, which attacked the aviation school and destroyed planes on the ground. It was the first encounter with the enemy for the recently graduated air cadets, now pilots. One of their cadet friends, Sub-lieutenant Kao, shot down a plane and chased others to the Kwangsi border, but the victory was clearly to the Japanese.

Some days later Kao was in a plane with a faulty gas gauge and had to make a forced landing. "He did not come back until the third morning by a slow train. We slept badly during the two nights he was missing but were more than elated to see him again with a slightly injured jaw and to hear first hand news of the battle and its results while the whole town is still rather vague about it.

"These eight young boys are courageous and pure-hearted with very direct and simple faith in our country and its war, and all of them have very enviable health of body. They are trained to use their skills simply and to give up their lives simply if need be. They are very reticent boys, every one of them.

"They have somehow grown attached to us in a very naive boyish way. Lots of affection has sprung up between us. They come to us or write to us as if to their closest family. Many we know are away doing active work; some are here protecting our very lives in Kunming. One of them I wrote to you about who plays the violin very well, a most affectionate and winning one, is now engaged to be married. Don't ask me what is going to happen to his girl if he marries and if something happens to him. We just can't answer things like that."

In the following years when one by one the airmen died in combat, their belongings were sent to the Liangs. Not one of the eight survived to the end of the war.

The Liangs had three rooms in a house, the main part of which was occupied by a family named Wong. Whei sketched a few glimpses of the household. "Sicheng smiling and stooping (for now he stoops more than ever) and Lao Jin who is just about to open our little cupboard trying to get something to eat, and children, now five — our two and two Wongs and one child of Ssu-yung [Sicheng's brother]. Bao-bao is getting very pretty with a peculiar demure smiling girlishness about her, while Hsiao-di is hard and ruddy with a pair of wide-awake-looking eyes, as much a boy as I have wished. He is quite an artist, drawing elaborate airplanes, anti-aircraft guns, ships and motor lorries, and thousands of other war inventions."

At about this time there arrived in Cambridge a manuscript of an article Sicheng had written in English on the sixth-century A.D. Great Stone Bridge of Chao Hsien. He had mailed it from Tientsin as they set out for the west hoping for its publication in the United States. I turned for advice to William Emerson, Dean of MIT's Department of Architecture, who was himself a historian of French architecture. By chance, one of his researches had concerned the earliest open spandrel bridge in France, which had been erected some ten centuries later than its Chinese forerunner. With mounting fascination he pored over the beautiful drawings and Leica photographs that accompanied the manuscript, and when he had finished reading the text he sent off the manuscript with his endorsement to *Pencil Points,* a leading architectural journal, which published it in two parts, in the January and March issues of 1938.

Pencil Points paid a fee to the author, but the real thrill for both Liangs was receipt of the reprints of the articles. These were printed on fine paper that enhanced the beauty of the illustrations, and the text appeared in an elegant and spacious layout. This success renewed Sicheng's contact with the American architects and scholars who had sought him out in his last years in Peking. Their response lifted his spirits.

With the Institute reestablished and funded in Kunming, though on a smaller scale, the architectural historians of the staff newly arrived from Peking began their systematic search for old Chinese buildings in the area. Among their discoveries were a few temples from the Sung Dynasty, but these were provincial versions of the great examples already studied and described in the Institute's *Bulletin*. While Liang was suffering from his spinal arthritis, Liu Tun-chen turned up in Kunming. He was able to start investigations in the Kunming neighborhood and then to lead a group for three or four months further west in Yunnan to Ta-li and Li-chiang to study pagodas, temples, and domestic architecture.

Up to this time, the Institute had paid little attention to studying the architecture of dwellings. This was because its researches were primarily aimed at discovering the stages of evolution of Chinese architecture as evident in buildings that had survived through the centuries. Domestic architecture barely contributed to this end for several reasons. Dwellings of the rich had been altered from their original form at the whim of the owner. Dwellings of the poor had disintegrated from the inability of their occupants to fight the elements or from pure neglect. As for the palaces of the Imperial Courts in the capitals, these were burnt down and destroyed by the successor regimes at the end of each dynasty.

However, the difficult and exhausting conditions of travel from Peking to Kunming across fifteen hundred miles of back country, putting up at night in villages, had opened the eyes of the Institute staff to the special architectural significance of Chinese dwellings. The distinct features of such dwellings, their relationship to the life-styles of the occupants, and their variations in different areas of the country were suddenly obvious and interesting.

In the autumn of 1939, Liang left Kunming for six months as leader of a wide-ranging Institute expedition to comb forty counties of Szechwan Province. He was accompanied by Liu Tun-chen, Mo Tsung-chiang, and Ch'en Ming-ta. They were making their accustomed investigations of temples and pagodas, measuring, photographing, and researching them. Not surprisingly, they found that the pagodas in the area, like the temples, reflected central Chinese developments, though later in date.

At the same time they were fascinated to encounter surviving architecture of the Han Dynasty (206 B.C.–A.D. 220) as represented in stone versions of wood-frame structures carved in the living rock in cliff tombs near Chiang-k'ou, in Peng-shan Hsien, western Szechwan. They were eager to make a careful examination of this relatively unknown early stage of Chinese architectural evolution. They had the expert knowledge but lacked the funds to finance new research or publish reports of it, or of the finds they had already made in the southwest.

In the spring of 1940, before Sicheng returned from his Szechwan trip, Whei saw to the completion of a three-room house they had planned together in the small village of Lung-t'ou Ts'un (Dragon-head Village), eight miles from Kunming. At that distance from the city they hoped to avoid the bombings. "It cost us twice the sum of money we thought we could afford," she wrote. "Now we are totally broke, feeling more wretched than ever. The price of rice has gone up to $100 a bag—it was $3.40 when we came—and everything else almost accordingly. This year nothing we do seems simple. I am at a loss to tell you what we are doing and how we are. Sicheng has been in Szechwan for five months. I have been very sick and am now well." Though bank checks we often sent had little immediate relevance, since the things the family needed were simply unobtainable, an exception was the matter of paying for the three-room house. By chance a check from us reached them in September 1940 to solve that problem.

Life was hard. There was no running water, hot or cold. Whei's very first purchase had to be a large earthenware crock three or four feet high in which water, carried into the house, could be stored. A water crock was so vital to a family that at the opening of a kiln women elbowed or even fought each other off in fear of losing out. Cooking was done bending over a three-legged earthenware brazier, its top just some eighteen inches above the unpaved kitchen floor. It could hold only a single wok. Fuel for the fire was coal balls made of coal dust and mud. These had to be coaxed to burn at cooking heat. If hot water was needed for washing people, clothes, or dishes, it had to be fetched from the crock and heated on this "stove" or a second one. Any family that had a large thermos to store hot water regarded it as their most precious possession. In addition there was the daily trudge into the village through dust or mud to find affordable food and carry it home. This had to be done each day because no refrigeration existed or had even been imagined. There were of course no telephones and no transportation. Lighting was by vegetable oil lamps, but that was expensive, too; so it was wise to go to bed, like the villagers, as the twilight was fading. Replacing worn out or outgrown clothing for the children was a major problem. Cloth was almost unattainable. In short, the Liangs were reduced by the war, the inflation, and the primitive life-style, to poverty.

Asked for an account of her day, Whei replied, "I get up to scrub and slave, then to buy and cook, then to tidy and wash, then to feel like hell, and have no time to feel at all between the three difficult meals, and then finally to ache and groan again back to bed wondering why I have lived. That is all."

Lao Jin, in two succinct sentences, gave his view of Whei at this period: "She is as usual very busy, only more so in these hectic days. In fact she has so little time to waste that she is in danger of wasting her life."

On the return of Sicheng after his six-month absence, Whei wrote:

"We are now residing in our newly built three-room cottage at the end of a fair-sized village eight miles northeast of Kunming city. It has considerable sceneries around and no military objective. Our house includes three large rooms and across our narrow lane a kitchen, where I am principally involved, and a maid's room, which has been vacant all these months. During the spring Lao Jin has added an extra 'ear-room' to one end of our main house. Thus the whole Pei-tsung-pu Hutung group is at present intact but Heaven knows for how long.

"Numerous friends including [Ch'ien] Tuan-sheng built similar cottages here. Our house was built last of all, so in the end we had to struggle for each plank, each brick, and even each nail required, and had to help in carrying material and in the actual carpentry and masonry.

"Some aspects of the house," she commented, "are not without beauty or comfort. In an amused way we are fond of it, even *proud*."

Strange to say, it was the only house these two architects ever designed for themselves. It stood at the outskirts of the village. It was on the edge of the open countryside next to a raised dike "lined with tall straight pines like those in old paintings." The beauty of the setting and the climate found ready response in Whei's heart: "The weather at this point is turning cool and with more and more autumnal glow of flooding light the scenery is glorious. Everywhere fragrance edges the air and wild flowers remind one of thousands of the nicest feelings long forgotten. Any morning or afternoon the sun steals in curious angles into one's aching sense of awareness of quiet and beauty amid a helpless world of confusion and disaster. Yet wars, especially our own, loom larger than ever, close to our very skin, heart, and nerve."

In November Whei wrote that the bombings were getting very bad. "Jap bombers or the machine-gunning from the pursuit planes are all like quick pains. Right overhead or far away, they are all the same—a sick sensation in the stomach, specially when one has not eaten a thing yet and is not likely to for a long time that day.

"Poor Lao Jin, who has to have classes in the morning in the city, often starts from this village at 5:30 in the morning only to run into an air raid before the classes have even started, then has to walk out with a crowd toward another city gate, toward another hill in another direction till 5:30 in the afternoon, and then to walk on roundabout routes to get back to this village without having food or work or rest . . . or anything, for that matter."

The intensified bombings in November resulted in the Liangs being uprooted again from their cozy house and dear friends. Sicheng on his return from the Szechwan trip had been made a Research Fellow of Academia Sinica and Dr. Y. T. Tsur, now President of the Institute, named Sicheng Director and attached his Institute to the Institute of History and Philology of the government-supported Academia Sinica. The Ministry of Education was now in charge. It ordered the Academia Sinica Institute to move from Kunming to Li-juang, a small town on the south bank of the Yangtze about two hundred miles west of Chungking in Szechwan.

A letter from Sicheng said, "We feel very sad about this moving. It means tearing away from a group of friends we have been with for over ten years. We shall be in an entirely strange place far away from any other center except the Academia Sinica Institute, and away from any 'big city.' The University will remain in Kunming; so will Lao Jin, Tuan-sheng, Shiro, and others. Wherever we go we shall spend many hours a day and many days a month dodging air raids, disrupting work and food and sleep and life in general. But I imagine conditions in England would be far worse."

18. Uprooted

With the two children and grandmother Whei left Kunming at the end of November 1940 in a truck with thirty-one other people who ranged in age from seventy years to a newborn baby. There was a skimpy luggage allowance per family. They rode "astride-wise" packed into the back of an open truck straddling their luggage rolls, a common means of transportation in China then. The journey lasted for two weeks, taking old and young "over mountains in mid-winter weather." On the day of departure Sicheng came down with a sudden fever and had to be left behind in Kunming; he arrived three weeks later.

"Soon after my arrival," he wrote, "I went to Chungking to raise some funds for the Institute. Then Whei had a terrific breakdown and has been in bed ever since, now already three months. Meanwhile on March 14th [1941] her brother, Lin Heng, the boy we called San Yeh in Pei-tsung-pu Hutung, was killed in an air battle over Chengtu. I had to go to Chengtu to settle his affairs and did not get home till April 14, to find Whei much sicker than she had told me in her letters. In spite of her illness she bore the painful news with great courage."

A short note from Whei came in the same envelope: "My young brother, who distinguished himself as an unusually skillful aviator, was killed in an air battle in which he had the satisfaction of shooting down one Jap plane, poor boy, before he was himself brought down, shot through the head."

Lao Jin wrote of him, "Since the beginning of the hostilities, he has been moving with the school from one place to another. He came to Kunming in the summer of 1939 and graduated, one might say *cum laude,* in the spring of 1940, ranking second in a class of more than a hundred. In the short interval of a few years, he had developed into an expert aviator, an army pilot. He had his chosen career, fulfilled his function, and died a dignified death."

Whei's grief at the loss of her young brother merged with the heartaches suffered in the loss of the eight "other brothers," the young cadets from Huang Hsien. Three years later she wrote a poem.

Elegy for My Third Younger Brother, Lin Heng,
Who Died in Air Combat in 1941

Brother Heng, I don't have
The language suitable to our age
To mourn your death.
Our age had asked you
And simply, you had given.
This cruel, simple, heroic sacrifice
Is the poem of our age;
This somber glory is you.

If this reality, supposedly unavoidable,
Has brought too much sorrow, I want to shout
This — you yourself understood, all too clearly,
Because you left too soon, ah, too soon, brother.
Your bravery got you into trouble:
The backwardness of technology,
The tragedy of chance!

It has been three years
Since you died in the skies over Chengtu.
If I tell you about them, please don't grieve
Because mostly it isn't our old nation
But others who are controlling this age.
Our souls bleed, they are bombed to nothingness.

Now we have allies, materials and arms,
Just as you had wished.
I remember how we used to discuss
And discuss, count and re-count.
Each day you waited, with such patience,
But each day passed, with nothing happening,
Slow as a camel!

Now the pursuit planes are not
What you had most hoped to pilot, like the "Hawk 75" —
So awkward and slow.
Ah, my brother, don't grieve;
You accomplished whatever could be accomplished.

Let's not talk about who wronged you.
It was the age, hopeless, unweighable.
China has yet to move forward; dark night
Waits its daybreak.

Brother Heng, I have used all these words
Not beautiful as poetry to mourn you.
Try to believe when I say my heart
Is too filled with bitterness, my throat too numb.
You will never come back I know. Blood young and warm
Became the substitute for science.
The sorrows of China forever
Sank into the bottom of my heart.

Ah. don't grieve.
If you do, I won't be able to comfort you.
Every day I thought through a hundred times:
You'd given all you had, like the other brothers
Who were gone the same way.
You made a gift of your life, freely:

Everything that was young, the future making its promises,
What might have been accomplished in maturity,
And the wisdom of the old.

All possibilities of love, family, children
And all the privileges and happiness life has to offer
As well as its confusions!
All of you, who have given so much, but for whom?
You believed the happiness of the Chinese people,
More important than yourself,
Must come before everything else.
That immortality that is the history of China
Must live on.

You believed—you also had your accomplishments;
In the end you delivered everything.
Since I can understand all this,
Why am I still mourning for you?

Is it because you who were so young
Left nothing of yourself?
When you were a child, I prayed for your happiness;
When war started, I prayed that you would be safe.
Today you've left no children
For me to look after or comfort.
And you yourself seem forgotten
By so many of your countrymen.
Ah, my brother, for whom did you make your sacrifice?
For whom?

Translated by Julia C. Lin

On his return from Chungking and Chengtu, Sicheng took up his scholarly career with renewed vigor. He now had Ministry of Education support. Momentarily, until caught by the ever-rising inflation, he could not only feed his family but also pay salaries to Liu Tun-chen and to his small group of junior colleagues. His recent field trip with all its hardships had yet reminded him of much interesting research still to be done.

The library of the Academia Sinica's Institute of History and Philology with its very important holdings of books for fundamental research written in Chinese and Western languages was the pivot around which the Li-juang academic community centered. He had colleagues in related fields who understood his work. His younger brother, the brilliant archaeologist Ssu-yung, moved there with his family, as did Li Chi and other old friends, who were pursuing investigations of their own that had meaning for Sicheng.

In addition to setting the household in order, Sicheng revived Whei's scholarly interests by bringing her from the excellent library books she could read in bed. His intention of pursuing researches on the Han cliff tombs discovered on the exploratory trip suggested that she could help by immersing herself in Han history. He wrote to me:

"Whei is specially interested in your interest in Han tombs and rubbings combined. Perhaps you do not yet know that she herself has wandered into the Han period. Very privately, with great diligence, she has made the acquaintance of prominent Han characters, emperors and empresses, generals and ministers, their favorites and their enemies—so much so that she talks about them like her best friends living next door! Moreover, she links them up, their customs, costumes, architectures, and even temperaments. If she keeps on at this rate, she will become an unusually well-informed young lady on Han. Even now she could tell you colorful and detailed stories on most of the interesting characters of the earlier Han dynasty.

"She plans to make you a list of quotations from Han history on wall paintings depicting scenes from life. It seems the Han people were unusually fond of painting pictures on their walls or screens and she has made notes of all of these. She rather thinks that the Han people had a greater ability to draw than we see in engraved stones or reliefs of the period. Execution of pictures on stone must sometimes necessarily make the representation of architecture and man seem heavy and less elegant in style, particularly when it is in low relief. From some of your restorations of rubbings we saw the beautiful linear drawings of horses and dogs in action. Just imagine what we would have seen when these lines were made on walls with brush strokes in some of the palaces mentioned in the Han history."

Just at this time, by odd coincidence, the Liangs received from me my first published work. It was on the Han stone reliefs from the Wu family burying-ground in Shantung Province, which I had visited in 1934. My notion of trying to bring some order to the scattered stones had finally produced a proposed reconstruction of three shrines.

Sicheng's reaction to the reprint I sent him gladdened my heart.

"It is of surprising interest to me because instead of dealing with the drawings as I thought you were doing, you have made a valuable contribution to the study of Han architecture. Not only is it a new approach to the Wu Liang Tz'u materials, it has also thrown a new light on the conception of a Han funeral monument. . . . I greatly admire you for your thoroughness and patience in getting the necessary materials, references, and the means to make your scheme realizable and beyond dispute. . . . You suddenly made us aware that this kind of small shrine, built in honor of the dead, is the embodiment of a religious conception of pre-Buddhist China. In it, the universe, orientation, ethics (the many good deeds done in the past), ancestor worship (rows of kings of the past), war glories (scenes of battle), the five-element idea, the love of learning, admiration for high position in officialdom, etc.: all hotch-potched with the concept of life, good living, death, and posterity. The hotch-potch of all these is the basic religion in China even today, so must have been the whole religion of China then. It is surprising that a little shrine like that could tell more than pages in history books. Whei thinks more significant than I do (but it is quite a point to bear in mind) — [and here Whei herself interpolates a line:] 'that the little shrine contains no central deity, nor all-important portrait or statue of the deceased, but a rhythmic flow of elements and humanity fused in one grand pattern.'

"At present your article has been lent out to many friends of Academia Sinica who want to read it. Li Chi saw it and was interested and wanted to read it. Tung Tso-pin, who himself once attempted to restore a tomb chamber from a set of rubbings with the aid of matchboxes and gave it up as a bad job in the end, poured out words of admiration at your perseverance and success."

Life in Li-juang, according to Sicheng, "is such that it is difficult to describe to you and difficult for you to imagine: under vegetable oil lamps, making children's cotton sole shoes, buying and cooking cheap coarse food, we live like our parents when they were in their teens but are doing modern work. Sometimes reading foreign magazines and staring at the colorful advertisements of modern streamlined facilities is like looking at miracles. The Kunming climate and sceneries were lovely and we loved them. Szechuan is dreary. We are situated on a rather uninteresting stretch of the upper Yangtze. However, my office force has, for the first time since we moved south, doubled in number and I have succeeded in raising a bigger fund than that we have had for the last two years. My salary covers only our food bills but we are thankful we are this well off. My charming sick wife is happy that we are still doing our work unshaken."

The letters from Li-juang tell so much beyond even the words written in them. The paper is of all shapes and sizes, much of it thin, yellow, and decaying, the kind that might have wrapped bits of meat or vegetables brought back from the market. Sometimes there are precious blue sheets given by friends. But all have in common that every inch is used. No empty space is afforded for margins or paragraphs, and the final page is often only a half or third of a page, the rest cut off for other use. Then the number of stamps on the surviving envelopes make one understand how costly — and therefore rash — correspondence, even inside China, was at that time. They explain too why one envelope may contain a number of letters accumulated through days for the one great splurge of stamp expenditures.

The Ministry of Education — or was it the Academia Sinica — may have envisioned Li-juang as a haven where scholars could work undisturbed by the war. Whei, writing in August 1941, conveyed her bitter comment.

"Even though I am almost 100% sure that the Japs will not drop any bombs over this little out-of-the-way village-town, Li-juang, yet the 27 planes that flew right over our heads an hour ago with their undescribable droning sound give me still the creeps — that queer sensation of being afraid of being hit any moment. They have gone upstream, bombed somewhere, probably I-pin, and are back again now over our heads on the same leisurely flight with that menacing drone and deadly purposiveness. I was going to say that this makes me sick, then I realized that I am already very sick, and this only makes me momentarily sicker with a slight rise of temperature and uncomfortable quickening of heart beats. . . . None of us can ever be remote from war, at any point in China today. We are integrally bound up with it whether or not we are doing the actual fighting."

They were now "fortunate enough to have a country maid who is good and faithful, very young and nice-tempered." Her only fault was that she was too vigorous. "If you have only seven old pillow cases and about that number of sheets of different sizes and strengths among five members of the family and know that white cloth is as unavailable as gold-leaf in the market, you wouldn't like the shock of seeing half the sheet [sic] and two pillow cases in shreds after one conscientious washing as well as half buttons dangling from shirt fronts and old shirts too strained and haggard after each washing when the price of any shirt is forty dollars and up. This problem applies to food as well as household articles in the hands of this maid. Of course wherever we can we use unbreakables, but nothing seems to be unbreakable and everything is either terribly costly or irreplaceable.

"Slow-tempered and always preferring to handle any work one item at a time, Sicheng is least capable of taking care of household odds and ends. And odds and ends there are galore, rushing at him like different trains pulling into Grand Central Station at any time. I am still the Station Master of course though he may be the Station! I might be run over, but he can never be. Lao Jin (here for a longish visit) is that sort of visitor who is either seeing people off or meeting someone at the train, slightly disturbing the traffic, but making the Station a little more interesting and the Station-Master a little more excitable."

Lao Jin added his testimony at the end. "In the presence of the Station-Master, and the Station typing, the passenger is too dazed to say or do anything except watch the trains rushing by. I have passed through Grand Central Station in New York many a time without having seen even once the Station-Master, but here both architecturally and otherwise the Station-Master and the Station may be mistaken for each other."

But Sicheng (dependent as always on his steel back brace) insisted at the bottom of the page, "Now it is the Station's turn. With the main ridge purlin considerably deflected due to faulty construction, and with ugly steel buttresses designed and executed by PUMC now considerably weathered after seven years of service, the heavy wartime traffic underneath seems to shake my very foundations."

The Institute's quarters in Li-juang were a simple L-shaped one-story farmhouse, its long arm oriented north and south. Running the full length of this arm on one side was an extended workroom with rough tables and benches provided for drafting and writing. A maid's room, a storeroom, and three bedrooms for junior researchers lined the opposite side. Across a narrow corridor lay the short arm of the L stretching toward the east. Directly across the corridor were two bedrooms, one for the grandmother and Bao-bao, the second for the son. Beyond these, two rooms for the Liangs, a bedroom and an office, completed the short arm. They faced south and looked into a pleasant courtyard rather heavily shaded with trees. Here Whei lived in her cot bed. (Plain boards or bamboo mats were the underpinnings for everyone else.) Opposite, along the west side of the long arm, was a larger courtyard dominated by a huge camphor tree and with a small grove of banana trees. Elsewhere in the compound were scattered shacks, one for the kitchen, one not very near for the dining room, with some space for Mo Tsung-chiang to sleep, and farthest from everything, the outhouse toilet.

The setting up and furnishing of the workroom was a great advance toward getting the Institute into action along the lines of the treasured workroom in the Palace courtyard in Peking. Liu Tun-chen was settled with his family not far away. Liang's longtime junior associates Mo Tsung-chiang, Liu Chih-p'ing, and Ch'en Ming-ta were at hand. Sicheng wrote that he would "like to bring out a presentable 'History of Chinese Architecture' one of these days." A playful letter from Lao Jin in Li-juang late that November of 1941 indicated in passing that Sicheng had already started work on the history he was contemplating: ". . . he remains very much as he always was, tinkering and pottering about before he goes to and after he comes out of his office in which his main business is divided between writing a short history of Chinese architecture and worrying over the Institute's finances. His duties as a historian are somewhat out of the ordinary: he bakes bread, builds kitchen stoves, weighs coal, and attends to such household duties that if he were transported overnight and dropped in America with nothing else but his body and soul, he probably would make a creditable living, possibly better than the one he now enjoys, by following the national profession of laundryman."

As for Whei, Lao Jin reported, "She is bathed, soaked, and saturated with Han Dynasty, so much so that if you touch anything whatever she pops off into that remote period from which she hardly ever returns of her own accord." He himself, the logician, had a philosophical approach to the inflation. "In these troublous times, it is essential to think of the things one possesses, the cash valuation of which is so staggering that one feels quite well off; at the same time one must never think of the things one has to acquire if one can help it."

19. The Capital and the Village

By the time the United States entered the war in December 1941, both John and I were government officials in Washington. We hoped and expected to go back to China, this time to the far southwest, Yunnan and Szechwan. Since the Japanese held the eastern provinces, "Free China" could be reached from the United States only via India and by plane from there over the Himalayas to Kunming. John went first, three years before I did. He left in mid-August 1942 and took nearly a month en route flying hops down the coast of South America, then to Ascension Island in mid-Atlantic, across Africa to Egypt, across the Indian Ocean to India, and finally over "the Hump" to Kunming.

There Tsinghua colleagues and other dear friends from our Peking days greeted him warmly at the Associated University. He drove a group of them out in a U.S. Army jeep eight miles to the village of Lung-t'ou Ts'un, where Ch'ien Tuan-sheng lived with his family in a house designed by Whei. Next door on the country lane was the house the Liangs had built for themselves and left so reluctantly. John found it charming: "local mud-brick walls and tiled roof with light wood interior and whitewashed plaster. Behind it was an attractive garden among eucalyptus trees."

At the end of a week he flew on to his post at the U.S. Embassy in Chungking.

The wartime capital was new to John and to many other Americans, the majority of whom had never been to China before being sent there on wartime assignments. It was not only on the other side of the globe but opposite in nearly every other way from the Washington they had left. A remote up-country river port on a steep-sided peninsula that jutted between the Yangtze River and its tributary, the Chialing, it had been the official wartime capital ever since late 1937. Heavy intermittent bombing by the Japanese air force had reduced much of it to rubble and the hasty rebuilding for emergency use had created a city where the new ramshackle office buildings and residences thrown up amid the ruins were not far superior to the mud-and-wattles slums that clung to the cliffsides. The extremes of climate added to the misery. Rain, penetrating chill, and slithery mud characterized the cold months. The summer heat and dampness were more ruthless than Washington's because there was no defense against them. Even water for washing was scarce and, for many households, had to be carried up from the muddy rivers hundreds of steps below.

The people of Chungking and its scattered village suburbs, like the rest of the Chinese population, were showing the strain of having been at war for the past five years. The patriotic fervor that had marked the early furious and heroic military resistance to the Japanese incursion in the east had sunk to a passivity appropriate to long-term endurance of the military stalemate. The endurance involved new routines of working and living from day to day. It required learning to live with the Japanese bombings by taking refuge routinely on signal in the cave shelters dug in the cliff faces of the city. It also involved learning to live with the Szechwanese, or, from the other point of view, the Szechwanese learning to live with the "downriver people."

The provinciality of West China up to recent years as noted in Yunnan was also evident in the hostility between the Szechwanese and their compatriots from the east coast cities who had come as wartime refugees 1,500 miles up the Yangtze River to the west. The Szechwan basin was rich, well-irrigated agricultural land dominated by conservative landlords. Its productivity could feed the sudden increase in population and its mountain walls abutting the narrow Yangtze gorges of its river gateway served as a functioning Maginot Line to keep out the Japanese armies. Through the first year of the war, government bureaus, institutes, and universities had been moved from the eastern cities not only to Yunnan but even more to Szechwan beyond the reach of the Japanese armies. At the same time a great flood of ordinary citizens had made their way westward as best they could by bus, rail, boat, or on foot to the western sanctuary. A few went to the Communist guerrilla areas in the northwest. Industrialists from Shanghai and the inland river ports had been encouraged to dismantle their factories and take the machinery by boat up the Yangtze to Szechwan. Still, despite heroic efforts, the mass influx from downriver managed to bring proportionately little in the way of goods or capital to the west. In such circumstances, like the Yunnanese the Szechwanese regarded the "downriver people" as unwelcome invaders.

Since Chungking was the wartime capital, Sicheng had to go there at intervals to obtain government funds for the support of the Institute. It was a difficult and time-consuming trip several days by boat downriver from Li-juang. His base when he reached the crowded city was the Academia Sinica hostel, which housed members coming temporarily into the capital from its outlying research centers. The hostel was bare, messy, and often crowded to the point of providing only dormitory accommodations — cots crammed together in one or another large room.

John described it as "the top intellectuals living in a state of squalor, clutter, bedquilts, pots and pans, children, oranges, and conversation. It is a slum but full of highly trained academicians, quite a subject for tragicomedy." Still, it furnished a roof over one's head and chance encounters with congenial associates from afar. Certainly nobody could expect a grand hotel or even a neat and clean "bed and breakfast" in wartime Chungking.

In late September 1942, when John went to the Academia Sinica hostel, he was met by Sicheng, who held his hand for five minutes with excitement. "He has come down to get funds and has been rather successful, getting increased grants from the Ministry of Education and the British Boxer Indemnity Fund."

Once John had settled down in Chungking, both the Liangs waited eagerly for his visit to them. Sicheng wrote, "Our meeting will mean your coming over to this damned little town so inconveniently off anybody's way. It takes three days on some rotten steamer upstream to reach Li-juang from Chungking and two days downstream to get back. There isn't any way to shorten the time or improve the means of transportation. . . . Still I'll give you a map of the location of our Institute compound in case you find yourself landed at Li-juang without anybody meeting you at the wharf. Boats don't run on schedule. Every arrival is an unexpected event here. But still, you can send us a telegram telling us the date and name of your boat. Telegrams are forwarded by mail via either I-pin or Nan-hsi, both sixty *li* [c. twenty miles] away from here, and may arrive either ahead of or after you."

John's visit to Li-juang was delayed until mid-November. He had an old friend, the sociologist T'ao Meng-ho, as a companion on the "rotten steamer upstream" trip. He was attacked en route by those Chinese respiratory germs that still disable Americans arriving in China without immunity. So several days of his week in Li-juang were spent in bed, running a fever, across the hall from Whei's sickroom. Sicheng was kept busy going back and forth between the two beds in this "ward" with food, medicines, thermometers, and so on. Was this long-awaited reunion a disaster, then? On the contrary, Whei wrote John after his departure that she was "still under the spell of your influence, which was considerable! Kidding and laughing was a treat to me, having gotten out of the habit myself for so long. As to the semi-serious, highly improper allusions and remarks that came between serious conversations, homey chats, or impersonal discussions, they were very touching, extremely flattering, altogether sweet."

Seeing for himself the family's problems, he was able to promise future help and to urge Sicheng to spend, not save, the money we had donated as well as other odd income from selling fountain pens, watches, and so on. A good maid, good food, and the powdered milk John was able to send them did wonders for Whei's health. By December 26 she wrote him that she now had "no fever, no cough, no indigestion, good sleep and appetite, good food and 'Klim.'" She particularly enjoyed the new frame built for her bed, which lifted it higher "ever so much nearer to human beings than to the ground and people don't have to stoop so low to give me anything."

Sicheng, who was none too strong himself, with the help of his colleagues completed twenty-six drawings of important architectural monuments with the necessary lettering and enlarged photographs to send to a National Art Exhibition in Chungking.

Whei wrote, "Sicheng's Institute has reached a very different status from those miserable, feebly struggling days when we first started to set up in the midst of war confusion and national plight. It has at last come into its own. Meanwhile I got out of the habit of creative writing, lost track of my poet-writer-author friends, and gave up all opportunity to do work for the new drama and stage that I had loved and for which I may have had some ability or aptitude.

"Sicheng is happy that his Institute is now on a firmer base, and is ever so much more known to the people in whose hands rest the means and power to uphold institutes of this kind. And incidentally Sicheng himself is now identified with the work, or is the person to whom such work is to be entrusted. He is not so happy now as in the old days; being the jack of all trades and the errand boy running between here and the war capital to gather funds, he is forced into the position of an administrator — the man looking after the business side of things, attending conferences, making contacts, etc. — instead of having all of his unhurried time devoted to his research, his drawings, and his field trips."

Her report that Sicheng's work was at last appreciated was matched by other good news. Sicheng wrote to John, "Our household arrangement has suddenly changed and improved so much that probably it is hard for you to believe. The routines are so normal that I attend to my work regularly without interruption, and Whei feels no strain about the housework. She claims that it is her philosophy that has changed, coincidentally with other minor changes here that make her so comfortable with many things that had irritated her before. Basically, of course, the change in our financial situation is doing the trick. Best of all, Whei has gained 8½ pounds in the last two months."

At last there seemed to be every reason to celebrate the turn-around in the Liangs' way of life and prospects.

20. The Stress of Poverty

However, life in Li-juang, "this damned little town so inconveniently off anybody's way," as Sicheng described it, was never going to run smoothly. By late February 1943, the refugee academic group including the wives had been afflicted with an epidemic of inflammatory gossip leading to jealousy, quarreling, anger, vituperation, and broken friendships. As Whei wrote, "This is a narrow-minded small town community. Some of the things happening here lately in the pleasant or comic form of squabbles have reached alarming proportions among really educated people. I wonder if people stranded on a lonely island with scanty supplies would in the end be hitting each other in such childlike manner."

To cap this, Liu Tun-chen, the head of research in historical documents for the study of Chinese architecture, announced he was leaving. He had been with the Institute for over ten years and shared the leadership with Sicheng.

In Whei's words, "Liu is a very capable person and very responsible. He has been entrusted with all the accounts and the management of all the odds and ends which are complicated and quite beyond Sicheng. Now Sicheng is going to be left with the whole lot!

"This is not all, as you know, there are only five of them in this Institute who have carried on the work since we came to the south. Now that Mr. Liu starts going himself there is a tendency for general breaking up."

The arrival of an eminent visitor from the outside world provided a break in the dullness and shifted attention from the daily bickerings. Professor Joseph Needham, distinguished British biochemist, was experiencing the Chinese land and people for the first time as wartime Science Attaché at the British Embassy in Chungking. (In later years, after his return to Cambridge University, his multi-volumed history of Chinese science brought him world renown.) Though she was lying in bed throughout the visit, Whei described the event to John.

"Professor Needham has been here and fed on fried duck and departed. At first most people were inclined to bet with each other on whether or not Professor N. was ever going to smile during his stay in Li-juang. I admit that Li-juang is not an over-exciting place, but still we might have reason to expect one little smile from so ardent a lover of Chinese early science who had taken all the trouble to come to China during such a war. Finally one smile broke through the conversation when the worthy professor was in the company of Mr. and Mrs. Liang (who sat up in bed). He was much delighted, he said, that Mrs. Liang speaks English with an Irish accent. I was not aware that the English like the Irish so much before. Later in the afternoon, on the last day of his visit, when tea was served with little cakes in the National Museum compound, Prof. N. was said to be even lively. Such was the proof of the English people's love of tea.

"Many have remarked that Liang Sicheng should be given the Nobel Prize for Peace this year for having successfully brought about a very friendly handshake between Dr. T'ao Meng-ho [China's senior sociologist, head of the Academy's Institute of Social Research] and Dr. Fu Ssu-nien [a vigorous humanist, head of the dominant Institute of History and Philology]. It was done dramatically too, before a large audience, since it was at a moment just before Prof. N. was to deliver a lecture in the Academia Sinica auditorium. Many clapped their hands in secret, according to report. Dr. Li Chi went up to shake Liang Sicheng's hand and awarded him privately the Nobel Prize for Peace. Mrs. Liang was to report to Dr. Fairbank in Chungking to assure him that there is still great hope for mankind in general.

"The preliminary work of the reconciliation should be credited to that certain person, who was known to have a habit ineradicable of getting seriously involved way inside the insides of every human situation.

"After reading Tolstoy's painstaking record of human beings between the years 1805 and 1812 in an area between Petersburg and Moscow, I have to admit that human beings in Li-juang and Chungking, or Kunming or Peiping [Peking] or Shanghai, between the years 1922 and 1943 are terribly similar to those described in *War and Peace* of a century ago in outlandish Russia even. So why not reconcile with it all — I mean life and people in general.

"The worst thing I can do is let myself in for bitterness. I am born a woman and it is wartime. My own mother happens to be an unusually incapable woman and very interfering, besides being the most impatient person God ever created. Just now it concerns the maid. The real trouble lies in my mother fussing with her when she should not, spoiling her when she should not, and being too impatient to let the maid do a steady routine every day like clockwork but must necessarily order her about precisely to change my orders, and so on — till no one can do a thing about anything. I used to argue and fight with mother but that is absolutely idiotic and suicidal."

The Liangs' mounting troubles had led John to write Lao Jin in Kunming for his insights and advice. The reply began, "Don't be discouraged with the Liangs," and went on to offer his view of the problems they faced.

"The difficulties of housing are small I suppose compared to the difficulties of human adjustments. The one who is most difficult to adjust is the mater. She belongs to an entirely different generation but lives in a comparatively modern household in which she has a good deal of ideas, some energy but absolutely no proper job, excepting the things that drift into her hands. She needs communication, being very, very lonely, but the only one with whom she might communicate is Whei and Whei can hardly communicate with her, being so alien to her general ideas and feelings. The result is that she can only get into any contact with her daughter through quarreling. They love each other and dislike each other. I have suggested separation ever so many times but it was never taken up and at present separation is quite impossible."

Perhaps it was a copy of one of John's family letters that inspired Whei to write him in a more extroverted vein.

"My reading, by the way, varies from *War and Peace, Passage to India, Disraeli, Queen Victoria, Palaces of the Yuan Dynasty* (in Chinese), *Palaces of the Ch'ing in Peking, The Sung Construction of Dams and Tomb Chambers, Official Chronicles of Hung, Indecent Tales of Anatole France, Memoirs of Casanova,* Shakespeare, André Gide, Samuel Butler's *The Way of All Flesh,* Liang Sicheng's manuscripts, Hsiao-di's compositions, and a Chinese translation of *Alice in Wonderland* that amuses the children."

The children, Tsai-ping ("Bao-bao") and her younger brother Tsung-chieh, still known by his childhood name Hsiao-di, though they played such an important part in the Liangs' life, had been somewhat neglected in her correspondence. A lively letter gives quick glimpses of them at ages fourteen and eleven.

"Tsai-ping has the happy combination of Sicheng's placidity and whatever virtue I have. She has made out wonderfully in school both in studies and in making friends. Her smiling radiance more than makes up for the lack of pep on her parents' part. . . . Tsung-chieh on the other hand is now a veteran country lad darkened like mahogany, wearing straw sandals, and using bona fide local dialect in dealing with the rough and the vulgar of his local schoolmates. But he is quite a little gentleman at home, very much concerned over my health and intensely absorbed in making all kinds of gadgets.

"I continue to be a 'juggler' managing economic acrobatics stunts so that everyone in the family and some among relatives and staff are well taken care of in small ways. I *have* to mend many almost unmendable underwear and socks for Sicheng and the two children continually. . . . Even Hsiao-di is made to sew on Sunday afternoons when we simply can't cope with the situation of mending. It is a greater job really than writing a whole chapter on Sung, Liao, and Chin architectural developments or an attempt to reconstruct pictures of the Sung capitals. Both these are jobs I have done with interest and conscientiousness for Sicheng while he was busy over other parts of his writing. Bao-bao is doing well but it is very strenuous for her to walk such a distance to school over the muddy lanes and she never can eat enough for lunch."

Sicheng had taken his son to Chungking, where the boy had passed entrance examinations for two middle schools. He had chosen, of the two, Nankai Middle School, where he had friends. Lao Jin commented, "His IQ is very high and the naughty boy has developed into an eager student."

21. New Hopes

In the spring of 1943, the Liangs suddenly came up with a scheme that charged the entire atmosphere with promise, hope, and, best of all, creativity. Whei wrote to John: "Sicheng has a plan of getting some plates drawn in black ink with lettering in Chinese and English and after completion sent to your place to have them microfilmed and sent to America for publication, or to find funds to get them published. The English texts would follow; the Chinese texts would be printed in China. Then one or two sets of our work might see themselves in print before the end of the war or as soon as the war is over. In that way the staff here would have something to look forward to, or there would be a definite aim for our next year's efforts. There are so many places that have written to us inquiring whether or not we have some new publications on Chinese architecture, it seemed a pity that we have never struggled harder to solve our printing problems."

Sicheng himself wrote separately to John, perhaps not knowing that Whei had written. "I have just completed a set of about eighty drawings. Could you be kind enough to photograph them with your microfilm so that we can have at least one set of duplicates before they are published?"

What they were proposing with such yearning — the microfilming of eighty architectural drawings — would be easy for John to arrange in Chungking. He was director of the American Publications Service, a wartime operation under the U.S. Embassy that collected Chinese and Japanese publications for the information of government bureaus in Washington and assisted the State Department   Cultural Relations program. Because of strict weight limitations over the Hump, the publications had to be sent in microfilm in both directions. For this purpose, John had an American photographic assistant to handle the technology. John sent the Liangs an encouraging letter promising his full cooperation in their project. Yet given the complexities of life in wartime Szechwan the process took months before the end was achieved.

Meanwhile Sicheng was spending long hours driving himself to finish his drawings. At night his light came from wicks in primitive vegetable oil lamps. Bending over his drawing board while working, he rested his chin on a small vase. This supported the weight of his head and with constant adjustment lessened the pressure on his spine, which had been stiffened from his Kunming bout with arthritis.

The history of Chinese architecture, on which he was working, he described as "considerably larger in size and scope than was required at first. But to make it shorter and still good requires even more time. To make it short and let it be bad would be without any point at all.

"Again, it is the first thing of its kind. I have waited all these years to bring one out. This is the maximum compromise I am willing to make. However, Whei and I are really happy in one sense, that at least the basic skeleton of our dream work has been constructed out of our chaotic field work and random research of the past years."

Sicheng arrived in Chungking in late November. John wrote, "He came over last night first and saw our microfilm on his history of architecture drawings which the boys had so enjoyed filming because they gave such a clear result. He weighs only 102 pounds and is plainly tired after completing his history of Chinese architecture in 110,000 characters, with a draftsman and Whei working till midnight too; but he is energetic and ambitious, as usual, and has that quiet dignity and charm which make him move through any scene like a nobleman."

The microfilming of the large and beautiful architectural drawings keyed to illustrate their architectural history was a small but vital contribution of a U.S. government office to promoting cultural relations. The drawings were copied in two identical reels, of which Sicheng immediately sent one to me in Washington for safekeeping. The other he kept in China.

Liang Sicheng's *History of Chinese Architecture,* written in Chinese, was in his words "an attempt to organize the materials collected by myself and other members of the Institute for Research in Chinese Architecture during the past twelve years." He had divided the previous 3,500 years into six architectural periods, defined each period by references to historical and literary citations, described existing monuments of each period, and finally analyzed the architecture of each period as evidenced from a combination of painstaking library and field research.

In addition to this architectural history, Sicheng had produced an abridged text written in English, to be illustrated with his drawings, captioned in both English and Chinese, and with the Institute's photographs. He acknowledged that both books would have to wait for publication until the war was over, but he chose not to postpone preparation of the texts and illustrations.

His years of research on the Sung architectural treatise *Ying-tsao fa-shih* had reached the stage where he was preparing a series of plates that translated the original drawings into modern graphic presentation and supplemented the original text with notes explaining both the terms and the methods of Sung architecture. Field studies of surviving Sung buildings had made this project possible. Photographs of existing structures contemporary with the text would also illustrate it. More than a hundred drawings had been drafted; inking and lettering them was in progress. This book, another unprecedented contribution to understanding Chinese architectural history, tentatively titled "Annotated Architectural Standards," would also have to be published after the war.

PART FOUR

Between War and Revolution, 1946–1948

22. War's End

Sicheng's downriver trips to Chungking to deal with the Ministry of Education were already seriously time-consuming, but a wartime appointment increased his periods away from home. He was named Vice-Chairman of the Chinese Commission for the Preservation of Cultural Objects in War Areas, which was responsible for listing, mapping, and compiling photographs of the important temples, pagodas, museums, and so on that were not to be destroyed. Two young men, Wu Liang-yung and Luo Chih-wen, were helping to draft English-language guides to be distributed to American airmen who were at that time still bombing Japanese bases in China's eastern provinces. Chinese-language versions of the same guides were also distributed. One set of these reached Chou En-lai and apparently caught his attention.

In Chungking to complete his responsibilities as vice-chairman, Sicheng was there to greet me when I returned to China as Cultural Attaché of the U.S. Embassy in the summer of 1945. By midsummer world events were speeding up. The Russians joined the war against Japan. The atomic bomb was dropped on Hiroshima. Headlines in the Chinese press on the "yuan-tzu-tan"—the unfamiliar name for the atomic bomb in Chinese— were mystifying. Rumor had it that it was huge, horrible, terrifying—but what was it? Professor Joseph Needham, the British Embassy's science attaché (about whom Whei had written), held an open-air seminar the following night to explain the dawn of the nuclear age and to answer the many questions of the still bewildered audience.

News of Japan's surrender reached Chungking about 8:20 on the evening of August 10, 1945. Sicheng and two young Chinese writers had joined me for supper at the U.S. Embassy mess. After eating, we dragged wicker chairs out onto the hilltop terrace before the Embassy portico to enjoy the cool breezes (on the very hot night) and watch the clusters of lights come out on the mountains beyond the Yangtze. Sicheng was telling the story of Tagore's long ago visit to Peking. Suddenly he stopped talking. He and the others stiffened into a vigilant tenseness almost like hunting dogs. I had to strain my ears to hear what they had heard. It was the far away sound of a siren. Could it be an air raid? Preposterous, and yet each of them was alert for the possibility after years of conditioning to the real thing. Could it, instead, be signaling the victory?

Far below us the news began to spread through the city. On top of the high hill we could almost follow its course. At first there were muffled murmurs, perhaps just people running through the streets, then individuals' shouts and the sputter of firecrackers, finally groups of shouting, cheering, clapping people, so widespread that the whole city seemed to be coming to life with a great roar.

Sicheng was desolated that after these eight long years of waiting he was away from his family when the news came. We all went down to mill around in the streets with the crowds. The occasion demanded symbols — flags, V-for-victory hand signs, thumbs-up, the noise of firecrackers, the red of rockets, the brilliance of searchlights making a five-pointed star over the city. There was an impromptu parade of jeeps, trucks, and buses loaded with celebrants. As one vehicle met another in the crowded streets, riders in each reached out to shake hands with co-victors across the way. When Sicheng finally got back to the Academia hostel he found the scholars there laughing and dancing with happiness and celebrating with nips from a single bottle of long-saved rare liquor.

A friendly U.S. army pilot offered to fly Sicheng and me in a C-47 to I-pin, which had the nearest airfield to Li-juang. After fifteen minutes in the air, Sicheng pointed to a walled town at a bend of the Yangtze far below and said, "That is the end of the first day's run upriver on the boat." In forty-five minutes the plane was over the compound in Li-juang — three-and-a-half days by boat. The I-pin landing field was knee-deep in grass but serviceable. Sicheng and I took a small steamer downriver the few miles to Li-juang.

Whei, confined to her bed, was pale and thin but indomitable. She and I had many long talks together sharing the stories of our lives in the years we had been apart. Her experience of hardships and illness had deepened her perceptions and emotions. I began to think, looking back, that the Chinese intellectuals we knew in Peking lived almost as remote from the real problems of China as we foreigners did. But these years had changed all that.

Her daughter, Bao-bao, had reached sixteen and was now known by her grown-up name, Tsai-ping. She was very petite, feminine, and introspective. In the drab routine of life in Li-juang she contributed a special lightness for the household when she came home from school every day bringing the news of the world (the only world she had known since she was eleven) to her mother's bedside. Whei, as always, lived in the sorrows, joys, troubles, and intrigues of the people around her even when they were at the puppy-love level of Bao-bao's contemporaries.

Whei celebrated by taking a sedan chair to a teahouse, I walking alongside. It was the first time she had been in the town in the entire five years of her stay. Though possibly unwise for her health, the foray stocked her full of new sights and sounds and faces to mull over in the weeks to come. She was keeping up her writing if possible every day — articles on architecture, on Han history and she even contemplated a novel.

To me the lack of even the most rudimentary conveniences in Li-juang was startling. Its only contact with the outside world was by riverboat. There were no telephones, no electricity, no radios, no wheeled carts or draft animals, and even the roads leading back into the hills from the shore were merely stepping stones through the terraced rice-paddies wide enough for two people to pass. There was every reason for the inhabitants of this isolated village to be backward, superstitious, poverty-stricken, and disease-ridden. When the Academia Sinica's Institute of History and Philology, famous for its excavations at Anyang and the resultant researches, which pushed Chinese recorded history back to 1500 B.C., brought its crates of Anyang skulls and bones, it was said they had difficulty for months in hiring local people. Word got around that they were cannibals.

In this environment nothing could have been more surprising than to go three miles up a stone path into the hills, come to a picturesque group of farmhouses, walk through several courtyards to an unlikely-looking inner building, and there find, shelved and in use, a remarkable Chinese library that also had all the rare and important publications in English, French, German, and Japanese on Asiatic archaeology, history, and exploration. This remarkable Academia Sinica library almost literally saved the lives of several of the refugees, including not only Whei but her brother-in-law, Liang Ssu-yung, the noted archaeologist, who was also flat on his back with tuberculosis for four years and kept his spirits up by reading and being read to during that period. These two protracted illnesses were not exceptions. Furthermore, in a remote town where there was no hospital and only one modern doctor, who could, in turn, travel only at foot pace, it is not surprising that there were tragic losses, especially of women and children. Among others, Li Chi of the Central Museum lost two teenage daughters in the five years there, and the wife of the sociologist T'ao Meng-ho died of tuberculosis.

Besides the physical suffering and the hostility of the local inhabitants, there had been the internal strains that such a community must be prey to, both jealousies and disputes. There was even the added refinement of cultural conflict. For example, T'ung-chi University, in exile from its Shanghai campus, had been German-founded and was staffed with German-trained students, whereas most of the Academia Sinica people had their scholarly roots in the United States. This created something of a chill between the two groups.

It was remarkable that scholars at work in such circumstances managed to pursue their researches and prepare them for postwar publication in Shanghai when decent paper and print-type should become available. But Sicheng had determined to publish *without* waiting, even though it involved making use of the local primitive technique described as "hand-stenciled lithography." Sicheng and all his younger colleagues used their manual skills to produce the two important final issues of the Institute's *Bulletin* in this manner, two hundred copies of each.

Whei continued, as always, to be torn between the unremitting pains of her body, the demands of running a household, and, necessarily in third place, her deep interest in writing and research. All three were vying for her attention at the same time. Of her health, she wrote me, "The troubles that bothered me are now just a little worse, especially the sharp pain connected with my bladder, which might be already serious." Yet she was working against a deadline on her domestic architecture article to be included in the forthcoming volume 7, no. 2 of the Institute *Bulletin*. Finally with the coming of the winter weather, "the gowns and the rags that have served us for nine or ten years have to be taken out and repaired. Since Sicheng is going to Chungking his things have to be mended first. He wore them so much last winter in Chungking that they are like the battleships that after an active service have to be taken to the dry dock to be overhauled, some so torpedoed and bombed that a good deal of ingenuity is required in the mending."

She added a poignant note, "You can't quite picture the contrast of the loneliness at present with the hilarious time we had in this very same compound when you were here." John was due to return to Chungking from Washington shortly and the fact that we both would be there made her long to come with Sicheng and join us. "This is beginning to be like the old times."

She wrote a welcoming letter to John later and added:

"Tell Wilma last Sunday I went to town again by 'chair' and took a boat punted by two of Tsai-ping's boy friends, and went to a restaurant to have noodles and sat in another teahouse to get a rest and then, returning by way of the football field, watched a volley-ball match from a tea-shed on the bank, etc.

"I also visited Tsai-ping's school the day before, wearing slacks, very elegant, and caused a sensation! But now those few sunny days are faded and forgotten. They seem utterly unreal viewed from the gray and rainy atmosphere this week.

"If the sun ever comes out again and if I could be restored to that state of fitness again, I would certainly take the risk to come to Chungking just for a lark, cold weather or no cold weather. Since I have all my clothes fixed and pieced together ready for the trip it would be no trouble to pack and come as the mood takes me. But it rains and rains . . . and there is no boat. It is certainly easier for you to come to China from the USA than for us to move over to Chungking from here."

And "just for a lark" she did come with Sicheng when a boat at last became available. It was the first time in five years that she had been out of Li-juang. Her health was so precarious that in Chungking she had to stay in bed most of the time in the Academia Sinica hostel dormitory. I took her out in a Jeep at intervals. One day we drove to the suburbs to pick up Hsiao-di at Nankai Middle School. Everything was new and exciting to her. Riding in the Jeep she kept her eyes peeled for the new dresses we passed, the traffic and the street life of the people of this (to her now) great city of Chungking. Several times I fetched her by Jeep to eat in the American Embassy mess. The military attachés in uniform, all of whom had served in the war on various fronts, fascinated her. Their conversation in which she soon took part was her first with the American allies. For her the war had been a sequence of tragic encounters with the Japanese enemies.

John's arrival and position as director of the newly established postwar United States Information Service had won us an enviable perquisite. In Chungking, where even a roof over one's head was hard to find, we were given two rooms in the USIS dormitory. It was a primitive building, a stretch of very small rooms side by side opening on a long veranda. Each room had barely space for a chair and wood-frame bedstead with a rush mat stretched across it, but one of our two rooms had the marvel of a tiny corner fireplace very like those we knew from New Mexico. We had pushed the narrow cot against a side wall to make a sofa, covered it with a hand-woven blanket, and hung above it a beautiful large rubbing of a T'ang horse brought back from Sian. With a little imagination one could see it as a cozy living room. Whei, when she first entered it, gasped, "It's just like walking into a magazine!" for it had been only in occasional foreign magazines that she had seen open fires and shaded lights these last years.

When she felt up to it we took both the Liangs to a play and a couple of movies. Sicheng had to return to his Institute in Li-juang and missed the most memorable evening, in which Whei and her young son participated. It was a reception at the USIS headquarters shortly after General George Marshall had arrived on his peace-seeking mission. Representatives of all leading Chinese parties and factions as well as a selection of diplomats including the Russians had been invited and accepted with alacrity. It was a magic moment. Japan had surrendered and the Chinese civil war had not recurred. A hope of real peace after the eight long years was in the air. For that one evening the very mixed crowd could forget their plans and fears and celebrate together.

As the drinks began to flow, the Russians, in character, started to sing. Perhaps it was this very unofficial light-heartedness that broke down the Kuomintang stiffness. A number of the Nationalist officials who had known the Communist leaders in their youth (for example, K. C. Wu [Wu Kuo-chen] and Chou En-lai had been schoolmates) were present and suddenly started exchanging toasts after so many years. Whei watched intently the startling reunions, as old friends and old enemies drank each other's health. Hsiao-di, Whei's handsome young son, attracted the attention of Feng Yu-hsiang, the warlord known as the "Christian General." He was very big and very stout, and the boy, leaning against his mother's knee, stared bug-eyed at this apparition. Whei talked with him briefly, but the Communist leaders were the focus of her scrutiny. They were visitors from another planet. She had heard and read nothing but evil of them from the KMT — yet they appeared in this setting to be human beings like any others.

Dr. Leo Eloesser, a famous American chest surgeon, was working in postwar Chungking for CNRRA, the Chinese National Relief and Rehabilitation Agency. When he heard about Whei's long struggle with tuberculosis, he kindly offered to see her at the hostel-dormitory. After making a simple bedside examination with his stethoscope and questioning her about her past history, he told me (not her) that he concluded both lungs were involved as well as a kidney and that in just a few years, perhaps five, her brief but vivid life must come to an end. I did not tell her and she did not ask me. I believe she knew all along.

23. Return to Kunming and Peking

After Dr. Eloesser's diagnosis, it was clear that Whei in her condition should not remain in this dank, wintry setting. She no longer romanticized her visit to the wartime capital. She made plain her aversion for "this hateful Chungking, this dreary dormitory, and this gray winter light. It is really quite unbearable." At the same time a letter from Sicheng informed us that a series of explosions to ease a dangerous rapid on the Yangtze had stopped all riverboat communication between Chungking and Li-juang. Even the postal service was maintained only by foot carriers. The option of Whei's returning to Li-juang was out.

By chance, at just this time I had to go to Kunming and decided to consult Lao Jin about this matter. He was, of course, very concerned. We both felt this was a heaven-sent opportunity for Whei to revisit Kunming as she had so longed to do. The doctor's grave conclusion, which I reported to him, persuaded us both that if it could bring happiness to her, it was worth the gamble on her health involved in the necessary airplane flight and move to a higher altitude. The plan was clinched when we found a charming small free-standing house near Chang Shiro's, on a hill just above the old ancestral home of the warlord T'ang Chi-yao, which had large windows, a profuse flower garden, and overhead several eucalyptus trees, from which hung fragrant long swaying branches. The house had just been evacuated by its departing "downriver" occupants and Lao Jin could move in to care for her.

When the plan was proposed to Whei she was obviously aware of the health risks involved. Yet she concluded after some hesitancy that "to get to Kunming once more and suddenly be given sunshine and scenery, a blossoming garden, and that mysterious atmosphere of the Kunming sky interposed with brilliant lights and luminous shadows, wild rain and wind-blown clouds, I think I shall feel better." The decision was soon made and she was packed off for her first airplane ride.

On her arrival in Kunming Chang Shiro and his wife insisted on her staying with them in their nearby house for the first days. The strain and exhaustion from her flight confined her to bed, but surrounded by her dear old friends again after the long separation, she was enraptured. Ch'ien Tuan-sheng and his wife and of course Lao Jin were the other intimate friends who gathered at her bedside for unending hours of conversation.

"Not even the most extravagant hopes I had entertained when I was alone in Li-juang," she wrote from her bed, "could be compared with the real and overwhelmingly delightful experiences of this reunion. It took eleven days to get all sorts of odd information both of the lives progressing under the special circumstances of Kunming and the lives lived in the Li-juang community straightened out for the convenience of the conversing friends who now meet and gather here. But the old bridge of deep mutual love and understanding was set up and expanded in less time than any of us had expected it to take. In two days or so, we knew very perfectly where each of us had been, emotionally and intellectually. Our views on national political situations, family economics, persons and societies in and out of wars in general were freely discussed and none of us had difficulty under-standing how each of us has come to feel and think that way. Even when the conversations were most rambling, there was always among the several of us that soothing flow of mutual confidence and interest and the added gratifications and fresh stimulations that are the result of this sudden coming together at an eventful time. . . .

"Not until this time was I aware of the delights of ancient T'ang or Sung poets who had lacked means to travel but while en route to their meager official posts suddenly encountered their friends here or there in a little inn or on some riverboat or in a temple with monks as their hosts. How they poured out their souls to each other in their long talks!

"Our age may be very different from theirs but our meeting this time has many similar points. We have all aged greatly, gone through a peculiar form of poverty and sickness, endured long wars and poor communications and are now apprehending great national strife and a difficult future.

"Besides, we meet at a place distant from our home, a place where we were compelled to live by circumstance and not by choice. The longing to go back to the place where we spent our happiest times is somewhat like the T'ang people's longing for their Ch'ang-an and the Sung people's for their Pien-ching. We are torn and shattered. We have emerged through various trials with new integrity, good, bad, or indifferent. We have not only tasted life but have been tested by its grimness and hardship. We have lost much of our health though none of our faith. We now know for certain that enjoyment of life and suffering are one."

As the spring weather improved, Whei recovered from the strain of the flight and Chang Shiro permitted her to depart to her "dream house."

"Everything that is most beautiful stands sentry around the garden, the clear blue sky and down below the cliffs and beyond where the hills are. . . . This is my tenth day in this new house. The room is so spacious and the window so large that it has an effect of early Gordon Craig stage design. Even the sunlight in the afternoon seems to have obeyed his instruction by coming through the window in a certain illusive manner with splashes of faint moving shadows thrown on the ceiling by the swaying eucalyptus branches outside!

"If only Lao Jin and I could invent dialogue to suit, it could have been a setting for a masterpiece of drama I am sure. But he sits at present at a little round table with his back against the light and myself, his hat on as usual, intent on his writing." [As he aged, he had to protect his sensitive eyes from sunlight and glare.]

"The altitude or whatever it is that is so trying to me makes me very short of breath; often I feel as though I had just run many miles. So I have to be much more quiet than I was in Li-juang in order to get the rest I need. I am not allowed to talk at all though I have a little more than my allowed ration. But the so-called 'conversation' doesn't do justice to the setting."

News of her shortness of breath was alarming, but the spark of vivacity in her writing style indicated she was enjoying herself even so. She included glimpses of the housekeeping that went on around her.

"I have been very lucky in getting just the kind of maid I need. The kind that has all the semblance of human intelligence and yet somehow remains much greater than just being a human being. She is a combination of log, rock, and all that is huge and indestructible. She is sufficiently dumb and good-natured to be a maid of the first order (that is, a maid who would stay), and is sufficiently capable and steady to be a maid nearer to the precious kind (that is, a maid one would not like to have leave). So you see how lucky I am!

"Lao Jin, who has lived so long in the professors' dormitory and acquired barbarous habits of internees in concentration camps, finds fault with our present standard of elegance, such as letting the maid do all the dishwashing. His usual habit is to keep a cup and a pair of chopsticks on his own windowsill so that he can mix his morning cup of cocoa himself by these devices. He was much upset once when he couldn't find these articles in his own room or on the dusty windowsill, but I reassured him that henceforth I would tell the maid not to wash them but place them under his pillow for his convenience!"

Six weeks later came a long letter from Sicheng, who was with his daughter in Li-juang. He reassured us that the apparently rash move had been the right thing to do.

"It is only a few days ago that the river project was finished. But still only very small boats can come up from Chungking. It will be the later part of May before a boat with cabins can come up. So Whei's trip to Kunming is the only solution to the problem. . . . In her first letter from Kunming, she wrote of a sense 'almost religious' in realizing that a deep prayer is fulfilled. She was overwhelmed by the welcome accorded her by our old friends, and mourned that she is 'taking' all the time without anything to 'give.'

"The visits you and John paid us in Li-juang relieved the monotony of her five years in this one room to such an extent that she was able to keep up her high spirits for a long time after your departure. And again, this visit of hers to Chungking would not have been even thought of if you were not there. The good psychological effect is tremendous.

"Although the high altitude of Kunming has a certain bad effect on her breathing and pulse, she is very happy there. She is surrounded by old friends who keep her company and keep supplying her with books, more than she can read. Lao Jin is staying with her (very Bohemian indeed) and she has a very good maid. So she is in good care and I have nothing to worry."

Meanwhile Sicheng and his few remaining colleagues were occupied packing the books, papers, drawings, and technical equipment of the Institute for shipping back to Peking whenever transportation became available. The Academia Sinica institutes were at the same time packing their invaluable library, research papers, and archaeological specimens, which, in the end, went to Taiwan. The Central Museum was returning its collection, library, and so on to Nanking, where its ambitious building had been left unfinished in the first chaos of the Japanese invasion.

The unhappy settlement at Li-juang was at last breaking up, many months after the Japanese surrender. The Yangtze River along its shore flowed directly eastward to Shanghai. It was the great thoroughfare for the "downriver people" to return home. But the government controlled all access to boats and planes. To avoid confusion, it assigned numerical priorities to its various offices and institutes to move them in orderly sequence. Inevitably, in the capital high-ranking officials and wartime prof-iteers could by devious means make their way ahead of schedule to the coast. There was no such option for the poverty-stricken wartime refugees in Li-juang. They were dependent on the government to get them home and had to wait through frightening inflation.

Liang's Institute was linked to the Central Museum. He wrote from Li-juang that the two institutions were jointly allotted No. 47 "while No. 1, the Central University, is still dubious of their time of departure. . . . Before the war ended, we thought we would throw away all our rags and fly back. But now we know that we shall have to hang onto them for a long time to come."

The return to Peking of the entire family including Lao Jin was finally accomplished by a direct flight from Chungking on July 31, 1946, but not before they had all waited more than a month in the Academia Sinica hostel slum, crammed together with some forty other marooned families. This hardship was a fitting climax to the miseries they had suffered in Li-juang and Chungking in the previous five years. Yet waiting in that seemingly hopeless present, Whei continued to live on her special capacity for aesthetic joy. "Kunming is eternally beautiful, sun or rain. The scenery outside my window was specially exquisite just before and right after a big thunderstorm. The atmosphere inside my room was indescribably romantic during the rain-pour — for the sudden darkening of heaven and earth while one was there in a lonely house within a big silent garden. It was something to be remembered all one's lifetime."

24. Honors, 1947

The war had been over for more than a year when the Liangs finally reached Peking. Sicheng had been appointed by the Ministry of Education to establish and head a new Department of Architecture at Tsinghua University. The Ministry planned to send him to the United States to study current architectural training in American universities.

Emerging from his years of poverty and isolation, overburdened with family and administrative responsibilities, he was comforted by the promised security of a prestigious job in his old university with housing provided for the family. On the other hand, the planned inspection trip sounded exhausting. It would involve constant travel to numerous campuses on a tight budget.

While he was contemplating this daunting scheme, he received letters of invitation from Yale and Princeton Universities. Yale invited him to come to New Haven for the academic year 1946–1947 as a visiting professor to teach a course in Chinese art and architecture. Princeton wanted him to take a leading part in an April 1947 international conference on "Far Eastern Culture and Society." Both invitations were tributes to his dogged persistence in researching and publishing his findings on the history of Chinese architecture despite hindrances of all kinds. His prewar publications had attracted international attention; his two wartime *Bulletins* had inspired admiration. He was suddenly a figure of international standing, in demand among his peers in the West. To go to the United States as an honored guest at two leading universities put a very different light on the project.

There were still complications of settling the family, and planning the Tsinghua department before he could leave. When he went to Tientsin to recover the negatives and other important materials belonging to the Institute that had been stashed away in the underground safe of a bank in 1937, he was shocked to discover that a flood in this port city had ruined all the precious treasures left there nine years before.

Fortunately, Sicheng had taken to Kunming and Li-juang prints of the

Institute's photographs he would now need for slides at Yale. With these and the large architectural drawings completed in Li-juang, he had the visual materials for teaching the history of Chinese architecture. In addition he packed for his trip to the United States the nearly completed text of the book he had written in English at Li-juang for which these were to be illustrations. He had entitled it "A Pictorial History of Chinese Architecture," and he hoped both to finish the text during his stay in the United States and to find an American publisher for it.

He was due at Yale in September but was again caught in the priority struggle, this time for space in a trans-Pacific vessel. This delayed his arrival at New Haven until late November. As soon as he had settled in Yale's Saybrook College, he got the university to copy his visual materials. These created for Yale's fine arts library an unprecedented collection of slides.

Not long after his arrival he met a junior faculty member of the Yale Department of Architecture, King-lui Wu. A 1945 graduate of the Harvard School of Architecture, Wu had returned to Yale to do research on town planning. Despite their wide differences in age, the two men found much in common. Wu had been appointed to redesign the Yale-in-China campus in Changsha, which had been destroyed in the war, and needed expert guidance. Sicheng for his part was not only eager to share ideas with Wu on new architectural expressions for postwar China but also to learn from this recent graduate what was currently being taught in two leading American architectural schools.

Wu attended Sicheng's course on Chinese art and architecture during the spring semester. He made a valuable contribution to Sicheng and to Tsinghua by listing from his own recent studies the preeminent books on American and European architecture and urban planning that should be available in the library of the new department. The books were purchased and sent and have survived to this day. Sicheng was so impressed by Wu that he asked him to join the Tsinghua Department of Architecture. However, Wu was obligated to Yale's Changsha architectural plans. He spent eight months of 1947–1948 working in Changsha for Yale-in-China, at the end of which time the civil war had so disrupted China that the project had to be abandoned. He returned to Yale, where he is now Professor of Architectural Design.

Sicheng's year teaching at Yale was truncated by unavoidable crises at both ends, limiting his time in the United States to barely seven months. The long wait in Shanghai for boat passage had lopped three months off the autumn semester. Serious news from home cut short his plans for the following summer. Yet in his limited time while he was giving Yale his course and his slides, he managed also to participate in activities outside New Haven that spread his influence and enhanced his own familiarity with current professional developments after his long isolation.

The first was the renewal of his old friendship with Clarence Stein, the noted architect and urban planner, in whose New York City apartment he was a frequent overnight guest. The second was his participation in the Board of Design Consultants for the United Nations headquarters buildings in New York City as the member appointed to represent China. The third was his attendance in early April as a leading figure at the Princeton University Conference on "Far Eastern Culture and Society" followed by the award to him of a Princeton honorary degree. The fourth was a collaboration that he and I undertook in order to put in final form the English-language text of the history of Chinese architecture he had written in Lijuang for submission to an American publisher.

Naturally there were also events scattered through the months that interested or delighted him in passing. These included his return to Penn and informal contacts with some former classmates, his visits to Cranbrook to see Eliel Saarinen, whose writings he had read in China, and to Tennessee to see the impressive architecture and engineering of the recently developed Tennessee Valley Authority. He went to Cambridge to lecture on his Chinese architectural discoveries at Harvard's Fogg Museum, where he had studied in 1927–1928, and there and elsewhere he came upon Chinese friends and relatives, resident or recently arrived in the United States, whom he had not seen for many years.

The happy reunion with Clarence Stein and Aline MacMahon after a decade's separation was very timely. Sicheng's appointment to develop a department of architecture at Tsinghua had inevitably dislodged him from his fifteen-year concentration on architectural history. He would never abandon this subject so dear to his heart, but he now faced the responsibility of organizing at Tsinghua a course of study that would prepare young architects and engineers to play their part in the modernization of China in the postwar world. From Stein he learned first hand about the possibilities and difficulties involved in urban planning. This guidance was to prove invaluable to him when, on his return to Peking, he added a concentration on urban planning to the curriculum of the Tsinghua department.

The United Nations involvement gave Sicheng contact with eminent architects from many parts of the world. His fellow members of the Board of Consultants included representatives of Australia, Belgium, Brazil,

France, Sweden, Britain, Soviet Russia, and Uruguay. Of these, Le Corbusier from France and Oscar Niemeyer from Brazil had the widest international reputations. Sicheng's teaching obligations at Yale limited his participation, but he spent what time he could in New York, staying with the Steins and learning much from the discussions of the Board. George Dudley, then a young American architect assisting Wallace K. Harrison, of the New York firm in charge of the U.N. headquarters project, wrote down in 1985 his memories of Liang from 1947:

"He was a fine addition to the U.N. Board of Design although regrettably few of us knew of him or his work. More than anyone he brought a sense of history to our sessions, far beyond the immediate history of Le Corbusier's insistence on his own version of the movement away from the Beaux Arts, or other still unresolved responses to the changes in our cultures. He did want the Secretariat building oriented east-west as the most important buildings in China over the centuries had been oriented in that way, providing for the long front entrance facade to face the warmer south. On the East River site this would mean the entire area to the north would be in continuous shadow from the 40-story building, which was best located at the 42nd Street end of the site where most of the office workers would reach it most directly. So he quietly (and generously) acceded to that reasoning."

Dudley added that Liang gave warm support to Niemeyer's scheme of a north-south high-rise slab, which finally achieved the unanimous approval of the Board.

Sicheng took his participation in the U.N. project very seriously. His new interest in urban planning and the relationship between architecture and the physical environment was greatly strengthened not only by the Board's general discussions but also by the opportunity to exchange ideas with individuals of such varied backgrounds. He was to encounter again some of his colleagues from this group in his later years as he traveled to architectural gatherings in Europe and Central and South America.

The Princeton Conference in early April 1947 on "Far Eastern Culture and Society" was part of a year-long celebration of the university's bicentennial. Some sixty specialists, principally concerned with Chinese studies, had been invited. The group included leading figures in the field from across the United States as well as some outstanding European and Asian scholars. Professor J. J. L. Duyvendak of Leiden University, Osvald Siren from Sweden, and Professor E. R. Hughes from Oxford University were matched by such distinguished Chinese scholars as Ch'en Meng-chia, Feng

Yu-lan, Ch'en Ta, Ch'ü T'ung-tsu, and Liang Sicheng. The ambitious program covered wide aspects of Chinese studies, but for the conference organizer, Professor George Rowley, who was Princeton's specialist in Chinese art, Liang Sicheng was the prize. Rowley had visited Peking in the mid-1930s and been deeply impressed with Liang's recovery of Chinese architectural monuments and his cultivated interest in the Chinese arts in general. Rowley's close collaborator, Professor Alexander Soper, the American specialist in architecture of China and Japan, had followed Liang's discoveries through the years in the Chinese texts of the Institute's *Bulletins,* including the two final issues produced in Li-juang. Both men admired Liang's pioneering and his later persistence throughout the wartime misery and destitution. They took pleasure in presenting him to this remarkable assembly of his peers, many of whom knew his work and some of whom had met him in Peking before his eight years of isolation. An exhibition of his drawings and photographs was held, and he gave a lecture on his architectural discoveries and another on the previously unreported sculptures in the living rock at Ta Chu in Szechwan. He also attended a number of the lectures given by others and took part in discussions.

At the end of the conference a special convocation was held in Nassau Hall at which Princeton recognized the notable researches of J. J. L. Duyvendak in classical Sinology and of Liang Sicheng in Chinese architectural evolution by the award of an honorary degree to each. An academic procession led by the president and faculty wearing the appropriate regalia opened the ceremony. There was a striking contrast between tall white-haired Professor Duyvendak in his medieval Dutch headdress and robe and the smaller, slender, and youthful-looking Liang engulfed in a too-large black commencement gown and cap, both kindly provided by Princeton. His citation read, "Ssu-cheng Liang, Doctor of Letters: a creative architect who has also been a teacher of architectural history, a pioneer in historical research and exploration in Chinese architecture, and a leader in the restoration and preservation of the priceless monuments of his country." His titles accompanying the citation, though they were only a few of the total he had accumulated, were impressive: Fellow of Academia Sinica, Director of the Institute for Research in Chinese Architecture, Chairman of Tsinghua's Department of Architecture and of its Institute for Architectural Research, member of the U.N. Board of Consultants, and Visiting Professor of Fine Arts at Yale University.

In the Princeton archives there is a letter that Sicheng wrote to President Dodds accepting his offer of an honorary degree. He added, with typical courtesy, modesty, and wit, "It is a reward much too high for one who did nothing more than spend a disproportionately large part of his time and energy in pursuit of perhaps the mere satisfaction of his idle curiosity."

I attended the Princeton conference and found Sicheng healthy and in good spirits. The recognition accorded him in the United States had coursed through his veins like an elixir.

Just before leaving China, I had made a hurried trip from Nanking to Peking for my farewells to Whei, the children, Lao Jin, and other friends. I could bring Sicheng reassuring news. In the small Tsinghua house he had never seen, Whei's bedroom was flooded with sunshine and she had not only a soft spring bed but even a bathtub with hot and cold running water. Dear friends were nearby; the "family gathering" had moved from Kunming to Tsinghua.

Other news was less heartening. Inflation had achieved frightening dimensions; householders living from day to day had to sell precious possessions to buy food and the civil war was going badly for the Nationalist government.

After his busy days at Princeton, Sicheng faced several weeks of winding up his responsibilities at Yale and going back and forth to New York for his U.N. Board meetings. Nevertheless he managed to spend some time with us in Cambridge. He told us that he intended to stay on in Peking no matter what the outcome of the civil war might be. His professional life had given him little interest or experience in politics. He knew nothing personally of the Communists. But like many fellow-citizens suffering from the extortions and corruption of Chiang's government he doubted that anything could be worse.

Finishing his English language "Pictorial History of Chinese Architecture" was the most urgent item on his calendar before returning to China, and he asked me to help. We worked together for several days, then and later, editing and revising the English text and planning its completion. I was to make inquiries to locate the most appropriate publishers. We planned that he would meanwhile be clarifying sections and adding others to put the manuscript in final shape.

At this point, without warning, Sicheng received a cable from Peking. Whei's tuberculosis had taken a very serious turn. An operation was under discussion and his participation in the decision was necessary. None of his involvements in the United States could take precedence for him over getting back to Whei as soon as possible. The Yale course, luckily, was already completed. The meetings of the U.N. Board continued, but he had made what contributions he could and Niemeyer's scheme, which he favored, appeared to be winning. The shipping of books for Tsinghua had already been arranged. Friends and relatives rallied to help him with his personal packing. Much of his luggage was devoted to gifts for his family. The Steins, who helped him with last-minute shopping in New York, were struck by his passion for gadgets or, as Sicheng might have termed them, "advanced American technologies" to surprise and excite the recipients in China. To handle whatever unfinished business might turn up after his departure, he gave me power of attorney.

He brought from New Haven the precious drawings and photographs intended to illustrate his book and left them in my care. The text on which we had been working he decided to take with him. As he explained, the two-week ocean voyage across the Pacific would be an ideal time to complete it, and he promised to mail it back. Neither he nor I thought of making a copy of the unfinished manuscript for me to have at hand. Today this may seem incredible, but of course this was more than forty years ago. In any case it was a fatal error. I put the large package of illustrations in storage in Harvard's Fogg Art Museum, but the text never came back to me.

When he made a quick trip to bid us goodbye, we talked hopefully, as old friends will, about a reunion. Yet we all knew how unlikely it was that we four would ever be together again. This realization made me want to learn from Sicheng before it was too late something more of those parts of his life and Whei's which lay outside the experiences we four had shared. Intuitively I felt that reliving those earlier years would lighten the sense of imminent loss that darkened our last hours together. He courteously agreed to my interviewing him along these lines and making notes of his replies. The interview could have taken a full day or, better, a week, but we had only hours — an afternoon and an evening. As I had hoped, his reminiscing was as spellbinding for him as for me. Many years later the notes from that interview provided the first framework for this book.

25. Worrisome Days

Despite the absence of Sicheng in the United States, the Architecture Department at Tsinghua had been activated. Two months after the end of the war he had invited Wu Liang-yung, his Chungking assistant, to join the faculty. He had already chosen his three closest colleagues at Li-juang — Liu Chih-p'ing, Mo Tsung-chiang, and Luo Chih-wen — for the department. All four of these young men were dependent on finding space on boats down the Yangtze to Shanghai and again northward to Peking. Wu managed to get to Shanghai first. Sicheng, who was there awaiting his trans-Pacific voyage, instructed Wu to do what he could to start courses at Tsinghua and, in a pinch, to turn to Whei for help.

Wu reached Peking in late 1946. The other three from Li-juang reached Nanking in early 1947 and were housed in the Nanking Museum until a Kailan Mining Company boat bound for Chinhuangtao agreed to take them. From there by train to Tientsin and eventually Peking, they finally reached Tsinghua. They were all promptly enlisted to teach architectural design along with Wu. Liu also taught construction and Mo, the skillful artist, taught watercolor painting. Liu Chih-p'ing, who had been an outstanding student in Liang's first class in Mukden and had worked with him all the years since, was named an associate professor on his arrival and a full professor the year following.

Whei, though housebound and obliged to spend much of her time in bed, played an important part in the establishment and operations of the department. Of course her previous close involvement with the analogous beginnings of the Northeastern University Architecture Department in Mukden made her advice invaluable. She had encouraged Wu and others to come to her with problems.

Sicheng was pleased to find on his midsummer return from the United States that, whatever might be his family worries, everything was in order in his professional life. His own joy on returning was tempered by the fact that Whei was running a low temperature, which postponed indefinitely the operation recommended by her doctors. They had discovered that one of her kidneys was seriously affected. At the same time the tuberculosis attacking her lungs had made her so short of breath as to raise questions about the use of anesthetics. Yet if and when the kidney operation could be undertaken, the removal of one source of infection might with luck restore to some extent her general health.

Sicheng resumed his role as nurse, confidante, and comforter in whatever free time he was spared. He was of course repeatedly called upon for public speeches about his UN advisorship and other aspects of his stay in the United States. A particularly influential talk was on "Technology and Humanity," in which he stressed the importance of social and cultural considerations in architectural design. With the start of the academic year, these private and public responsibilities were augmented by the demands of administration and teaching.

The gifts that he had hurriedly gathered to bring home to family and friends arrived some time after he did. Whei, who was longing for dainty garments and colorful fabric as well as pretty baubles to reward devoted friends, was shocked to discover that the majority of his purchases had been American electronic gadgets intended to ease and improve her life in bed. She wrote this scenario: "On one grand occasion, Mr. Liang showed me off fully equipped with collapsible, reversible, and connectable and disconnectable mechanisms to the teeth. Sitting in bed with an adjustable canvas back support, fitted in front by an adjustable writing-and-reading stand, with a recording machine plugged into an electric transformer that was duly plugged into an ordinary plug of this house, a magnifying glass in one hand and a microphone in the other, I was to behave like a carefree young lady of the modern age, much like Charlie Chaplin eating a piece of corn on the cob with the help of ingenious machinery."

Later she added regarding the recording machine: "Yes, we did hear all the greeting speeches recorded in the discs used. I must say they were confusing. Sicheng sounded like Mr. Mei Yi-ch'i, Wilma sounded like John, and John's throaty voice was approaching Paul Robeson's. The best and most distinct of all the speeches is that of Aline's, and no wonder. I feel terribly proud to have a professional artist's 'broadcast' in my collection. So far I have done very little with this machine in the way it was intended to be used but let my children record playful conversations when there were gatherings. I felt like Emperor Ch'ien Lung on occasions when he was presented with various foreign clocks. I dare say he let his court ladies play with them for a while."

But everyone approved of the small Crosley automobile Sicheng had bought. After the infinite complexities of getting it through Chinese customs and licensed, it turned out to be a godsend to the entire family and particularly to Whei, who could be driven to see friends or have friends driven to see her with an ease formerly inconceivable.

Whei's physical condition improved in the cooler weather of autumn. Her doctors decided to take the preliminary steps to determine her ability to tolerate the kidney operation. She wrote us from her Peking hospital room on October 4: "I'd better tell you why I am here in this hospital. Don't get uneasy. I am only here for a general overhauling; just to mend a few hinges here and there—perhaps stop a few roof-leaks and put in a few mosquito screens—to put them all in our architectural terms. Yesterday evening, troops of interns, young resident doctors, went over with me the history of my case, like going over the history of two wars. We drafted agendas (as John so often did) and formed various subcommittees on the problems of my eyes, teeth, lungs, kidneys, diet, amusements, or philosophy. We left out nothing, so we came to as much conclusion as all the big conferences about the world situation today. Meanwhile a great deal of work has been started, to see what is wrong and where; all the modern forces of technical knowledge are to be employed. If tuberculosis is not cooperating, it should be. This is the logic of it."

She turned from critiques of her own architecture to comments on the building of the Central Hospital at West Ssu-pai-lou, where she was lying abed. "This is a beautiful creation of the Early Republic: a 'Min-kuo'—'Yuan-Shih-kai-ish'—foreign contractor—German baroque four-story building! My two tall and narrow formal windows face the south and overlook the entrance court, where one sort of expects 1901 automobiles, carriages, and Chinese Early-Republic-Mandarins to adorn the cement baroque steps and paths."

In a burst of high spirits, she had visited the Summer Palace with Bao-bao and her young friends. "Inside the Summer Palace I had to take a sedan chair, costing 70,000 *yuan* for a round trip; going right through on top of the ridge of the hills at the back of the Palace, the place I loved most and where I took the Steins once. It was a success; the weather was marvelous after a night of rain. We could see miles around. The kids were very happy accompanying me on foot. I felt royally important to have so much service and attention from them. Lao Jin and Sicheng were sweet enough to keep house for us while were gone for the day. . . . You see, I emerge from under deep waters and take what may be termed 'unnecessary activities'; without these I might have passed out long ago, like an oil lamp in exhaustion—sort of faded away, winked, blinked, and gone!"

In the end the operation was performed but not until December 24,

1947, after two months of apprehension, brief recurrence of fever, further tests, blood transfusion complications, and, finally, waiting for the hospital heating system to be turned on. Before the operation she took the precaution of bidding me farewell. "Goodbye, dearest Wilma. How nice it would be if you would suddenly drop in and present me with a pot of flowers and a whole torrent of nonsense and laughter."

A cable from Sicheng reported that the operation had been successful. Shortly after the operation Sicheng and Lao Jin both wrote asking us to get some of the new wonder drug streptomycin. It was not easily obtainable, but we managed to send two separate shipments in care of American friends assigned to Peking. Finally we had news that Whei was settled at home, on the Tsinghua campus in her warm and snug bedroom, which she described wistfully as "sound-proof and friend-proof."

By mid-February she had thrown off a post-operative fever, and her strength was gradually returning. Sicheng commented, "With it her mental activity returned, which, as a nurse, I do not welcome. She bursts into verse after verse, and recently she also dug up a few old poems from her piles of manuscript and sent them to various magazines and literary supplements of newspapers. Sixteen poems sent out within a few days! And, as usual, they are very good."

A postscript asked us to send him a New Year's present of a five-hundred-sheet box of lightweight typing paper. "It costs 10,000 *yuan a sheet* here; one box is half a month's pay." Inflation of that scale was hard to imagine. Lao Jin, too, wrote that Whei was much better, but added, "The trouble is and has always been her incapacity for suffering boredom. She doesn't have to be amused, but she has to be occupied." Her correcting and rearranging of her poems for publication was motivated by her conclusion that "when the iron curtain finally hangs they would be out of date." Lao Jin encouraged her plan "to place them in their proper historical perspective so that whatever future standard of criticism there may be, it simply doesn't apply to them."

In March 1948 Liang was elected to membership in Academia Sinica as a representative of Art History in the Humanities Division. He flew in August to Nanking to attend a celebration of the twentieth anniversary of the organization's founding and the first plenum of its members to be held at the Academia Sinica headquarters there. It was a last gathering with many old friends. The civil war was reaching a crisis and within a short period Generalissimo Chiang would resign and move to Taiwan. The Academia Sinica as a government-supported institution followed him there. Liang had no such intention.

26. Final Letter

March 31, 1948, was the twentieth anniversary of Sicheng's and Whei's wedding in Ottawa. A few intimate friends celebrated the occasion with the Liangs over tea and cakes in their Tsinghua house, and Whei dazzled the group with an impromptu lecture on the Sung capital. But Lao Jin worried about the "bride and groom." Whei's incision had ruptured about an inch but was being treated with streptomycin. Meanwhile, Lao Jin wrote, Sicheng himself was very thin, maintaining a heavy schedule of classes Monday through Friday at Tsinghua, and "living a daily life as a telephone switchboard—so many threads converge on him."

In that year, which was only the second since the founding of the Department, the classes naturally included only freshmen and sophomores, a total of forty-one students. Sicheng took responsibility for the main historical course, presenting the evolution of Western architecture followed by that of Chinese. He was also involved in the design-criticism sessions that twice a week examined and appraised the students' drawings. He wrote in May 1948 near the end of his first year at Tsinghua, "I never liked teaching very much. I prefer research work. But I am compensated by the good work of the students. On the average they are very bright and conscientious, and I enjoy it as a whole. But it keeps me extremely busy and prevents me from research. It is a real dilemma."

Field studies were out of the question during the civil war, and his Institute for Architectural Research had not reestablished a program of work since the return to Peking. Moreover, his months in the United States had intensified his interest in urban studies and the social aspects of architecture. These preoccupations led him to reorganize the Architecture Department into two parts—Architecture and Urban Design. Clarence Stein had contributed two hundred volumes for the use of teachers and students in this new division.

Sicheng must have wanted free time to study this new field and its application to China. He was looking beyond the immediate requirements of construction. Providing a population with a livable and healthy total environment was at the forefront of his thinking. He wanted to make sure that his students would not be technically qualified only. They must be sensitized to human needs for beauty, comfort, space, health, safety, and neighborliness.

In mid-1948 a new friend entered the Liangs' lives. Lin Zhu was a young girl recently graduated from her Shanghai high school. She had come to Peking hoping to enter Tsinghua, and her father had given her a letter of introduction to Whei. Her first impressions of the Liangs bring them to life and also give us a glimpse of the writer herself at that early age, quiet and shy, intelligent and sensitive. That she became a close friend is not surprising.

"I couldn't help feeling nervous when I thought about meeting the famous Liangs. What could I talk to them about? I had never socialized on my own with members of my father's generation. But as soon as I met them, all my worries vanished in a flash. Professor Lin warmly arranged to have me stay at the house of a Professor Wu. When she realized that it was my weakest subject, she offered to help me study English and arranged that we would meet twice a week, on Wednesdays and Fridays. Because I wasn't good at making conversation, I was terrified of getting together with strangers. But when I went to see Professor Lin, all I had to do was bring my ears — she was so talkative and interesting. I could never get a word in edgewise except for an occasional giggle. She was the most beautiful and elegant woman I had ever met in my life. Of course when I met her she was already more than forty years old and the tortures of her disease had already reduced her to a near skeleton. But once you came near her the physical Lin Wheiyin disappeared. What you felt was only the brightness of her spirit, her wisdom and her beauty. I was often intoxicated with admiration for her.

"At that time her health was extremely poor and every afternoon she had a low-grade fever, but she insisted on teaching me — this undiligent student. I felt very guilty, but I was so attracted by her that I was unwilling to give up any chance to be near her. We always began our lesson at 3:30 in the afternoon and had tea at 4 o'clock. If Professor Liang was at home he would join us for tea and sometimes the room was filled with guests. When there weren't many guests, Professor Lin would talk to me about urban planning for Peking, or discuss architecture or literature or art. It seemed as though she never thought that I was still a blank when it came to architecture and that compared to her I was only an ignorant child. But it was these conversations that increased my knowledge about architecture and made me begin to be interested in it.

"One day Professor Lin asked me what ancient buildings I had seen in Peking. I said that I'd seen all of them inside the city. She wanted to know which places I liked best. I said I was fondest of the Altar of Heaven and the Great Ancestral Temple. 'When you visit the Altar of Heaven you have to pass along a long spirit path before reaching the pure-white round altar under the blue sky. This really gives you a feeling of going toward Paradise. And the large grove of ancient pine trees near the entrance to the Ancestral Temple is so peaceful and solemn.'

"Hearing mention of these ancient pine trees, Professor Lin laughed and asked me whether I had ever heard the story of Sicheng's and her visit to the Ancestral Temple. I shook my head. She then told me: 'At that time I was only about eighteen or nineteen. When I first went out with Sicheng I put on airs of being a young lady, but not long after we entered the Ancestral Temple courtyard he climbed a tree and left me standing underneath all alone. He really made me so mad!' I turned my head to look at Professor Liang. He raised one eyebrow and smiled mischievously: 'But you still fell in love with that stupid boy!' They both laughed and so did I.

"Another time after our English lesson, Professor Lin asked me which field most interested me. I said: 'I love literature, but I also know that I'm not right for this field. Therefore I'm not planning to develop myself in that direction; I just like it, that's all.' She asked me which writer's work I liked. I answered, 'There are countless foreign writers, but the only Chinese writers I like are Shen Ts'ung-wen and then Ts'ao Yü's plays.' She was very glad to hear this and talked on and on about Shen's works. She also said: 'The way Shen is being treated right now isn't fair. Chao Shuli, the famous writer from the revolutionary zone, was strongly influenced by Shen.' She suggested that I read Chao Shuli's works. In fact, it was from his works that I learned about the Communist Party in this period.

"Lin Wheiyin was my teacher as well as the guiding spirit of my life. Even my wedding was arranged by her from her sickbed. Shortly after that her illness grew more critical. We stopped my English lessons, but because at that time her daughter had gone south and her son was in college, I still often went to the Liangs' home. I was most impressed by the Liangs' love of Chinese culture, their firm attachment to their careers, and their optimistic spirit toward life.

"During that period Sicheng's workload grew very heavy every winter because the Tsinghua dormitory had no central heating and they depended on a coal stove for heat. Wheiyin was very weak and sick and couldn't bear the cold. Their house had to have three or four large stoves about half as tall as a man. Sicheng had to personally make sure that these stoves kept burning. I often heard them describe to me battles in which they saved a stove that was about to go out. Only now do I realize that, in Wheiyin's condition, the stove going out would have meant the end of her life. But whenever they talked about it they were always witty and good-humored; they never grumbled or complained."

These intimate concerns of one family were taking place in a time of political and military upheaval. Northeast of Peking the Chinese Communists were overpowering the Nationalist forces. Chiang Kai-shek's crack troops with their American arms had been flown in American planes to the Three Northeastern Provinces to take over the major cities while the Communists from North China had moved into the countryside as the Japanese surrendered. Chiang in Nanking retained personal control and directed his armies from a great distance without reference to or advice from local commanders. He pursued a policy of hoarding troops and equipment by gathering them in supposed strong points inside the major cities of the northeast. The Communists, controlling the surrounding countryside and organizing support among the people, besieged these garrisons and picked them off one at a time between May and November. Changchun fell on October 20, 1948, and Mukden on November 1. By December 1 in the key battle north of Nanking at Hsuchou, Kiangsu, the Communists captured whole armies of Nationalist troops with their equipment. The end was in sight.

Neither Whei nor Sicheng appeared to have the slightest interest in politics. Brought up in the world of the arts, rational in thought, single-minded in their determination to achieve their personal ambitions in architectural history and poetry, they had found no time for political involvement or speculation. Even their wartime hardships did not ignite in them the political outrage felt by many of their friends. They were to enter the communist world with all the hope and innocence of childhood.

A political commentary from Whei was therefore most unusual. "The stupid thought-control of the right, the purposeful thought-manipulation of the left are enough to leave one very thoughtful and speechless for a long time. The kind of liberalism your country has enjoyed is a long way from us, and our economic life, for those who are lucky enough to be above starvation, means counting tens of thousands of *yuan* merely where one is that day, for the next day one will be penniless again. When life in general is a huge mismanagement, mine in bed is rather meaningless."

At last, even correspondence had to come to an end. Whei's final letter was written between November 8 and December 8, 1948, in the very month of the Communists' arrival. She wrote it soon after receiving the first copy of John's book, *The United States and China* (first edition). It was, in effect, a book review, containing both praise and criticisms as good book reviews should.

"Now that I feel that we have perhaps only a month or two to write freely to you all in the U.S.A. without postal service difficulties or whatever hitch there might be, I feel a bit choked or tongue-tied. Even this letter. . . . I only hope that it will get to you before Christmas or for Christmas.

"Many many thanks for all the books you sent us, specially the last, which is John's own masterpiece and what a book! We certainly enjoyed and admired and gaped and discussed and were all very very much impressed. Sometimes we said to each other in affectionate patronizing phrases that John certainly grasps our 'special celestial' complications here, or feels 'that feel of things' there and anyway certainly this is no 'foreign devil' stuff — not even the *slightest,* to a modern Chinese — this time. [Chang] Shiro said affectionately that he enjoyed John's book and [in Chinese] that 'There truly is not a single sentence that is an outsider's misinterpretation. . . . He understands a lot,' etc. Lao Jin said that it is a very 'sane and scientific' summing up of us and that 'there are some things John fundamentally understands. He is truly different from other foreigners.' And I must say that Sicheng and I are surprised that it is so *absolutely free* from foreign happy misunderstanding and well-wishing-wish-hope-or-despair. What I particularly admire in it is the way John puts Western things in Western terms and Chinese things in Chinese terms and yet in the *same* Western language intelligible both to the American who reads about China in his own tongue and the Chinese who reads about his own country in the other tongue. We all enjoy this enormously.

"Besides, we often point out to each other with the greatest admiration and without the least shame that we learned this and that fact about China from John and for the first time in our lives (!). For instance, 'It is interesting — I never knew that corn or sweet potato came to China this late, or, specially, so many events among Sino-Western relations.'

"In other words, we all so very much enjoyed what John must have enjoyed writing. The Liangs have not been so pleasantly surprised since Wilma Fairbank's reconstruction of the Wu Liang shrines.

"My only regret, if I have any, is that no Chinese *art* has been touched on in the summary though I don't quite see what art has got to do with foreign relations issues! Still, art is so much a part of us that when talking *about us* in general it is still somehow '*there* too,' mixed with semi-conscious complications in us. . . . When I say '*art*' I mean '*poetry*' also of course, and by that I mean also perhaps the particular sensitivity and aesthetic-emotional experiences aroused by or reached through our *language* — our peculiar written characters, word-pictures, phrase structures, *literature,* and literary traditions and heritages. Our peculiar language is really three parts *rhetoric* and *poetry* and only one part clear and precise speech! . . . What I mean is perhaps that this rich self-contained 'language-poetry-art combination' also made us what we are and think and feel or dream. . . .

"In short, I think art is at least as important in influencing our mental make-up as diet is over our physical make-up. I am sure the fact that we eat rice and bean curd can't help making us a little different from those who take great big pieces of steak and drink several glasses of milk, often with cream cake or pie. In the same way, the man who sits grinding his ink-stone patiently making up a landscape is almost a different species from the young rebel who stays in the Paris Latin Quarter familiar with his Balzac type or postimpressionist paintings and the latest Matisses and Picassos (or the young man who travels down to Mexico to have a look at the Mexican frescoes). . . .

"All the above was my private bit of book-reviewing for the sake of arguing — affectionate argument worked up to tease John. It is going to cost me hell to send this letter!

"As far as political views are concerned I agree with John entirely this time. This means that I have come up closer to his views since we last argued in Chungking — or rather, I have changed a bit by following the day-to-day issues at hand in the last two years and I feel John is fairer too. I am very very happy that this is so. By the way, being very ignorant of many things, I am very grateful to John's instructive, informative bird's eye view of so many many phases of Chinese life, system, or history. Being familiar with ourselves, we don't often try to get a clear perspective or to articulate about it, so John's book is fascinating reading to us all and we are going to make the younger generation read through it too.

"Maybe we won't see each other for a long time now. . . . Things will be very different for us, though we don't know how different, next year or next month. But as long as the younger generation have something interesting to do and can keep fit and have work, that is all that matters."

Advance units of the Communist People's Liberation Army "liberated" Tsinghua a few days after Whei's last letter was mailed, and Peking was surrendered to the Communists in the next month, January 1949. Exchange of letters was no longer possible; our worlds did not touch.

PART FIVE

Under the Communist Party, 1949–1972

27. Defeats

A full account of the Liangs' lives in the succeeding years under the Communist government is out of the question. Only bits and pieces, unassayed, reached the Western world. What follows is a collection of these.

Before Peking surrendered, the People's Liberation Army infiltrated the Tsinghua campus area. An officer brought Sicheng a map of the city and explained that Professor Liang was asked to designate areas where precious buildings and cultural relics must be preserved if artillery should be called into action. Sicheng, impressed, remembered that he had sent Chou En-lai in Chungking copies of his analogous lists for wartime preservation.

After the surrender the new government cleaned up the city. Between 1949 and 1951 piles of trash and tons of garbage and stinking scum littering the streets and byways of Peking were carted away. Miles of sewers were cleared and the lakes, which were clogged with mud, debris, and rank growth of weeds, were dug out and the water purified.

Two other moves by the government made this a honeymoon period for the average citizen. The inflation that had oppressed the people throughout the eight years of war was controlled. The century of foreign special privilege in China was ended, and the citizens' humiliation replaced by national pride.

Sicheng was named Vice-Director of the Peking City Planning Commission. He early formulated his recommendations for transforming Peking into the new national capital.

1. The city should be a political and cultural center, *not* industrial.
2. Industry must be absolutely barred. It would result in traffic congestion, environmental pollution, rapid growth of population, and shortage of housing.
3. The Forbidden City should be strictly preserved.
4. New buildings inside the old city wall should be limited in height to two or three stories.
5. A new administrative center for government buildings with a north-south axis should be established west of the Forbidden City.

The Party spurned every one of these recommendations except the third; the Forbidden City was saved. As for industry, Mayor P'eng Chen early told Sicheng as they stood on the T'ien An Gate looking southward, "Chairman Mao wants a big modern city: he expects the sky there to be filled with smokestacks."

We must assume that this news depressed Sicheng. He had every reason to love the old city of Peking. Not only was it his home; he and Whei had studied all its beauties in the course of his career. To save the Forbidden City was not enough. The great walled city itself must not be desecrated.

He turned his attention to his fifth recommendation, that an administrative center for the new government should be established on a north-south axis west of the Forbidden City. This would permit important new construction without disturbing the traditional central axis of the city. With the help of Ch'en Chan-hsiang, a British-trained urban planner, Sicheng prepared a presentation of his scheme. He had it printed and distributed at his own expense. He also published an article entitled "Peking — a Masterpiece of Urban Planning," hoping to win the support of the general public.

However, Soviet advisors coming to China in large numbers between 1950 and 1960 insisted that the government had to center on T'ien An Men. Furthermore, a huge area in front of the gate had to be cleared and paved for mass gatherings and parades. They envisioned a close imitation of their own Kremlin-with-Red-Square in Moscow.

Though hostile or at least unresponsive to Sicheng's proposals, the Party turned to him for help in its projects. Both Liangs were appointed to the groups designing the new national symbols, including the national flag and national emblem. The Liangs urged that the emblem should have Chinese characteristics (not a hammer and sickle) and in the end a representation of the facade of the T'ien An Gate in red and gold became the emblem that is still used today.

An important historical symbol required by the new government was a monument to People's Heroes, honoring the martyrs in previous revolutionary movements that eventuated in the communist victory. Planning for it began in 1951, and it was finally erected in the center of T'ien An Men Square in 1958.

What form should it take? A pagoda? A pavilion? Sicheng's advice that it should resemble the stone memorial stele universally found throughout China swayed the design group. Since the slab could not be small in the vast T'ien An Men Square, he figured a height for it appropriate to the gate itself. Whei took part in the design of the base and introduced the egg-and-dart motif she had studied in the Yun-kang caves. Nearby according to Chinese custom evergreen pines were planted to mark the undying remembrance of the dead heroes, but these were later removed.

The Party's decision to tear down the great walls and gate towers of the city horrified the Liangs. The arguments for this plan were that the walls were defense fortifications of a feudal empire of no use any more, that they obstructed traffic and restricted the development of the city, and that they were a source of bricks potentially valuable for building structures or paving roads.

In May 1950 Sicheng put forward a counterproposal that the walls and gates must be preserved to serve the health and recreation of the people. He pointed out that the flat tops of the walls "ten meters or more in breadth" could become a continuous public park with flower beds and garden seats. The gate towers and corner towers with their upswept double roofs could become museums, exhibition halls, refreshment kiosks, and teashops. The moat surrounding the walls at their base and the strip of land between the two could make a beautiful "green belt" and provide boating, fishing, and skating "for the great masses of the working people." He added a vigorous paragraph citing a relevant instance of preservation by the Soviets, the Big Brother that China was emulating in 1951.

"The city wall of Smolensk in the Soviet Union, seven kilometers in circumference, called 'The Necklace of Russia' was destroyed during the Second World War, and the whole Soviet People took loving care of its repair. The city walls of Peking cannot only be called 'The Necklace of China,' but 'of the world.' They are our national treasure, but also the cultural relic of the people of all nations. We have inherited the priceless and unique historical property, how can we now destroy it?"

The Party was not convinced, and it rejected even Sicheng's most simple and practical suggestion that traffic could be eased and controlled by opening traffic entrances and exits in the city wall on either side of each gateway without disturbing the gate towers and the integrity of the wall. In the next twenty years the wall itself was destroyed in its entirety. All the magnificent towers were torn down with the minor exception of the southeast corner tower and two gate towers, the front gate on the south and the west gate on the north, both of which had already suffered demolition of their barbican sections. With the disappearance of the moat, urban sprawl erased even the contours of the once famous capital of the Mongols, the Ming, and the Ch'ing.

In 1953 the Party adopted a slogan to guide and control architectural design: "Utility, economy, and, if conditions allow, beauty." Sicheng was given the responsibility to develop a national style of architecture that would meet these requirements. The need for new structures was great after the years of wartime devastation and the establishment of a new government. But experienced practicing architects were few, and Sicheng himself, though a distinguished architectural historian, was not in that category.

He faced a daunting problem. Though he was a recognized expert in the national styles of Chinese architecture over the past two thousand years, the norm through that period had been buildings of not more than one or two stories centered around courtyards and expanded if necessary by additions at the ground level. The only structures on a larger scale were palaces and tomb-halls of the imperial family and Confucian, Buddhist, or other temples.

Now in the twentieth century the government needed office space for the bureaucracy in its many ministries and other large structures for students' dormitories at its many universities, for hotels, assembly halls, institutes, museums, factories, and so on. Limited space in urban locations dictated high-rise construction. What to do?

To meet such needs, notably in Shanghai and Nanking, foreign architects in the 1920s had designed and supervised construction of a few modern steel and concrete structures four or five stories high on commission from Western or Chinese firms. Not uncommonly such buildings were capped by large temple-style concave curved roofs and overhanging eaves to denote their Chinese origin.

Sicheng had been critical of such mismatched structures "wearing a Western suit and a Chinese skullcap." Still, to create a national style for construction of large modern semi-high-rise buildings, the use of steel and concrete was essential. He had long been struck by analogies between the steel framing of modern construction and the post-and-lintel skeleton of Chinese traditional wooden architecture, both designed to support the weight of the roof and eliminate the need for bearing walls, thus permitting complete freedom in fenestration.

His proposals for a national style are not clear, but the criticisms that bore down on him in 1955 were that he had neglected "economy and utility" for "formalism and reactionism." Large roofs covered with glazed tiles "wasted the nation's money" as did painted beams. The ancient style was ironically applied to modern buildings. The Party called for a "three antis" attack on Sicheng: "anti-formalism, anti-reactionism, and anti-waste." He was the target of severe blows from opponents and supporters, colleagues and students, all required to carry on a bitter criticism campaign against him. None dared to defend him openly.

By 1955 his years of unremitting toil for the Party and also of struggle against it for what seemed to him its follies had led him to the brink of exhaustion. Early in the year he was hospitalized. There he was discovered to be a victim of tuberculosis; he would have to be a bed-ridden patient for many months.

Shortly after Sicheng's hospitalization Whei was taken to the same hospital and settled in an adjoining room. She had been as deeply involved as he in the struggle. She had suffered with him and for him as their great hopes for the future dimmed. Despite her lifelong precarious health, her will and determination had survived the Party's hostility. In 1945 Dr. Eloesser had told me that her condition was very serious and that she had perhaps only five years to live. That she lived for ten additional years seemed an incredible feat on her part. But by 1955 her untimely end was near. She died on April 1 at the age of fifty-one.

For Sicheng, shattered by his illness and disgraced by order of the Party, the death of his beloved wife after their twenty-seven years together was a crushing blow. He fell into a deep depression. How was he to live on without her?

Later that same year he was transferred from the hospital to the Summer Palace for three months' convalescence. Much of his time there he spent (like so many others) writing and rewriting for the Party confessions of his guilt. This was the more poignant because in the course of the thought reform movement of 1952–1953 he had been required to write a self-criticism in which he severely criticized his father's conservative reformism, which had influenced him profoundly. He admitted that he had once nursed the feudalistic idea of "pledging to myself that I would one day make my famous father proud of me."[1] Through the next years he studied Marxism-Leninism and in January 1959 was finally accepted as a Party member.

In view of his international reputation, it was advantageous to the Party to send him abroad as a representative in delegations to international gatherings. As early as 1953 he had been sent to the Soviet Union with a delegation from the Chinese Academy of Sciences. In 1956 he attended architectural meetings in Poland and East Germany. In 1958 he went to Prague and again to Moscow. The next year he attended a Stockholm meeting on world peace. An extended trip in 1963 took him to Cuba, Mexico, and Brazil, where he enjoyed a reunion with architect Oscar

Niemeyer. His final trip abroad was to Paris in 1965 for an international architectural conference.

Between the interruptions of this foreign travel schedule, and of the many meetings in China of committees, societies, and conferences, not to mention recurrences of illness, Sicheng continued his teaching at Tsinghua and chairmanship of the Architecture Department. Until 1953 he had no textbook for his course on the history of Chinese architecture, but in that year Tsinghua reproduced by offset the hand-written Chinese manuscript he and Whei had researched in Li-juang. Because it was not a Marxist treatise, it was considered not worthy of printing and was distributed for internal use only without attribution to Liang or the Institute. By 1955 Tsinghua had reproduced, from Sicheng's microfilm reel photographed in Chungking, a pamphlet of the Institute's architectural drawings. These were also unattributed and limited for student use only. Some of these reached Europe, where certain drawings were published by writers on Chinese architecture without credit to Liang or the Institute. It seemed at the time a shameless case of plagiarism.

Sicheng's life was complicated in that period due to long absences for travel and for official commitments. At his departmental office, numbers of unopened letters and journals piled up. He needed help. To cope with such problems, he turned to the young woman, Lin Zhu, who had been devoted to Sicheng and Whei ever since her arrival in Peking from Shanghai in 1948. Her subsequent marriage to a member of the Tsinghua Architecture Department had ended in divorce in 1957, leaving her with a small son and daughter to support and raise. Her mother in another part of the city took charge of the children as she continued her employment in the Department. When Sicheng asked her for assistance with his paperwork, she gladly accepted and arranged to stop in at his home every other day for the purpose. She tells the story herself:

"About the second week, I opened a letter and burst out laughing. I rushed to Sicheng to congratulate him because a representative from the People's Congress had proposed marriage to him on her own behalf. Attached was a picture of this middle-aged woman. Sicheng also laughed. That day we talked about the problems in our lives. After that we would have short conversations following every day's work. We talked about everything from our lives and work to literature and architecture. I'm not a talkative person, but he always listened quietly to me and exchanged opinions with me. This was the first time in my life that I found a soulmate to whom I could really pour out my heart. It had been seven years since Wheiyin had passed away. Sicheng lived alone and he was in poor health and very lonely. This led us to draw close emotionally and made us care about each other. We fell in love and decided to marry.

"After we married in June 1962, because of our differences in age, education, and life experience, many people, including members of Sicheng's family, didn't understand or support our marriage. If such a great social pressure confused me for a while, several years of living with Sicheng made me understand and value him more profoundly. Our fates had already become inseparable."

28. Lin Zhu's Story

The last years of Sicheng's life, which ended in 1972, were spent as a target of the Cultural Revolution. Lin Zhu wrote a first-hand account of this tragic period in 1986 for a Tsinghua memorial occasion honoring Liang. Excerpts from it constitute this final chapter and the last two paragraphs of the preceding chapter.

In 1966 [four years after her marriage to Sicheng] I was sent to Yenching County on the outskirts of Peking. Along with other students and teachers from Tsinghua University, I joined a work team carrying out the "Four Purifications Campaign" in the countryside. In June we received an order to return to the university to join the Cultural Revolution.

Prior to this, I had received letters from Sicheng saying that he was suffering from high blood pressure and serious dizziness. This made me worried and eager to see him. [He was sixty-five years old and frail.] The June weather was turning hot and the depressing atmosphere enveloping the work team made me feel a nameless fear. When our bus entered the Tsinghua campus I saw numerous big-character posters with people crowded around them making Tsinghua seem unfamiliar. As soon as I got off the bus somebody told me there were posters in the architecture department attacking him—"Liang collaborated with P'eng Chen [the former Mayor of Peking] against the Communist Party: Liang is a 'reactionary academic authority'" [a term used in the Cultural Revolution for well-known intellectuals]. Suddenly I felt the luggage I was holding weighed like a stone pressing heavily upon my heart.

Numbly, I went home. Pushing open the door, I saw the curtains in the room were drawn as usual and all was dark. Sicheng was writing something. He looked so thin and small and haggard. When he saw me, he stretched out his hands but then immediately let them drop. In a low, hoarse voice he said, "I've been longing for you every day but I was afraid. . . ." I had never seen such a painful expression on his face, and he was so demoralized it frightened me. I patted him lightly, hoping to comfort him a little. Secretly, I hoped this was only a momentary dark cloud and that everything would be cleared up and pass soon. At that time I could never have realized that this dark cloud would envelop the whole of China for an entire decade and that he would never have the chance to see blue sky over China again.

I returned to my department "to receive training." All my colleagues kept silent. Outside the window, teams and teams kept passing by, beating drums and gongs and parading cadres wearing dunce caps through the streets. I was scared that Sicheng would be treated the same way. But I had to force myself to conceal my fear and pretend to be calm and relaxed.

The Central Party Committee sent a work team to Tsinghua and order was temporarily restored. Then some people pasted up a big-character poster saying "Liang Sicheng is a die-hard follower of P'eng Chen and a major rightist who has infiltrated the Party." As a result, he wrote detailed confessions recounting how he entered the Communist Party and his relationship with P'eng Chen [who had since been repudiated by Mao]. All of this was in fact common knowledge and his repeated confessions were never accepted.

One day, he finally understood what they wanted from him. They believed that the article he had written during the anti-rightist campaign [1957] in support of the Communist Party was written at the suggestion of P'eng Chen's faction in order to disguise rightists as leftists and help them infiltrate the party. One Sunday, Comrade Liu Jen (Vice-mayor of Peking and P'eng Chen's right-hand man) came to see me and asked me what I was thinking these days. I showed this article to him. He read it and was very pleased. He immediately put it in his pocket and said, "This will appear in tomorrow's paper." The next day the article was indeed published without a word changed.

He continued: "Anyway, I believed that only the Communist Party could make China strong. I was willing to follow it and so I wrote an application to join the Party. But at that time I didn't understand any of the Party's modus operandi, so I sent my application directly to Prime Minister Chou En-lai and asked him to forward it to Chairman Mao. After I joined the Party I may have committed some mistakes, and this includes my articles, but all of my behavior was open and aboveboard. I never engaged in any intrigue or conspiracy."

He frankly but painstakingly wrote about every issue the work team demanded that he confess. His account of every issue was honest and detailed. He didn't hold anything back. I always felt I was naive in every respect, especially politics, but even I was amazed to find how politically naive and pure he was. He was completely loyal and completely trusted the Communist Party. Even I couldn't imagine how a person who had lived in the old society all his life could keep such a childlike heart, never suspecting that others had evil intentions.

At the end of July, the Central Committee decided to remove the work team from the university. This made me very anxious [because there would be no one in control]. But the students were very excited. They kept singing, "With our pens as weapons, we'll fire on the black gang. . . ." Listening to their singing, I felt a bone-chilling shiver from the back of my neck spread over my whole body. After the work team withdrew, the masses elected the leading committee of the Cultural Revolution. Every day people were writing big-character posters criticizing the university Party committee and every departmental committee on down. Everyday Sicheng and I were trying to figure out why "Chiang Nan-hsiang (the former president of Tsinghua) was a revisionist," what a "bourgeois educational line" was, and what a "proletarian educational line" was. These questions, which seemed to have been resolved by the revolutionary masses, still confused us and we were afraid to ask. And every day more counter-revolutionaries were ferreted out and struggled against.

I didn't dare to think about it, but I had a premonition that they'd never let Sicheng go. Finally the thing I had most feared came about. That day I was reading a big-character poster in front of my department and suddenly someone was pushed out the door. A huge black placard was hanging on his chest on which were written some white characters: "Reactionary Academic Authority, Liang Sicheng" with a big cross over his name. The crowds in front of the department burst out laughing. Stooped over, he tripped and almost fell but forced himself onward. I raised my head and for a moment our eyes met. My god! I cannot describe the expression of utter humiliation and shame in the eyes of that upright scholar whom I loved so much. Even now, if I were given a chance to relive my youth in exchange for looking again into his eyes at that moment, I would say no.

That day when we got home we almost didn't dare to talk for fear of striking the other's wounds. From then on, whenever he left home he had to put on that black placard.

In August Mao's campaign of destroying the "Four Olds" began. One evening, after a rapid banging on the door, a group of Red Guards burst into our home. The leader ordered me to open all our closets and valises and then demanded that we stand in one place without moving. They rifled through everything as they pleased and confiscated all our bankbooks and art objects. They also gathered together all the knives from our silverware including twelve dinner knives, twelve butter knives, and twelve fruit knives. They asked Liang Sicheng very sternly why he had collected so many knives: "You certainly must be planning to revolt!" I was about to explain, but I was immediately struck in the face.

At this crucial moment, two Red Guards rushed out shouting from Wheiyin's mother's room. They were holding a short sword inscribed with the words: "Presented by Chiang Kai-shek." At that moment, I froze on the spot. After roaring, "Liang Sicheng must confess the truth!" they rushed out holding a whole pile of stuff and refused to hear any word of his explanation. After they had left, Wheiyin's mother cried and howled and only then did I learn that the sword had been worn by Lin Heng when he graduated from the Airforce Academy in 1940. I remembered that Wheiyin had once sadly told me the tragic story of how her younger brother and other pilots had sacrificed their lives in the war against the Japanese. The next day everyone at Tsinghua knew that Liang Sicheng had concealed a sword presented to him by Chiang Kai-shek. From then on anyone wearing a red armband could break into our home at any time they pleased and take away or destroy anything they felt belonged to the "Four Olds."

One day I came home after work and discovered that the drawings of a floral wreath pattern that Sicheng and Wheiyin had designed for the Monument to the People's Martyrs had been thrown all over the place and were covered with footprints. I was just about to put them in order when Sicheng said: "Forget it!" Then he had me move them to the courtyard, where he set fire to them in silence. He held the last piece in his hand and stared at it for a long time, but in the end he still threw it onto the fire. I had never seen him cry after we were married, but now in the fire's reflection I saw tears in his eyes.

To avoid more trouble, we inspected all our things, mainly his published and unpublished manuscripts and the letters he had written in the early fifties to various Chinese leaders, including Mayor P'eng Chen, concerning the new construction and city planning for Peking. There were also some letters between Sicheng, Wheiyin, and the Fairbanks recounting their long friendship and the Fairbanks' support of their academic careers during the Sino-Japanese war. We thought about it over and over but finally decided to destroy all these letters.

Other manuscripts included Sicheng's *Annotated Architectural Standards* on the *Ying-tsao fa-shih,* the fruit of Sicheng's labors over several decades. No matter what, we couldn't destroy them, but still we had no way to keep them. Faced with this dilemma, I decided to give them to our maid Li Aiyi. She came from a poor peasant background and the Red Guards never entered her room. I told her: "These materials will prove Mr. Liang's innocence. Please take good care of them for me. Hide them under your trunk." She nodded her head and said: "I understand."

For the next several days the Red Guards came every night on raids, asking us to surrender any "feudal, bourgeois, or revisionist" writings. I insisted that all writings had been confiscated by previous Red Guards. Because I couldn't produce the names of those Red Guards, in the end I was often beaten. (During those days I was beaten at night, but I still had to go to work during the day as though nothing had happened. I was afraid that if I didn't, the revolutionary masses would look down on me even more.) I must thank our good-hearted housekeeper that *The Collected Writings of Liang Sicheng* and *Annotated Architectural Standards* could be published today.

Red Guards came day in and day out to "instruct" Sicheng and me. One day they said to me: "You should seriously consider how to draw the line between yourself and Sicheng. Will you follow the Party or a reactionary academic authority? We give you three days to make your choice." They were clearly ordering me to divorce Sicheng. This made a thousand confused thoughts swim in my brain. I thought back over the twenty years that I had known Sicheng. I also thought about his long-term companion in life and work and my teacher and guiding spirit, Lin Wheiyin. Divorce? No! I'd rather be beaten to death along with him by the Red Guards than abandon him.

Because Sicheng's health was getting worse and worse and he could no longer hold himself up to go out and read the big-character posters, I copied the relevant posters for him every day. Like a starving man, he devoured the posters as well as the leaders' speeches and the "exposés" printed by various revolutionary groups. We were trying hard to assimilate the revolutionary approaches in these posters, desperately hoping to catch up with the masses.

One day I saw an eye-catching big-character poster with the title "Liang Sicheng — the dregs of the KMT, forfeiter of national honor, wily old anti-communist." This poster exposed four major crimes. First, in April 1966, when Liang Sicheng greeted a delegation of French architects, he kissed the female leader of the delegation on the cheek and thus had "forfeited our national integrity." Second, he served as an advisor on the design of the United Nations building. Third, he served as vice-director of the KMT's "preservation committee of cultural relics in war zones." Fourth, he opposed Chairman Mao's directives on urban planning.

So that was it!

I asked him what the story of his kissing the French woman was all about. He said: "That day, the Society of Architects held a banquet for the delegation of French architects. After the leader of the French group finished her speech of thanks, she came to me and kissed me on the cheek. As the host, after I had made my speech in return, I also kissed her on the cheek. This is just a common gesture of politeness."

"Why didn't you shake her hand in the Chinese custom?" I asked.

"What Chinese custom? Do you think we didn't learn to shake hands from the West? China is a land of many peoples each of whom has its own customs. We should respect the customs of the different peoples in our own country, and of course on the international level, we should also respect the customs of foreign allies. If I'd followed the Manchu custom of greeting, I'd have had to shake my sleeves out flat and bend one knee while placing one hand on the ground. If I'd followed Han Chinese custom, I'd have had to join my fingers together and salute or else kneel down to kowtow. Or should I have followed Tibetan custom to present her with a white piece of silk? Would I have preserved 'national integrity' then?" Even in such a serious atmosphere, I couldn't help laughing at his answer.

As for the problem of opposing Chairman Mao's directives on urban planning, I was reminded of Professor Hou Jen-chih's recent quote from the essay "Miscellaneous Records of Peiping Suburban Architecture," which Sicheng and Wheiyin had written together.

"All around the outskirts of Peking are numerous buildings dating from the last two or three hundred years. If you happen to go on an outing, everywhere you look you'll see ancient buildings rich in flavor. . . .

"No matter whether you come across a towering ancient city gate or an abandoned palace foundation, all are silently telling you or even singing out to you the unbelievable changes wrought by time."

It was exactly this second paragraph quoted by Professor Hou that was taken as a model for Liang Sicheng's antiquarian ideology and criticized again and again. Once I tried to figure out with Sicheng what exactly was the problem with this paragraph. I told him that when I first read this essay, I knew nothing about architecture but I was moved by his poetic-sounding words.

He laughed and said: "This proves that your emotion, interest, and taste fit perfectly with a 'reactionary authority' like me! Architecture is history made of stone. It faithfully reflects the politics, economics, ideas, and culture of a given society. Even now, I maintain this approach, which I believe accords with dialectical materialism. We cannot deny history, and what's more, we cannot cut ourselves off from history. People always draw experience from the successes and failures that they themselves have encountered — that's what history is. If we deny or cut ourselves off from history, the human race can never make any progress. It's impossible!

"My plans for the city of Peking were proposed exactly from such a historical approach," he continued. "We couldn't simply barge ahead with Peking, this masterpiece left by history. Peking was the essence of feudal society, and completely reflected this society's politics, economics, culture, and ideas. It was a gigantic museum. I wasn't saying Peking couldn't be touched or that we couldn't build in the city, but before any act or action, we had to first have a tight, coherent, far-sighted, and comprehensive plan. Areas of filth or refuse certainly had to be cleaned up, but why did places like the Twin Pagodas at the Chin Dynasty Ch'ing-hsiu temple on West Ch'ang-an Avenue have to be torn down? Why couldn't we try to preserve it as a small city park? If this didn't work out, we'd still have time to tear it down later. What I meant was we had to be prudent! . . .

"At the beginning of Liberation, standing on the T'ien An Gate, the mayor of Peking told me that Chairman Mao had said in the future from here we'd be able to see smokestacks everywhere. I was dumbstruck. Wasn't this exactly what we wanted to avoid? What would a city that had 'smokestacks everywhere' be like? This picture was really terrifying. So I honestly opened my heart and told them all my ideas. I considered that as a capital, Washington, D.C. was a good model to borrow from the capitalist countries. Peking, a city with a concentration of ancient buildings, was not a suitable place to develop industry. The best way was to make it like Washington, a political and cultural center with beautiful scenery and a lot of greenery. And its abundant famous sites and ancient buildings could make it a tourist city. When I brought up these ideas I never meant to oppose anybody. I also deeply believed Chairman Mao's words, 'because we are serving the people, we will follow good opinions no matter from whom they come.' At that time I didn't realize that 'every word of Chairman Mao's is the absolute truth,' but even today I still don't get his statement about 'smokestacks everywhere.'"

That night, I saw him write in his notebook: "I feel as though the whole world is flying forward. I really can't catch up. What can I do?"

During those days, what we discussed most were still problems about the art of architecture. For example, were "big roofs" [traditional wide-eaved Chinese tiled roofs] antiquarian or not? . . . He said, "The 1955 campaign only made me realize that big roofs required high building costs, and therefore didn't conform to the economic principles of socialist construction. But I don't think that the experiment of using big roofs to represent a national style was antiquarian. I was always opposed to uncreative mechanical formulas such as sticking a big roof on top of a modern structure. We cannot replicate those mismatched buildings that appeared in the 1920s, 'wearing a western suit and a Chinese skullcap.' I cannot deny that I still think the old big roofs are very beautiful. But none of the big roofs constructed after Liberation reached the standard of beauty that I imagined. I therefore became more and more discouraged and began to doubt whether big roofs suit modern architectural forms.

"After what we went through from 1950 to 1955, the question of how to represent our national style in new architecture was again placed on the agenda and a series of theoretical problems waited to be resolved. At that time, the eyes of the entire nation were focused on me. Should I keep silent? Give up my pursuit? Or should I lie about what I really thought? I could do none of these. Therefore I set forth my own rationale in a speech on the art of architecture to a seminar in Shanghai. It was then published in the *Architectural Journal* (1959, no. 6). In 1961 I again published several views concerning architecture in the same journal. These are exactly the things that the Red Guards are criticizing as 'launching a counterattack against the Party for a second time, and trying to revive capitalism.'

"If free scholarly debate is synonymous with being anti-Party, and if promoting national style is synonymous with capitalist revival, then I can only say I'm anti-Party and trying to revive capitalism. But I still believe that the 1959 Shanghai seminar was a normal discussion of theoretical problems that one inevitably runs into and needs to solve during the course of creating architecture.

"At that time, I heard Prime Minister Chou En-lai's and Vice-Premier Ch'en Yi's speeches after the Canton conference. Their speeches deeply moved me. I thought all I could contribute to my country was my knowledge, and therefore I offered my entire range of knowledge to China's future masters (my students) without holding anything back.

"I'm now very perplexed. I often think that if you had me study architecture all over again, I might still reach the same conclusions. Does this mean that I can never be reformed in my lifetime? I regret that I took up architecture, this profession. It would have been better if I had studied mechanics or radio."

He and I had many such conversations. At that time I understood some of what he was saying, but not always. I was most impressed by his rational attitude: he always tried hard to find the positive elements in the masses' criticism and never lost his temper. Although we had lived together for several years, only at this time did I realize clearly what a genuine scholar he was. I was often scared by his talk, however, and cautioned him over and over that he couldn't say these things to anyone but me. Sometimes he smiled mildly, "You're really the loyal wife of a 'reactionary authority.'" Only when I began to compile *Liang Sicheng's Collected Writings* in 1978 and systematically read works by him and Wheiyin did these points of his resurface more clearly in my mind.

I remember Wheiyin's somewhat flushed complexion because of the low fever caused by TB and I remember how troubled and anxious she was about those mismatched buildings going up. Their whole life was one of courageous exploration. They went forth along a path of thorns, never paying attention to the tempests hitting them in the face, never giving any thought to personal gain or loss, glory or humiliation. I think of how people only bother to congratulate those who succeed, but in science when we celebrate the achievements of the victors, we shouldn't forget the explorers who preceded them. It is these men and women who, with their brave spirit, hard work, and even precious lives, marked the road with signs reading "go this way" or "dead end" for those who came after.

But at that time, I was very troubled. Why were my ideas and feelings always so different from the masses'? Why did I always feel Sicheng's words were reasonable? Why couldn't I staunchly criticize his words as 'the revolutionary masses' did? Why? . . . Was I really a 'reactionary' or a 'counter-revolutionary'? I had to be on guard every second, not against other people, but against the emergence of my own 'counter-revolutionary' ideas.

Not long after the Cultural Revolution began, Sicheng's salary was cut off and his bank account was confiscated. Our family of five, Sicheng, myself, Wheiyin's mother [who had lived in the Liang household since 1929], and my two children now depended solely on my monthly salary of six Chinese *yuan*. Sicheng paid no attention to the abrupt drop in our standard of living.

All kinds of "revolutionary" organizations came to take him out for public struggle meetings. Often they made him stand in the "airplane position" for four hours at a stretch. [In the airplane position two people pulled his arms straight out behind him, forcing his head down. Retaining this position for hours unsupported was both painful and humiliating.] But instead of being angry, he was glad because he naively believed that this meant that the students were beginning to undertake the important tasks of "struggle, criticism, and transformation" assigned to colleges in the Cultural Revolution and that the students were no longer fighting each other but were really engaged in an "educational revolution." He would willingly "be trampled underfoot by the masses" if it would help the educational revolution to succeed and help prevent a revival of capitalism or if it could help the nation become stronger. He thought the question he had never understood — what a "proletarian educational line" was — would soon be answered.

However, frequent public struggle meetings made his health visibly deteriorate. Since he had no medical ties with Tsinghua, I had no choice but to take him to Peking Medical School's number 3 hospital. I will always be grateful to Dr. Ch'en Shih-chi, who treated him. When Dr. Ch'en saw Sicheng's name on the medical file, he didn't disdain him like the others. Instead, he told his assistants in a low voice, "He's an architect who often used to publish articles in the newspaper." He examined Sicheng very carefully and found a number of other doctors to make a team diagnosis. For an entire morning, I watched them as they repeatedly examined him, looked at the results of all sorts of tests, and conferred in low voices. I was extremely nervous.

Finally, Dr. Ch'en pulled me aside and whispered to me: "His illness is very critical. The best way is for him to remain in the hospital, but I guess Tsinghua's Red Guards won't agree to this. How about this — let's keep in close contact. Don't bring him here again. Such extensive activity could be fatal to him at any moment. He must stay in bed. Do you have a blood-pressure gauge at home?" He was glad that we owned a blood-pressure gauge, a stethoscope, and a hypodermic needle. He asked me to measure Sicheng's blood pressure, count his pulse every day, and keep a record. He also instructed me how to give him medicine and what to pay attention to in great detail. He especially cautioned me to prevent him from catching cold at all cost. From then on, I was not only Sicheng's wife, maid, and barber, but had a new job added to the list — nurse.

In 1967, the Cultural Revolutionary Leadership Committee of Tsinghua University notified me that I had three days to move my whole family into a room measuring twenty-four square meters in the northern part of the campus. It was February and the cold of winter hadn't yet passed. I went to see that room and started shuddering before I had even passed through the door. It was a dark and damp room; since no one had lived there for the whole winter, a thick layer of ice and frost covered the walls and ground. This would be fatal to his health.

Again, we sold off any "extra" furniture, but the most troublesome thing was what to do with such a huge number of books. I picked up some valuable architecture books and magazines and asked to put them temporarily in the library of the architectural department. But the Cultural Revolution Committee member glared at me with bulging eyes: "You want to turn the library into your family's private storage room? No way!" I said to him: "Then I will sell these books. Please sign this application form, so that afterwards you won't say I destroyed materials that we could be criticized for." He was beside himself with anger, but all he could do was wave his hand and say: "Leave them there for the moment." The department office became the headquarters during the fighting between different factions. Most of these books were torn up or lost; only a few of them survived. Afterwards I donated what remained to the department library.

Other books, including a full set of "Harvard Classics" in English and Liang Ch'i-ch'ao's collected works, could be only sold to the junkyard. Preparing for possible questions by the Red Guards I recorded the following in my notebook: "To get rid of these feudal, bourgeois and revisionist books, I hired a bicycle-ricksha to make 45 trips and sold the books for 35 yuan."

I cleaned up the small kitchen as a bedroom for Wheiyin's mother, but it was really a difficult problem how Sicheng, I, and two grown-up children could live in this room measuring only twenty-four square meters. I made a floor plan and had pieces of paper cut to scale to represent our furniture, but no matter how I tried to arrange the plan, I couldn't get all the pieces of paper to fit. This was the last time that Sicheng's talent as an architect had a chance to shine: soon he had made bookcases and wardrobes into partitions; our "bedroom" appeared, including a desk for him to write self-criticisms at. And then we were able to plan something for the son and daughter. In this tiny space of twenty-four meters there miraculously appeared a well-regulated, clearly subdivided tiny design.

The day we moved into this room, a cold spell suddenly set in. The temperature plummeted to −10 degrees centigrade. Even though we kept the stove burning, the room temperature was still around zero degrees. Just at that moment, we suddenly heard several continuous crashes, as one after another, our windows were all smashed. In the cold wind, my children and I urgently glued newspaper over the windows, but no matter what we did, we couldn't get them to stick — as soon as we applied the glue, it froze. The room temperature started rapidly dropping: −2 degrees, −3 degrees, −5 degrees, −7 degrees. Only after struggling for two hours did we finally manage to stick the newspaper on when the wind subsided. I didn't sleep the whole night, constantly adding charcoal to the stove and changing Sicheng's hot water bottle, but he still caught cold. This kind of "game" occurred once every several days. Even when spring came and the flowers were blooming, he was still struggling with his illness, tenaciously fighting for his life.

Sicheng was eventually hospitalized. Prime Minister Chou En-lai made inquiries about his condition and ordered that he be admitted to the Peking Hospital. Still, even there his first duty was to "confess his crimes" and write self-criticisms. But no matter how hard he tried, he couldn't write them well. As the deadline got closer and closer, I got horribly anxious. One day, the Workers' Propaganda Team ordered me to go to the hospital to get his self-criticism. I went to the hospital and found that his self-criticism was a mess, the sentences unconnected by logic. I was very anxious, but Sicheng said timidly: "I don't know why, but my mind won't obey me." I started to sob. A nurse patted me on the shoulder and called me away. "Don't blame him," she said in a low voice. "His brain lacks oxygen." Her words reminded me what the problem was. I went back in to try to comfort him and asked him to go to sleep.

I then added to his inconsistent writing the charges against Sicheng that I'd read in other people's big-character posters and produced a new self-criticism, which I took back to Tsinghua. My heart was thumping violently as I handed it in to the army representative there. He took it and flipped through it a moment. "Did you write this for him?" I was startled, but instantly denied it: "No, no — I copied it for him." Less than an hour after this self-criticism was posted on the wall, numerous big-character posters appeared around it criticizing it as "a false self-criticism but a real counter-attack."

Shortly after this, Sicheng joined a study group of Chairman Mao's thought made up of patients in the hospital. He was very glad that he had a chance to come near other people. He told me that one day when they were discussing some problems in the study group he said that a pound of pork was selling for sixty cents and everyone in the room laughed at him. One old lady said, laughing: "See! This old man has been hoodwinked by the revisionist gang to the point that he doesn't even know how much a pound of pork costs."

During the period in which he was struggled against, only his son and my two sisters sometimes came to see us. All other people kept their distance. (At that time his daughter was abroad.) But when I ran into some ordinary people, such as some old Tsinghua postmen, they often asked me about Sicheng. A young carpenter came to our house, insisting that he see Sicheng and ask him some questions about *Ch'ing Structural Regulations*. He said urgently that if he didn't learn it now, no one would know later. Another day, a white-bearded old man holding a big watermelon came to Peking Hospital to see him. It turned out to be Old Wang, who'd been Sicheng's rickshaw puller before the Sino-Japanese war. Sicheng's health had taken a turn for the better after he was hospitalized, but when he left the hospital the doctor still told me: "Don't let him catch cold under any circumstances."

The Tsinghua campus was still enveloped in an atmosphere of tension and terror. The Workers' Propaganda Team clearly knew that I had someone critically ill at home to take care of, but they wouldn't give me a minute off from morning till night. Even though there was nothing to do in the evening, I had to sit idly in the study group of Chairman Mao's thought until midnight, or even one in the morning. Every day I'd return home with my heart thudding. The first thing was to see if the stove had gone out. Because we lived far away from the hospital I once again became nurse and intermediary (between Sicheng and his doctors). Each time I took him to the hospital I had to struggle to get the time off. Finally, Sicheng caught a cold and was again hospitalized.

When Tsinghua relayed a report regarding the policy toward intellectuals, the Workers' Propaganda Team regarded it as a great favor to my family and asked me to talk about my response. I replied: "This great policy of Chairman Mao's has so profound a significance that I must think it through very carefully." But what could I say? Only one line of it remained in my mind: "We will keep these counter-revolutionary academic authorities alive as negative examples for us to learn from." To us intellectuals hardship in livelihood was not the most terrible thing. The most unbearable thing was personal humiliation and nasty mockery.

Not long afterward, Sicheng was readmitted to the Party and again became a member of "the proletarian vanguard." This totally confused him. He was still isolated, waiting for the students whom he cared for most to come. He wanted to discuss problems of educational revolution with them. But his hopes came to nothing. He was still "a contemptible pile of dog-shit." How could he know that Tsinghua had been labeled "a small temple with bigshot gods, a small pond overrun with perverted turtles" and that most of its intellectuals had been forced to a Carp Island in Kiangsi Province to be reeducated through labor? Students always occupied first place in Sicheng's mind. He rarely bothered with relatives and acquaintances, but a student was always welcome. As a teacher he had done everything to help them without a shred of hesitation. Now, however, he lived in lonely isolation. His son was forced to a cadre school far away from Peking. I will forever be grateful to Ch'en Ch'an-hsiang, Wu Liangyung, Luo Chih-wen, and Du Erzhe. They were the ones who brought him warmth and pleasure in the final days of his life.

Sicheng was still concerned about important national affairs. Every day my first job was to read him *The People's Daily* and *Reference News*. During New Year's 1969, after listening to the leading article in *People's Daily,* he said to me: "I won't be able to see the day when Taiwan returns to the mainland." Then he quoted some lines from the Sung poet Lu You: "'The day the imperial army recaptures the north, don't forget to inform me in the family shrine.' When that day comes, please don't forget to cheer for me." The tears welled up in my eyes. I held his hands tightly: "No, you promised me you'd never leave me."

If somebody asked me what he needed most during these final days, I could only say that it was the answer to the question: "What is educational revolution?" But he never found it. He lost hope. The sadness of losing Wheiyin didn't crush him, the criticism against big roofs didn't crush him; but now, he felt deeply grieved. In this last and most painful period, how much he hoped to discuss educational revolution and "how to prevent the revival of capitalism in the field of architecture" with his friends and students. But no visitors came to see him in the hospital and his number hung untouched in the reception room. Could it really be true that people had already forgotten this scholar and teacher who had unselfishly and without reservation offered up all his knowledge? No, I don't believe it! Only history will tell us.

I remember a little poem that he made up in the early sixties when he was climbing a mountain in Kueilin:

> I'll take the lead in climbing the mountain,
> but how can I pretend to be young?
> Only because I'm scared to fall behind,
> Must I fight till the bitter end.

Yes, I saw with my own eyes how he "fought till the bitter end" during his last ten years. But at that time, how could someone as honest and naive as Sicheng know that the Great Teacher whom he trusted so deeply was leading him along a road that ran backward? No matter how hard he tried to follow this road, he could never find progress. His tragedy encapsulates the tragedy of the entire nation.

Written by Lin Zhu, late at night, April 20, 1986. Translated by Judith Zeitlin and Wu Hung.

Liang Sicheng died on January 9, 1972 at the age of seventy.

Fourteen years later, on what would have been his eighty-fifth birthday, a commemoration of Liang's life was held at Tsinghua University. A large group of colleagues and students, family and friends, and a number of officials attended. Tributes to his character and admiration of his accomplishments were delivered by some forty admirers to a gathering of nearly seven hundred in attendance.

Texts of these tributes were published in 1986 by the Tsinghua University Press in a White Book entitled *Collected Essays in Commemoration of Liang Sicheng on his 85th Birthday (1901–1986)*.

Afterword

One strange story has yet to be told. Though the Liangs had died, their work lived on and I was caught up in it in a curious fashion.

In March 1957, eight years after the bamboo curtain had cut off all contact between us and the Liangs, I received in Cambridge through a party unknown to me a message from Sicheng in Peking. It was concrete and brief. I was instructed to send the architectural drawings and photographic prints he had left with me in 1947 to him in care of a "Miss C. Lau" at a street address in Newcastle, England, who would forward them to him through the Britain-China postal service.

I knew how he treasured these drawings and prints, which he dreamed of presenting to the West as illustrations of his "Pictorial History of Chinese Architecture." Could I be sure that his message was genuine? Did he really want me to send these irreplaceable materials to a stranger, barely named, whose address was as remote from China as my own?

At the time, the United States had no postal or other connections with China. I could not check with Sicheng the authenticity of the message nor could I mail the package directly to him.

Since I had no options, I packed the treasures with great care and mailed them to Miss Lau in early March 1957. My letter to her, sent ahead, stressed their importance and Liang's need of them. After a worrisome six weeks, I received a letter from her assuring me that the package had arrived "safely and undamaged." She added that she would forward it, insured, as soon as possible and was meantime "writing a letter to mention it to Prof. Liang." Her delay in replying to me was, she wrote, due to "pressure of work at college." What college, I wondered. Was she a student or teacher? I heard nothing further from her.

Twenty-one years later, in 1978, a European friend of mine visiting the Tsinghua Architectural Department mentioned to a professor my longtime friendship with Professor Liang. The professor countered with a sharp query, "Why, then, did Mrs. Fairbank not return to Professor Liang his drawings and photographs as he directed her to do?"

I was stunned to read in Cambridge this account in my friend's letter from Peking. Those beautiful drawings and the photographic prints, sole survivals of the Leica negatives destroyed in the war, were the fruits of Sicheng's life as I had known it. What could he have thought of me as his last fourteen years went by without recourse to these basic illustrations of his researches?

In an old file box, I found the carbon of my March 7, 1957 letter to C. Lau and with it her laggard reply of April 20 the same year. I sent off Xerox copies of both letters to Tsinghua with an explanatory note. I could defend my reputation, but it was cold comfort.

Who was this C. Lau? If I could not trace the lost package I should at least be able to trace *her*. She would now, I imagined, be a middle-aged woman. But where? Would she, could she have the key to the tragic loss?

At my request Liang's son, Tsung-chieh, inquired in Peking among his family and his father's colleagues for the identity of C. Lau. His conclusion was distressing. "Since none of us have heard of this student in England, my father must have taken an unlucky chance on her (whoever she was) being a responsible person. The mistake was his if the package was not just lost in the mail. In any case, twenty-one years have gone by. It's too late now."

Yes, if the package was lost in the mail it was certainly too late now. And if she too had disappeared without alerting either him or me, the unwise choice had been Sicheng's. For the moment I accepted this finality. Yet as time went on I found myself visualizing the precious package lost and forgotten but existing somewhere — that recurring dream we all have about lost treasures. I had to make one more try.

Having failed to find C. Lau through Peking sources, I turned to London. I spelled out the complex problem in detail in a letter to our dear friend, Sir Anthony Lambert, a retired ambassador, and begged him to help me. At once a magic began to work. He handed my letter to Tim Rock, a member of the Society of Architectural Historians of Great Britain. Rock remembered that up to two years earlier the Secretary of the Society was a lady who lived in Newcastle and had been registrar at the School of Architecture there. He phoned her. She happened to remember a student, Lau Wai-chen, as a senior two decades earlier. She called back to report she had found that Lau had become a chartered architect and was thought to be practicing in Singapore. Rock then phoned the U.K. Architects' Registration Council to get her registration number. With this in hand he got her current Singapore address from the Royal Institute of British Architects.

He summarized the magic for me, "Three telephone calls, fifteen minutes and a Registrar with a memory."

Sir Anthony's letter of November 13, 1979 gave me Lau's Singapore address. Of course I wrote her at once. Enclosing copies of our 1957 exchange of letters to refresh her memory, I told her that our package had never reached Liang and added that one or two of his colleagues were suspicious that I had never intended to return the materials to him. The questions that had been haunting me took up the second page.

"Assuming you forwarded the package to Peking. . . . When? By what route? Did you insure it? Did you write Prof. Liang that you had received it from me? Did *you* ever know it did not reach him?"

And, finally, the big question, "Where might it be now? Lost? Destroyed? or somewhere gathering dust on a shelf? Let me know if there is ANY way I can trace it."

Her reply, slow in coming, paid no attention to my questions. "Twenty years is really a long time and it is difficult to recall all the past events. After receiving your letter I have started looking all over and finally found a parcel containing the drawings and photographs. If I can remember, after some exchanges of letters there was no reply from Prof. Liang so the parcel was remained."

The parcel "was remained" for two decades? With no word to me or Liang, both of whom had entrusted it to her? Why was it valuable enough to transport halfway around the world but not to return it to its rightful owner in all these years? I never understood, and she never explained to me what she had had in mind.

For over six months after the package was rediscovered she clung to it, refusing to send it either to me or to Peking. As she wrote, she regarded it as her responsibility [after twenty years] "to hand over the parcel to the Liang family personally."

Despite my increasing exasperation, I maintained a polite correspondence with her. Then in May 1980 she wrote me that her plan to deliver the parcel to the family in the spring had had to be put off until autumn. This was too much. I sent her a sharp letter saying, "For whatever reason you ignored your responsibility in 1957, you have no excuse for continuing to keep the parcel now." I directed her to send the package at once by registered mail to Mrs. Liang (Lin Zhu) and told her I was sending copies of this letter to her and to Liang's successor, Professor Wu Liang-yung, whose addresses in Peking she had had for some months. She wrote them for sympathy, but they backed my prodding. So, finally, nearly two months later, Sicheng's precious materials reached Lin Zhu by express mail from Singapore on July 17, after twenty-three years.

I later spent that October in China and with Lin Zhu examined the drawings and photographs in detail as we made an inventory. The paper for the drawings, which had been acquired in wartime West China, was not of the best and had browned in thirty-nine years, but the black ink lines and their captions were as clear as the day they were drawn. These and the Leica prints were complete and in good condition. For this we owed C. Lau a grudging gratitude in the end. Meanwhile Liang's manuscript of the text had turned up at Tsinghua. The scattered parts of this lost work were at last reunited.

Four years later Liang's book *A Pictorial History of Chinese Architecture* was published in the United States by MIT Press. At Professor Wu's request, I had resumed my role as editor and found the appropriate publisher. Despite the lost decades, Liang's careful analysis of China's architectural development had no rival. The book was welcomed by the public in this country and abroad, favorably reviewed, and so handsomely presented that the Association of American Publishers awarded the MIT Press its 1984 Medal for Excellence in Professional and Scholarly Publishing.

The Architecture Department of Tsinghua University was as pleased as I at the recovery of the treasured illustrations and the publication of Sicheng's *Pictorial History*. As an expression of gratitude, they invited me to travel over the length of Shansi province with Lin Zhu as my guide and companion to visit the sites Sicheng had researched there. Some, in the south, were revisits to places John and I had seen with the Liangs in 1934. Fifty years later, journeying north of Taiyuan by car, we could search out important buildings with ease. The high point for Lin Zhu and me was our first view of Sicheng's great discovery, the superb T'ang Buddhist temple Fo Kuang Ssu in the remote Wu-T'ai mountains.

At several stops along the way, former students of Sicheng who were continuing his work in their areas greeted us warmly. I was encouraged to find that his influence had survived despite the ferocious attack on him ordered by the Party in the Cultural Revolution.

After our architectural expedition in China, I invited Lin Zhu to come to America. She stayed with John and me in Cambridge for two months. Here she and I traveled rather widely from New England south as far as Charlottesville, Virginia, visiting interesting American architecture along the way. Inevitably we made a special stop at Philadelphia to see where Sicheng and Whei had studied architecture at the University of Pennsylvania. Her letters since lead me to believe that the wooded hills, blue mountains and farmhouses of New Hampshire were her special delight.

Lin Zhu's love and care for Sicheng throughout his painful last years save that period from being a total tragedy. Her memoir, printed here, is a moving expression of undying devotion. How fortunate Sicheng was in both his wives and how I cherish them both.

In the 25 years that China was closed to us, the Liangs' children grew to adulthood. For her English language skills, the daughter, Tsai Ping, spent years in London and elsewhere abroad in the interests of the Party. We met very seldom. The son, Tsung Chieh (Congjie), became a gifted scholar. He loyally stood by his father and Lin Zhu throughout their suffering. We had been fond of him as a boy and meeting him again in his maturity in Peking our fondness grew. MIT's publication of his father's English language *Pictorial History of Chinese Architecture* impressed him deeply. He was inspired to make it available to Chinese readers by adding Chinese characters to the text to produce a bilingual edition of the book. For his cherished father, he interrupted his own work to spend months translating under the supervision of Chinese architectural historians since he, himself, was not trained in the field. The bilingual edition was published in 1992 in Beijing by China Architecture and Building Press. It sold out within a few months of its appearance in Beijing bookstores. The Publishers' Association of China awarded it a prize in 1992. Tsinghua University keeps some copies of it to give to honored foreign guests welcomed by the president.

Congjie has visited us in Cambridge on several occasions, most recently in 1991 a short time before John's death two years ago. He and I share our sorrows as well as our pride in the achievements of Sicheng, Whei, and John, those three beloved intimates whom we have lost. I hope that the tie between our families will be lasting, carried forward by his and our children and grandchildren.

Notes

Introduction

1. *Proceedings of the American Philosophical Society* 137, 2 (June 1993): 282.

Chapter 1: Favorite Son

1. *Jimmin Chugaku* (Tokyo), June 1964, pp. 79–81.
2. Chuang Tzu, *Jen Chien Shih*, Book 4, Part 1, Section 4.
3. V. K. Ting, ed., *Chronicle Biography of Liang Ch'i-ch'ao* (Taipei: World Publishing Company, 1958), November 5, 1923, p. 650. Hereafter designated as *NP* [*Nien P'u*].

Chapter 2: Favorite Daughter

1. Jonathan Spence, *The Gate of Heavenly Peace: The Chinese and Their Revolution, 1895–1980* (New York: Viking Press, 1981), p. 154.
2. Leo Ou-fan Lee, *The Romantic Generation of Modern Chinese Writers* (Cambridge, Mass.: Harvard University Press, 1973), p. 133.
3. Spence, *Gate*, p. 156.
4. Spence, *Gate*, pp. 159–161.
5. Hsu Kai-yu, *Twentieth Century Chinese Poetry: An Anthology* (New York: Doubleday, 1963), p. 67.

Chapter 3: Their Teens

1. *NP*, June 28, 1922, p. 618.
2. Letter, January 2, 1923, in Hsu Kai-yu, *Twentieth Century Chinese Poetry*, p. 68; quoted from Hu Shih's preface to *The Completed Works of Hsu Chih-mo*, pp. 4–5.
3. Their own publication, *Hsin Yueh*, "Crescent Monthly," was not established for several years and then in Shanghai.
4. In Oscar Wilde, *The Happy Prince and Other Tales* (London: D. Nutt 1888; reprint Overbrook Press, 1936).
5. *NP*, May 8, 1923, p. 642.
6. *NP*, May 11, 1923, p. 643.

7. *NP,* July 26 and 31, 1923.
8. Lee, *Romantic Generation,* p. 146.
9. Lee, *Romantic Generation,* 146.
10. Stephen N. Hay, *Asian Ideas of East and West: Tagore and His Critics in Japan, China and India* (Cambridge, Mass.: Harvard University Press, 1970), p. 195.

Chapter 4: Professional Studies

1. *NP,* August 12, 1924, p. 662.
2. *NP,* July 10, 1925, pp. 676–678.
3. *NP,* February 16, 1927, p. 722.
4. *Montana Gazette* (Billings), January 17, 1926.
5. According to the Penn Archives, she graduated February 12, 1927.
6. *NP,* December 12, 1927, p. 751.

Chapter 5: Homecoming

1. *NP,* December 18, 1927.
2. *NP,* February 12, 1928.
3. *NP,* p. 758; the first of the quotes is from an April 26, 1928 letter.
4. *NP,* p. 760; the last of the quotes is from an April 26, 1928 letter.
5. *NP,* p. 761, May 4.
6. *NP,* p. 762.
7. *NP,* June 10, p. 763.
8. *NP,* p. 765.
9. *NP,* May 13, p. 762.
10. *NP,* August 28, p. 768.
11. *NP,* p. 778.
12. January 21, 1929 issue. *NP,* p. 779.
13. Vol. 2, p. 402.

Chapter 6: A Professorship

1. T'ung Chun, author's interview, 1981.

Chapter 7: In Peking

1. *NP,* October 4, 1926, p. 710.
2. Lee, *Romantic Generation,* p. 161.
3. Excerpted from *Ta-kung Pao,* December 8, 1935; trans. Julia Lin.

Chapter 9: Search for Surviving Buildings

1. Yang T'ing-pao, to author, December 6, 1979.
2. An extensive report on the Kuan-yin Hall and Gatehouse of Tu-le Ssu was published in the June 1932 issue of the Institute's *Bulletin*.

Chapter 11: Further Searches

1. Extracts from S. C. Liang, unpublished MS, "In Search of Ancient Architecture in North China," written in Kunming, 1940, in my possession.
2. On his return to Peking Liang immediately wrote and soon published in the Society's *Bulletin* for September 1933 his preliminary survey of these and other old monuments that he had found in Cheng Ting. He led another group there two or three years later to make extensive researches of his Cheng Ting finds. Careful measurements and photographs and a full account were prepared and sent to the printer, but the manuscript and illustrations were lost when the Japanese invaded Peking in 1937.
3. Quoted from "In Search of Ancient Architecture," pp. 24–25.
4. Wilma Fairbank, "The Offering Shrines of 'Wu Liang Tz'u,'" *Harvard Journal of Asiatic Studies* 6, no. 1 (March 1941): 1–36; reprinted in *Adventures in Retrieval* (Cambridge, Mass.: Harvard University Press, 1972).

Chapter 12: A Joint Expedition in Shansi

1. *Bulletin of the Society for Research in Chinese Architecture* [YTHS] 5, 3 (March 1935).
2. See L. Sickman, "Wall Paintings of the Yuan Period in Kuang-sheng Ssu, Shansi," *Revue des Arts Asiatiques* 10, 1–2 (1937).

Chapter 13: Japanese Encroachment

1. Liang Sicheng, *Ying-tsao suan-li* (Calculation rules for Ch'ing Architecture) (Peking: YTHS, 1934).
2. *Ch'ing-tai ying-tsao tse-li* (Ch'ing Structural Regulations) (Peking: YTHS, 1934).
3. Edgar Snow, *Journey to the Beginning* (New York: Random House, 1958), pp. 143–144.

Chapter 14: Interval of Reprieve

1. Extract from Liang, "In Search of Ancient Architecture," p. 2.

Chapter 15: Triumph and Disaster

1. Extracts from Liang, "In Search of Ancient Architecture."
2. Shortly after the devastating Buddhist persecutions of A.D. 845–847.

Chapter 27: Defeats

1. Tsui Shu-chin, *From Academic Freedom to Brainwashing* (Taipei, 1953), p. 18.

Selected Bibliography

WESTERN LANGUAGES

Boorman, Howard L. *Biographical Dictionary of Republican China*. New York: Columbia University Press, 1967–1971.

Chu Ch'i-ch'ien. Inaugural address, February 16, 1930, Society for Research in Chinese Architecture [Ying-tsao hsueh-she, YTHS]. English translation published in *Bulletin of the YTHS* 1, no. 1 (July 1930): 1–10.

Demieville, P. Review of the *Ying-tsao fa-shih*. *Bulletin de l'École Française d'Extrème Orient* 25 (1925): 213–264.

Dudley, George A. *The Workshop for Peace: Designing the UN Headquarters*. Cambridge, Mass.: MIT Press, 1994.

Fairbank, John K. *The United States and China*. Cambridge, Mass.: Harvard University Press, 1948. Fourth ed. 1979.

———. *Chinabound: A Fifty-Year Memoir*. New York: Harper and Row, 1982.

Fairbank, Wilma. "The Offering Shrines of 'Wu Liang Tz'u.'" *Harvard Journal of Asiatic Studies* 6, 1 (March 1941): 1–36. Reprinted in Wilma C. Fairbank, *Adventures in Retrieval* (Cambridge, Mass.: Harvard University Press, 1972), pp. 43–86.

Glahn, Else. Article on the Sung Dynasty *Ying-tsao fa-shih*. *T'oung Pao*. Leiden: E. J. Brill, No. 61, 1975, 232–265.

Guy, R. Kent. *The Emperor's Four Treasuries*. Cambridge, Mass.: Harvard University Press, 1987.

Hay, Stephen N. *Asian Ideas of East and West: Tagore and His Critics in Japan, China and India*. Cambridge, Mass.: Harvard University Press, 1970.

Hsu Kai-yu. *Twentieth Century Chinese Poetry: An Anthology*. New York: Doubleday, 1963.

Knapp, Ronald G. "Bridge on the River Xiao." *Archaeology* oo (January/February 1988): 48–54.

———. *Chinese Bridges*. London: Oxford University Press, 1993, pp. 24–43.

Lee, Leo Ou-fan. *The Romantic Generation of Modern Chinese Writers*. Cambridge, Mass.: Harvard University Press, 1973.

Liang Ssu-ch'eng. "Open Spandrel Bridges of Ancient China." *Pencil Points* 19 (January 1938): 25–32; 19 (March 1938): 155–160.

———. *A Pictorial History of Chinese Architecture*, ed. Wilma Fairbank. Cambridge, Mass.: MIT Press, 1984.

Pelliot, Paul. *Les Grottes de Touen-Houang: Mission Pelliot en Asie centrale*. Paris: Geuthner, 1924.

Snow, Edgar. *Journey to the Beginning*. New York: Random House, 1958.

Spence, Jonathan. *The Gate of Heavenly Peace: The Chinese and Their Revolution, 1895–1980*. New York: Viking, 1981.

Tsui Shu-chin. *From Academic Freedom to Brainwashing*. Leaflet. Taipei, 1953.

Wilde, Oscar. *The Happy Prince and Other Tales*. London: D. Nutt, 1888. Reprint 1936.

CHINESE AND JAPANESE

The White Book. *Collected Essays in Commemoration of Liang Sicheng on His 85th Birthday, 1901–1986*. Peking: Tsinghua University Press, 1986. In Chinese.

Li Chieh. *Ying-tsao fa-shih* (Building Standards). Shanghai: Commercial Press, 1918, 1920, 1925. In Chinese.

Liang Ch'i-ch'ao. *Nien P'u, Chronicle Biography of Liang Ch'i-ch'ao*. V. K. Ting, ed. Taipei: World Publishing Co., November 5, 1958. In Chinese.

Liang Sicheng. *Annotated Architectural Standards* (On the *Ying-tsao fa-shih*). N.d.

———. *Ying-tsao suan-li* (Calculation Rules for Ch'ing Architecture) and *Ch'ing-tai ying-tsao tse-li* (Ch'ing Structural Regulations). Jointly issued by *YTHS*, Peking: Ying Tsao Hsueh Shih, 1934. In Chinese.

———. "A Discussion of the Questions Concerning the Preservation or Destruction of the City Walls of Peking." *Hsin chien she* (New Construction) 6 (1950). In Chinese.

———. "Japan in My Memory." *Jimmin Chugoku*, pp. 79–81. Tokyo: Kyuokuto Shoten, June 1964. In Japanese.

———. *Collected Works of Liang Sicheng*. 4 vols. Beijing: Chinese Architectural Works Publishing Co., 1982. In Chinese.

Lin Whei-yin. *Collected Poems*. Beijing: People's Literature Publishing Co., 1985. In Chinese.

———. *Lin Whei-yin: Collected Works of a Contemporary Chinese Writer*, ed. Chen Yu and Chen Chung-ying. Hong Kong: Joint Publishing (H.K.) Co., 1990. In Chinese.

Tokiwa Daijo and Sekino Tai. *Buddhist Monuments in China*. 5 vols. and 5 portfolios of plates. Tokyo, 1925. In Japanese.

Index

This book has been set in Linotron Galliard. Galliard was designed for Mergenthaler in 1978 by Matthew Carter. Galliard retains many of the features of a sixteenth-century typeface cut by Robert Granjon but has some modifications that give it a more contemporary look.

Printed on acid-free paper.